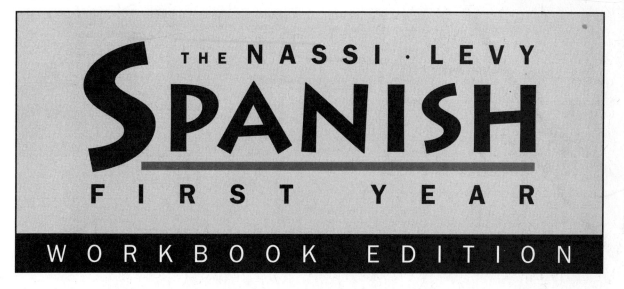

THE NASSI·LEVY SPANISH FIRST YEAR
WORKBOOK EDITION

(New Edition)

Stephen L. Levy
Head, Foreign Language Department
Roslyn (New York) Public Schools

Robert J. Nassi
Former Teacher of Spanish
Los Angeles Valley Junior College
Los Angeles, California

When ordering this book, please specify *either* **R 510 W** *or*
NASSI/LEVY SPANISH FIRST YEAR, Workbook Edition

AMSCO SCHOOL PUBLICATIONS, INC.
315 Hudson Street / New York, N.Y. 10013

To Sergio,
    You are the wind beneath my wings!
        Q.E.P.D.

                        S.L.L.

Cover photograph of Casares, Spain by Super Stock, Inc.
Illustrations by Felipe Galindo

ISBN 978-0-87720-139-7

19 20 21 22 23 24 25   08 07 06

Preface

The NASSI/LEVY SPANISH FIRST YEAR is designed to give students a comprehensive review and thorough understanding of the elements of the Spanish language that are normally covered in the first year of study. Highlights of Spanish and Spanish-American cultures are provided to familiarize students with the background of native speakers of the language. Abundant and varied exercises help students master each phase of the work.

ORGANIZATION

For ease of study and reference, the book is divided into six Parts. Parts One to Three are organized around related grammatical topics. Part Four provides a comprehensive review of vocabulary, presented thematically. There are also chapters on cognates, synonyms and antonyms. Part Five covers Spanish and Spanish-American Civilizations. It includes the geography, history, lifestyle, science, literature, music, art and architecture of both Spain and Spanish America. Part Six provides materials for comprehensive practice and testing of the speaking, listening, reading, and writing skills.

Each grammatical chapter deals fully with one major grammatical topic or several closely related ones. Explanations of structures are brief and clear. All points of grammar are illustrated by many examples, in which the key elements are typographically highlighted.

Care has been taken in this text that reviews the first stage of a basic sequence to avoid the use of complex structural elements. To enable students to concentrate on the structural practice, the vocabulary has been carefully controlled and is systematically "recycled" throughout the grammatical chapters.

EXERCISES

For maximum efficiency in learning, the exercises directly follow the points of grammar to which they apply. Carefully graded, the exercises proceed from simple assimilation to more challenging manipulation of elements and communication. To provide meaningful practice to the students of a grammatical topic, the exercises are set in contexts that are both functional and realistic. Many are also personalized to stimulate student response and internalization of the concepts under study.

While the contents of the exercises afford extensive audiolingual practice, the book's format also encourages reinforcement through written student responses, including English to Spanish exercises intended to sharpen composition skills, The grammatical chapters conclude with Mastery Exercises, in which all grammatical aspects in the chapter are again practiced in recombination of previously covered elements. All directions to exercises at this level are in English.

FLEXIBILITY

The topical organization and the integrated completeness of each chapter permit the teacher to follow any sequence suitable to the objectives of the course and the needs of the students. This flexibility is facilitated by the detailed table of contents at the front of the book and the comprehensive grammatical index at the back. Both teachers and students will also find the book a useful reference source.

CULTURE

The cultural chapters in Part Five are presented in English. Students gain a wealth of knowledge and insight from the information provided as they proceed from Spanish influence in the United States, to Spain, to Spanish America. Each cultural chapter includes exercises designed to facilitate and check learning.

OTHER FEATURES

The Appendix features complete model verb tables and the principal parts of common irregular verbs, along with basic rules of Spanish punctuation, syllabication, and stress. Spanish-English and English-Spanish vocabularies and a comprehensive Index complete the book.

The NASSI/LEVY SPANISH FIRST YEAR is a thoroughly revised and updated edition. Its comprehensive coverage of the elements of Spanish, clear and concise explanations, extensive contextualized practice materials, and functional vocabulary, will help students strengthen their skills in the Spanish language. As they pursue proficiency, they will also gain valuable insights into the cultures of the Spanish-speaking world.

Thanks are due to our consultants, who reviewed substantial parts of the manuscript and made valuable suggestions.

Contents

Part One
Verbal Structures

Part Two
Noun and Pronoun Structures

Part Three
Adjective / Adverb and Related Structures

Part Four
Word Study

Part Five
Spanish and Spanish-American Civilizations

Part Six
Comprehensive Testing
Speaking, Listening, Reading, Writing   *437*

Part one
Verbal Structures

MÉXICO

REPÚBLICA
DOMINICANA

PUERTO RICO

CUBA

HONDURAS

GUATEMALA
NICARAGUA

EL SALVADOR

COSTA RICA
VENEZUELA

PANAMÁ
COLOMBIA

ECUADOR

PERÚ

BOLIVIA

PARAGUAY

CHILE
URUGUAY

ARGENTINA

ESPAÑA

Islas Baleares

Islas Canarias

FRANCIA

PORTUGAL   ESPAÑA   ITALIA
○ Madrid   Barcelona •
Islas Baleares
• Sevilla

Chapter 1
Present Tense of -ar Verbs

[1] REGULAR -AR VERBS

a. The present tense of regular -ar verbs is formed by dropping the infinitive ending -ar and adding the personal endings -o, -as, -a, -amos, -áis, -an.

b. The present tense has the following meanings in English:

usted canta	*you sing, you're singing, you do sing*
él canta	*he sings, he's singing, he does sing*

cantar *to sing*			
(I sing, I'm singing, I do sing)			
yo	cant*o*	nosotros, -as	cant*amos*
tú	cant*as*	vosotros, -as	cant*áis*
usted ⎫		ustedes ⎫	
él ⎬ cant*a*		ellos ⎬ cant*an*	
ella ⎭		ellas ⎭	

NOTE:

1. The subject pronouns *usted (Ud.)* and *ustedes (Uds.)* are usually expressed in Spanish. The other subject pronouns *(yo, tú, él, ella, nosotros, vosotros, ellos, ellas)* are usually omitted, unless they are required for clarity or emphasis.

Canto bien.	*I sing well.*
Cantan bien.	*They sing well.*

BUT

Ud. canta bien.	*You sing well.*
Ella canta bien pero él canta mal.	*She sings well but he sings badly.*
Ella y yo cantamos bien.	*She and I sing well.*

2. The feminine forms of *nosotros* and *vosotros* are *nosotras* and *vosotras*.

3. *Tú* and *vosotros* (the familiar forms) are used when addressing close relatives, intimate friends, or small children. In many Spanish-American countries, the *ustedes* form is used instead of the *vosotros* form.

[2] COMMON -AR VERBS

admirar *to admire*	buscar *to look for*
arreglar *to arrange, fix*	cambiar *to change*
ayudar *to help*	caminar *to walk*
bailar *to dance*	cantar *to sing*
bajar *to go down, descend; to lower*	celebrar *to celebrate*
borrar *to erase*	cocinar *to cook*

comprar   *to buy*
contestar   *to answer*
cortar   *to cut*
dar   *to give*
decorar   *to decorate*
descansar   *to rest*
desear   *to wish, want*
dibujar   *to draw*
enseñar   *to teach*
entrar (en)   *to enter (into)*
escuchar   *to listen (to)*
esperar   *to wait; to hope*
estudiar   *to study*
explicar   *to explain*
ganar   *to win*
gritar   *to shout*
hablar   *to speak*
invitar   *to invite*
lavar   *to wash*
llamar   *to call*
llegar   *to arrive*

llevar   *to carry, take, to wear*
mirar   *to look at*
montar   *to ride* (a horse, bicycle)
nadar   *to swim*
necesitar   *to need*
pagar   *to pay (for)*
pasar   *to pass; to spend* (time)
patinar   *to skate*
practicar   *to practice*
preguntar   *to ask*
preparar   *to prepare*
regresar   *to return*
sacar   *to take out; to take* (photo)
terminar   *to finish, end*
tocar   *to touch; to play* (a musical instrument)
tomar   *to take; to drink*
trabajar   *to work*
usar   *to use; to wear*
viajar   *to travel*
visitar   *to visit*

EXERCISE A

Enrique is telling his cousin what they and their friends are going to do after school. Express in complete sentences what he says.

EXAMPLE: Alfredo / montar en bicicleta
Alfredo **monta** en bicicleta.

1. Sarita / tocar la guitarra [plays]
Sarita toca la guitarra.

2. Lewis / trabajar en el supermercado
Lewis trabaja en el supermecado.

3. Carol y Gloria / bailar el flamenco
Carol y Gloria bailan el flamenco.

4. tú / practicar el piano
Tú practicas el piano.

5. Uds. / mirar la televisión
Ustedes miran la televisión.

6. yo / visitar a mis amigos

Yo visito a mis amigos.

7. Roberto y yo / escuchar discos

Roberto y yo escuchamos discos.

8. nosotros / pasar un buen rato en la biblioteca

Nosotros pasamos un buen rato en la biblioteca.

EXERCISE B

Saturday is a day of chores at the Ortegas. Gloria is explaining what each family member does. Tell what she says.

EXAMPLE: Carlos / lavar el carro
             Carlos **lava** el carro.

1. mi mamá / comprar la comida

Mi mamá compra la comida.

2. yo / usar la aspiradora

Yo uso la aspiradora.

3. mi papá / trabajar en el jardín

Mi papá trabaja en el jardín.

4. Eduardo y Clara / arreglar la casa

Eduardo y Clara arreglan la casa.

5. mis hermanitos / sacar al perro

mis hermanitos sacan al perro

6. mi abuela / cocinar la cena

mi abuela cocina la cena

EXERCISE C

You and some friends are planning a party. Mario wants to know who's doing what. Tell him.

EXAMPLE: comprar el pastel *(Iggy)*
             Iggy **compra** el pastel.

1. decorar el salón *(Gunther y Paco)*

Gunther and Paco decorate the room.

Gunther y Paco decoran el salón.

2. comprar los refrescos *(tú)*

Tú compras los refrescos.

You buy the soft drinks.

3. buscar los discos *(yo)*

Yo busco los discos. *You look for the record*

4. tocar la guitarra *(Marta)*

Marta toca la guitarra. *Marta plays the guitar.*

5. preparar la comida *(Estela y yo)*

Estela y yo preparamos la comida.
Estela and I prepare the food.

6. ayudar con los preparativos *(todos)*

todos ayudan con los preparativos
All help with the preparations.

7. cortar las flores *(Silvia e Inés)*

Silvia e Inés cortan las flores.
Silvia e Inés cuts the flowers,

EXERCISE D

You received a note from a friend who's taking a cruise in the Caribbean. Complete the note with the present tense of the verbs in parentheses.

Dear Lucy:

Querida Lucy:

Greetings from the Dominican Republic we are spending a great amount of

¡Saludos de la República Dominicana! Nosotros ___pasamos___ ratos agradables aquí: yo
1. (pasar)

I swim in the Carribean see, my brothers and I ride on the

___nado___ en el mar Caribe; mis hermanos y yo ___montan___ en motocicleta
2. (nadar)   **3.** (montar)

motorcyde all afternoon; my dad visits the store and my mom

todas las tardes; mis padres ___visitan___ las tiendas y mi mamá ___compra___ *buys*
4. (visitar)   **5.** (comprar)

many seuveniers. At night, all of the family gives at me

muchos recuerdos. Por la noche, toda la familia ___da___ un paseo por la playa.
6. (dar)

on the beach, My brother doesn't wishes to return to the house

Mis hermanos no ___desean___ regresar a casa, pero nosotros ___regresamos___
7. (desear)   **8.** (regresar)

but we wish to next sunday. the vacation ends and

el próximo sábado. Las vacaciones ___terminan___ y tú y yo ___entramos___ en la
9. (terminar)   **10.** (entrar)

you and I enter in the school monday.

escuela el lunes. Es todo por ahora.

It is for all the time

Hasta la vista,   *Until next time,*
Rick   *Rick*

[3] -*AR* VERBS IN NEGATIVE CONSTRUCTIONS

A verb is made negative by placing *no* before it.

María **no habla** español.   *María doesn't speak Spanish.*
Yo **no bailo** bien.   *I don't dance well.*

EXERCISE E

Ana and her sister often disagree with each other. Tell what Ana says and what her sister responds.

EXAMPLE: dar un paseo
      ANA: Nosotros **damos** un paseo.
      VIOLETA: **No damos** un paseo.

1. montar en bicicleta

    ANA: Rafael _____ .

    VIOLETA: _____

2. visitar el museo

    ANA: Nosotros _____ .

    VIOLETA: _____

3. mirar la televisión

    ANA: Mis amigas _____ .

    VIOLETA: _____

4. comprar un helado

    ANA: Yo _____ .

    VIOLETA: _____

5. descansar un poco

    ANA: Tú _____ .

    VIOLETA: _____

EXERCISE F

Look at the people in the following pictures. Say that they are *not* doing what they're doing.

EXAMPLE: Pedro *(tocar)* _____ .
Pedro **no toca la guitarra.**

1. Las amigas *(mirar)* _____ .

2. Yo *(nadar)* _____.

3. Carolina *(patinar)* _____.

4. La familia *(viajar)* _____.

5. Ellos *(arreglar)* _____.

[4] -*AR* VERBS IN INTERROGATIVE CONSTRUCTIONS

In a statement, the subject usually comes before the verb. In a question (an interrogative sentence), the subject usually comes after the verb.

Ud. contesta correctamente.	*You answer correctly.*
¿Contesta Ud. correctamente?	*Do you answer correctly?*
Juan habla inglés.	*Juan speaks English.*
¿Habla Juan inglés?	*Does Juan speak English?*

EXERCISE G

Raúl's little brother always questions everything Raúl says. Tell what his little brother says in response to the statements below.

EXAMPLE: Gloria viaja mucho.
             ¿Viaja Gloria mucho?

1. David baila bien.

_____

2. Mis amigos patinan en el parque.

_____

3. Tú visitas el museo.

_____

4. Nosotros miramos el cielo.

_____

5. Uds. caminan por la ciudad.

_____

6. Yo canto mal.

_____

7. Wong desea comprar un suéter.

_____

EXERCISE H

Luis never remembers what his friends ask. Write Luis's questions based on the answers given.

EXAMPLE: Yo arreglo bicicletas.
             ¿Arreglas tú bicicletas?

1. Esteban visita la biblioteca todos los días.

_____

2. Los hermanos lavan el carro los sábados.

_____

3. Yo nado en la piscina cada tarde.

_____

4. Nosotros practicamos el béisbol.

_____

5. Luz desea ir al cine.

_____

6. Mi amigo y yo miramos un programa a las ocho.

_____

7. Yo viajo por avión cada verano.

_____

MASTERY EXERCISES

EXERCISE 1

While visiting Madrid with a group, you took many pictures. Upon your return, you show the slides to some friends. Describe what's going on in each slide.

EXAMPLE: Alice *(bajar)* _____ .
Alice **baja del autobús.**

1. Nosotros *(visitar)* _____ .

2. Javier, Arthur y Cristina *(entrar)* _____ .

3. Javier *(pagar)* _____ .

4. Tú *(mirar)* _____ .

5. Nosotros *(tomar)* _____ .

6. Gregorio *(escuchar)* _____ .

7. Kyoko *(comprar)* _____ .

8. Este señor *(trabajar)* _____.

9. Nosotros *(llegar)* _____.

10. Yo *(sacar)* _____.

EXERCISE J

A new classmate is asking you about yourself and your friends. Answer the questions as indicated.

EXAMPLE: ¿Deseas tú mirar la televisión? *(sí)*
Sí, deseo mirar la televisión.

1. ¿Trabajas tú después de las clases? *(no)*

_____

2. ¿Visitas tú a tus parientes a menudo? *(sí)*

_____

3. ¿Sacan Uds. fotografías? *(sí)*

_____

4. ¿Baila bien Alfredo? *(no)*

_____

5. ¿Toman Uds. el autobús al centro? *(sí)*

_____

6. ¿Dan Elena y Joe un paseo por el parque? *(sí)*

_____

7. ¿Escuchas tú discos de rock? *(no)*

_____

EXERCISE K

While watching a Spanish-language TV show with some friends, José makes the following comments. Express them in Spanish.

1. I'm watching an interesting program.

_____

2. This group sings well.

_____

3. They don't dance well.

_____

4. She's wearing a horrible dress.

_____

5. This group is returning to Venezuela tomorrow.

_____

6. They travel a lot.

_____

7. He doesn't play the guitar well.

_____

8. I admire their talent.

_____

9. I listen to their music a lot.

_____

10. At what time does this program end?

_____

Chapter 2
Present Tense of -*er* and -*ir* Verbs

[1] REGULAR -*ER* VERBS

a. The present tense of regular -*er* verbs is formed by dropping the infinitive ending -*er* and adding the personal endings -*o*, -*es*, -*e*, -*emos*, -*éis*, -*en*.

b. The present tense has the following meanings in English:

usted come — *you eat, you're eating, you do eat*

ella come — *she eats, she's eating, she does eat*

comer *to eat*			
(I eat, I'm eating, I do eat)			
yo	com**o**	nosotros, -as	com**emos**
tú	com**es**	vosotros, -as	com**éis**
usted		ustedes	
él	come	ellos	com**en**
ella		ellas	

[2] COMMON -*ER* VERBS

aprender	*to learn*	esconder	*to hide* (something)
beber	*to drink*	leer	*to read*
comer	*to eat*	prometer	*to promise*
correr	*to run*	responder	*to answer*
creer	*to believe*	vender	*to sell*

EXERCISE A

Mike and a friend describe their first day at school. What do they say?

EXAMPLE: el señor Bilbao / vender libros
El señor Bilbao **vende** libros.

1. los alumnos / comer en la cafetería

Los alumnos comen en la cafetería

2. David / beber jugo

David bebe jugo

3. tú / aprender el español

Tú aprendes el español

4. Angel y yo / correr en el patio

Angel y yo corremos en la patio.

5. la maestra / leer una novela

La maestra lee una novela

6. yo / responder en la clase

yo respondo en la clase

7. ustedes / comprender la lección

ustedes comprenden la lección

8. nosotros / prometer estudiar mucho

nosotros prometemos estudiar mucho

EXERCISE B

Tell what each person is doing in the pictures below.

EXAMPLE: Guillermo **esconde la tiza.**

1. Phil *lee el libro.*

2. Shakeela y Víctor *comen la almuerza*

3. Yo _corro ahora_ .

4. Cristina _bebe el jugo de naranja_ .

5. El hombre _vende el perriodico_ .

6. Enrique y yo _estudiamos matematicos_ .

EXERCISE C

Alfredo is baby-sitting his younger brother, who asks a lot of questions. Answer his questions according to the cues provided.

EXAMPLE: ¿Quién vende helados? *(el señor Rossi)*
El señor Rossi **vende** helados.

1. ¿Quién aprende a nadar? *(Rafael)*

Rafael aprende a nadar.

Claire Alvey

2. ¿Quién comprende el japonés? *(los señores Uchida)*

Los señores Uchida comprenden el japonés.

3. ¿Quién bebe una leche batida? *(tú)*

Tou bebes una leche batida.

4. ¿Quién debe comprar unos dulces? *(mamá)*

Mama debe compra unos dulces.

5. ¿Quiénes comen en el restaurante? *(Grace y Rocío)*

Grace y Rocío comen en el restaurante

6. ¿Quién responde a todas mis preguntas? *(yo)*

Yo respondo a todas mis preguntas.

[3]   **-ER VERBS IN NEGATIVE AND INTERROGATIVE CONSTRUCTIONS**

a. A verb is made negative by placing *no* before it.

Felipe **no bebe** leche.   *Felipe doesn't drink milk.*
Yo **no leo** novelas.   *I don't read novels.*

EXERCISE D

Pedro's sister often disagrees with him. Tell what Pedro says and what his sister responds.

EXAMPLE: aprender a jugar al tenis
            PEDRO: Luis **aprende** a jugar al tenis.
            GLORIA: Luis **no aprende** a jugar al tenis.

1. leer el periódico todos los días

PEDRO: Tony _____ .

GLORIA: _____

2. vender tortillas

PEDRO: El señor Galán _____ .

GLORIA: _____

3. comer en un restaurante elegante

PEDRO: Nosotros _____ .

GLORIA: _____

4. correr en el parque

PEDRO: Gabriel y Yuri _____ .

GLORIA: _____

5. esconder el dinero

PEDRO: Mi hermano _____ .

GLORIA: _____

6. prometer ayudar en casa

PEDRO: Yo _____ .

GLORIA: _____

b. In a question (an interrogative sentence), the subject usually comes after the verb.

Felipe corre todos los días.   *Felipe runs every day.*

¿**Corre Felipe** todos los días?   *Does Felipe run every day?*

EXERCISE E

Jorge's grandfather is hard of hearing and often repeats what Jorge says in the form of a question. Tell what his grandfather asks after Jorge makes each of the statements below.

EXAMPLE: Mis amigos aprenden el japonés.
              ¿**Aprenden** el japonés **tus amigos**?

1. Mi papá promete llegar a casa temprano.

_____

2. Yo como demasiado.

_____

3. Tú comprendes mis preguntas.

_____

4. Uds. leen todos los días.

_____

5. El señor Robles vende árboles.

_____

6. Graciela no responde a mis cartas.

_____

7. Los niños beben mucha leche.

_____

8. José corre en el parque todos los días.

_____

[4] REGULAR *-IR* VERBS

a. The present tense of regular *-ir* verbs is formed by dropping the infinitive ending *-ir* and adding the personal endings *-o, -es, -e, -imos, -ís, -en*.

b. The present tense has the following meanings in English:

usted vive   *you live, you're living, you do live*

ella vive   *she lives, she's living, she does live*

vivir *to live* *(I live, I'm living, I do live)*			
yo	viv**o**	nosotros, -as	viv**imos**
tú	viv**es**	vosotros, -as	viv**ís**
usted		ustedes	
él	viv**e**	ellos	viv**en**
ella		ellas	

NOTE: The endings of *-er* and *-ir* verbs are the same in the present tense except for the *nosotros* and *vosotros* forms.

[5] COMMON *-IR* VERBS

asistir (a)   *to attend*   insistir (en)   *to insist on*

cubrir   *to cover*   partir   *to leave, depart*

decidir   *to decide*   permitir   *to permit, allow*

describir   *to describe*   recibir   *to receive*

descubrir   *to discover*   subir   *to go up, climb; to raise*

dividir   *to divide*   sufrir   *to suffer*

escribir   *to write*   vivir   *to live*

EXERCISE F

Rosita and a friend are visiting some cousins in Mexico. Tell what goes on during their visit.

EXAMPLE: sus primos / vivir en la capital
            Sus primos **viven** en la capital.

1. ellas / decidir visitar Tenochtitlán

   ellas deaden visitar Tenochtitlán

2. el autobús / partir a las nueve y media

   El autobús parti a las nueve y media

3. Rosita / insistir en visitar las pirámides

   Rosita insisti en visitar las pirámides

4. Amelia y yo / subir a las pirámides

   Amelia y yo subimos a las pirámides

5. el guardia / permitir cámaras en las pirámides

el guardia permiti cámaras en las pirámides

6. yo / descubrir muchas cosas interesantes

yo desubro muchas cosas interesantes

7. tú / escribir muchas tarjetas postales

Tú escribes muchas tarjetas postales

8. Uds. / describir la experiencia a los primos

Ustedes describen la experiencia a los primos.

EXERCISE G

Yusef tells a sick classmate about the day at school. Write what he says.

1. la maestra / dividir la clase en grupos

La maestra dividi la clase en grupos

2. yo / escribir en la pizarra

Yo esribo en la pizarra

3. nosotros / asistir a una asamblea

Nosotros asitimos a una asamblea,

4. Rogelio / decidir ser cómico en la clase

Rogelio decidi ser cómico en la clase

5. todos los alumnos / subir al laboratorio

todos los alumnos subien al laboratorio

6. tú y yo / recibir buenas notas en el examen

Tu y yo recibimos buenas notas en la examen

7. El equipo de béisbol / partir para México mañana

El equipo de béisbol partite para México mañana

[6] -IR VERBS IN NEGATIVE AND INTERROGATIVE CONSTRUCTIONS

a. A verb is made negative by placing *no* before it.

Luz **no escribe** cartas.	*Luz doesn't write letters.*
Nosotros **no cubrimos** la mesa.	*We don't cover the table.*

EXERCISE H

Gabriel meets a friend he hasn't seen since he moved away. He asks about people in his old neighborhood. Answer his questions negatively.

EXAMPLE: ¿Todavía vives en la calle Londres?
No, ya **no vivo** en la calle Londres.

1. ¿Asiste Peter a la escuela contigo?

_____

2. ¿Escriben Pola y Anita muchas poesías?

_____

3. ¿Insistes tú en jugar al béisbol los sábados?

_____

4. ¿Viven tus abuelos en Guadalajara?

_____

5. ¿Permiten tus maestros radios en la escuela?

_____

6. ¿Reciben Uds. tarjetas de Larry?

_____

b. In a statement, the subject usually comes before the verb. In a question (an interrogative sentence), the subject usually comes after the verb.

La madre divide el pastel. *The mother divides the cake.*
¿**Divide la madre** el pastel? *Does the mother divide the cake?*

Tú sufres mucho. *You suffer a lot.*
¿**Sufres tú** mucho? *Do you suffer a lot?*

EXERCISE I

Kim never remembers the questions her friends ask. Write the question asked based on the answer given.

EXAMPLE: Clara y yo asistimos a la misma universidad.
¿Asisten Clara y tú a la misma universidad?

1. Nosotros vivimos en un apartamento.

_____

2. Sanjeetah insiste en alquilar un apartamento.

_____

3. Yo divido los gastos con ella.

_____

4. Nuestras amigas no suben al apartamento por la escalera.

_____

5. Yo parto en autobús el sábado por la mañana.

_____

MASTERY EXERCISES

EXERCISE J

While waiting in line with a friend to buy tickets for a concert, Marisol's conversation jumps from one topic to another. Complete her statements with the appropriate form of the verbs given.

1. *(vivir)* Mi amigo Tomás _____ en el campo. Nosotras_____ en

una ciudad grande. ¿Dónde_____ tus primos?

2. *(comprender)* Este señor no _____ el español. Tú y yo_____ el

español y el italiano. ¿Qué lengua_____ ellas?

3. *(responder)* ¿ _____ tú bien? Sí, yo siempre_____ bien. Alberto

no _____ en voz alta.

4. *(asistir)* Carlos no _____ a los conciertos. Tú _____ a los

conciertos. ¿ _____ tus hermanas también?

5. *(leer)* Mi madre _____ el periódico en casa. Yo no _____ el

periódico en la escuela. ¿ _____ tú el periódico los domingos?

6. *(recibir)* ¿ _____ tú muchos regalos? Pedro y Alfredo no

_____ regalos. Yo _____ regalos en mi cumpleaños.

EXERCISE K

A new exchange student at your school is asking you questions about yourself, your friends, and the school. Answer the questions as indicated.

EXAMPLE: ¿Comen Uds. en la cafetería? *(sí)*
Sí, **nosotros comemos** en la cafetería.

1. ¿Aprendes tú mucho en tus clases? *(sí)*

_____

2. ¿Sufren de alergias Uds.? *(sí)*

_____

3. ¿Recibes tú buenas notas? *(sí)*

_____

4. ¿Venden comida española en la cafetería? *(no)*

_____

5. ¿Beben tus amigos café con leche? *(no)*

_____

6. ¿Permite el maestro dulces en la clase? *(no)*

_____

7. ¿Corren Uds. en el parque después de las clases? *(sí)*

_____

8. ¿Parte el autobús a las cuatro? *(no)*

_____

EXERCISE L

You are describing a new friend to your parents. Express the following sentences in Spanish.

1. Pedro lives on Fourth Street.

_____

2. He attends my school.

_____

3. He's learning English while I'm learning Spanish.

_____

4. In school, Pedro writes everything in Spanish first.

_____

5. His parents insist on speaking Spanish at home.

_____

6. He responds in English.

_____

7. They don't understand English well.

_____

8. Pedro and I read the Spanish newspaper together.

_____

9. Pedro decides to do gymnastics.

_____

10. I'm discovering many new things.

_____

[1] REGULAR STEM-CHANGING VERBS (*O* TO *UE*)

a. Many verbs that contain *o* in the stem change the *o* to *ue* in the present tense, except in the forms for *nosotros* and *vosotros*.

b. This change occurs in the syllable directly before the verb ending.

c. These verbs have regular endings in the present tense.

	mostrar *to show*	**volver** *to return*	**dormir** *to sleep*
yo	m**ue**stro	v**ue**lvo	d**ue**rmo
tú	m**ue**stras	v**ue**lves	d**ue**rmes
Ud., él, ella	m**ue**stra	v**ue**lve	d**ue**rme
nosotros, -as	mostramos	volvemos	dormimos
vosotros, -as	mostráis	volvéis	dormís
Uds., ellos, ellas	m**ue**stran	v**ue**lven	d**ue**rmen

NOTE:

1. All stem-changing verbs that change *o* to *ue* are identified in the end vocabulary by (*ue*) after the verb.

2. The verb jugar (to play) follows the same pattern in that the stem vowel changes in all present-tense forms except those for *nosotros* and *vosotros*: *juego, juegas, juega, jugamos, jugáis, juegan.*

[2] COMMON STEM-CHANGING VERBS (*O* TO *UE*)

almorzar *to eat lunch*

contar *to count*

costar *to cost*

devolver *to return, give back*

dormir *to sleep*

encontrar *to find; to meet*

morir *to die*

mostrar *to show*

poder *to be able; can, may*

recordar *to remember*

resolver *to solve; to resolve*

sonar *to sound; to ring*

volar *to fly*

volver *to return, come (go) back*

EXERCISE A *w/ English*

You're working at the returns desk of a department store. Tell what items various people return. Use the verb *devolver* in each statement.

EXAMPLE: yo / los libros de mis amigos
Yo **devuelvo** los libros de mis amigos.

My mother returns the new dress.

1. mi madre / el vestido nuevo

Mi madre devuelve el vestido nuevo.

2. Dolores / el regalo

Dolores returns the gift.

Dolores devuelve el regalo.

3. los niños / los juguetes

The boys return the toy.

Los niños devuelven los juguetes

4. tú / una cámara

You return the camera

Tú devuelves una cámara.

5. Ana y José / los discos de María

Ana and José return María's disks

Ana y José devuelven los discos de María.

6. Uds. / la cinta

You all return the tape.

Ustedes devuelven la cinta

EXERCISE B

Tell what each of these people counts.

EXAMPLE: el profesor / los exámenes
           El profesor **cuenta** los exámenes.

1. los alumnos / los minutos

The students count the minutes.

Los alumnos cuentan los minutos.

2. Sarita / sus blusas

Sarita counts the blouses

Sarita cuenta sus blusas.

3. el niño / de uno a cinco

The boy counts ~~from~~ from one to five

El niño cuenta de uno a cinco.

4. yo / los días

I count the days

Yo cuento los días.

5. el señor Chomsky / su dinero

Mr. Chomsky counts his money.

El señor Chomsky cuenta su dinero

6. tú / hasta mil

You count up to one thousand.

Tú cuentas hasta mil.

7. Luigi y yo / los libros

Luigi and I count the books.

Luigi y yo contamos los libros.

EXERCISE C

Tell what each of these people does.

EXAMPLE: el niño / contar de uno a diez
           El niño **cuenta** de uno a diez.

The students count to have lunch in the cafeteria
1. los alumnos / almorzar en la cafetería
Los alumnos cuentan almorzar en la cafetería

the math counts to solve the problem
2. el matemático / resolver el problema
El matemático cuenta resolver el problema.

I tell my friends to meet in the park
3. yo / encontrar a mis amigos en el parque
Yo cuento encontrar a mis amigos en la parque

We count to return to the store
4. nosotros / volver a la tienda
Nosotros contamos volver a la tienda

Elsa plays in the park.
5. Elsa / jugar en el parque
Elsa cuenta juga en el parque

You return the books to the library.
6. tú / devolver los libros a la biblioteca
Tú cuentas devuelves los libros a la biblioteca

My brother sleeps twelve hours.
7. mi hermano / dormir doce horas
Mi hermano duerme dormi doce horas.

My mother is able to speak two languges
8. mi mamá / poder hablar dos lenguas
Mi mamá puede hablar dos lenguas.

The clock rings at six in the morning.
9. el despertador / sonar a las siete de la mañana
El despertador cuenta sonar a las siete de la mañana.

The tourists fly in the plane to Madrid.
10. los turistas / volar en avión a Madrid
Los turistas volar en avión a Madrid

EXERCISE D

Some of your friends are excited about going on a youth trip to Spain. Write what each one says.

EXAMPLE: yo / no poder esperar más
Yo **no puedo** esperar más.

1. Gloria y Lourdes / contar los días

_____

2. nosotros / volar el sábado

_____

3. Clara / resolver hablar solamente en español

_____

[handwritten: I know that ~~what~~ I should study more. I don't watch tv programs]

Yo ___*sé*___ que debo estudiar más. Yo no ___*veo*___ programas de
  1. (saber)   2. (ver)

[handwritten: during the week. When I arrive at school I put my books in]

televisión durante la semana. Cuando llego de la escuela, yo ___*pongo*___ mis libros en el
  3. (poner)

[handwritten: my locker and do my homework. I don't go out with friends for late.]

escritorio y ___*hago*___ la tarea. Yo no ___*salgo*___ con mis amigos por las tardes.
  4. (hacer)   5. (salir)

EXERCISE C

María is having a terrible day. Everything around her is falling. Describe what's happening.

EXAMPLE: la botella de leche / al suelo
          La botella de leche **cae** al suelo.

1. las monedas / detrás del escritorio
   Las monedas detras caen del escritorio.

2. el niño / en el jardín   *[handwritten: The boy falls in the garden]*
   El niño cae en el jardín.

3. yo / en el sillón   *[handwritten: I fall in the chair]*
   Yo caigo en el sillón

4. la cuchara / al suelo
   La cuchar cae al suelo

5. Carmen y yo / en el patio   *[handwritten: Carmen and I fall on the patio.]*
   Carmen y yo caemos en el patio

6. tú / en la calle   *[handwritten: You fall in the street]*
   Tú caes en la calle.

EXERCISE D

Jorge is organizing a picnic at the beach. What do his friends bring to the picnic?

EXAMPLE: Mario / los refrescos
          Mario **trae** los refrescos.

1. Gilberto / los platos   *[handwritten: Gilbert takes the plates.]*
   Gilberto trae los platos

2. Susan y yo / los sándwiches   *[handwritten: Susan and I take the sandwiches.]*
   Susan y yo traemos los sandviches.

3. Virginia / los vasos
   Virginia trae lo vasos
   Virginia brings the glasses

You take the cake.

4. tú / el pastel

Tú traes el pastel

5. Vicente y Gerardo / el estéreo

Vincenta y Gerado brings the stereo

Vicente y Gerardo traen el estéreo.

6. yo / las palomitas

I bring the popcorn

Yo traigo las palomitas.

[2] IRREGULAR PRESENT-TENSE FORMS

The verbs *oír, decir, tener,* and *venir* are irregular in the present tense.

oír	*to listen*	**oigo, oyes, oye, oímos, oís, oyen**
decir	*to say*	**digo, dices, dice, decimos, decís, dicen**
tener	*to have*	**tengo, tienes, tiene, tenemos, tenéis, tienen**
venir	*to come*	**vengo, vienes, viene, venimos, venís, vienen**

EXERCISE E

Several friends are discussing the types of music they listen to. Tell what they say.

EXAMPLE: Roberto / la música clásica
   Roberto **oye** la música clásica.

1. Yusef y Luis / la música rock

_____

2. yo / la música de jazz

_____

3. mi padre / la música clásica

_____

4. tú / la música de guitarra

_____

5. Alicia y yo / las sinfonías

_____

6. Josefina / la música romántica

_____

EXERCISE F

Tomás is helping his younger sister master the rules of etiquette. Tell what she says in each situation Tomás presents to her.

EXAMPLE: Tú quieres otro pedazo de pastel. *(por favor)*
Yo **digo** «por favor».

1. Juan recibe muchos regalos. *(gracias)*

   Él _____ .

2. Nosotros saludamos al maestro. *(buenos días)*

   Nosotros _____ .

3. Tú conoces a un amigo de tus padres. *(mucho gusto)*

   Yo _____ .

4. Elena sale de su casa. *(adiós)*

   Ella _____ .

5. Los niños pasan delante de una persona. *(con permiso)*

   Ellos _____ .

6. Tú entras en la casa. *(hola)*

   Yo _____ .

EXERCISE G

Some young people are talking about what they and their friends have to do on Saturday. Using the expression *tener que* (to have to), write what they say.

EXAMPLE: Isabel / ir al supermercado
Isabel **tiene que** ir al supermercado.

1. yo / arreglar mi cuarto

   _____

2. Pablo / trabajar

   _____

3. Ramona y yo / devolver los libros a la biblioteca

   _____

4. tú / ayudar en casa

   _____

5. Lorenzo y Esteban / ir a un partido de fútbol

   _____

EXERCISE H

Tell at what time these people come home.

EXAMPLE: Rosa / 4:00
             Rosa **viene a casa** a las cuatro.

1. yo / 5:30

_____

2. mis padres / 6:00

_____

3. tú / 12:00

_____

4. Laura y yo / 9:15

_____

5. Antonio / 11:00

_____

EXERCISE I

Answer the following personal questions.

1. ¿Qué oyes tú en la radio por la mañana? *(las noticias)*

_____

2. ¿Qué dices cuando tus amigos vuelven a sus casas? *(hasta luego)*

_____

3. ¿Qué tienes que hacer después de las clases? *(estudiar)*

_____

4. ¿A qué hora vienes a casa todos los días? *(4:30)*

_____

5. ¿Quién tiene que preparar la comida en tu casa? *(mi mamá)*

_____

6. ¿Quién tiene que lavar los platos cada noche? *(mi hermana y yo)*

_____

7. ¿Quién oye el pronóstico del tiempo en tu casa? *(mi papá)*

_____

[3] IRREGULAR VERBS *DAR* AND *IR*

		dar *to give*	**ir** *to go*
yo		doy	voy
tú		das	vas
Ud., él, ella		da	va
nosotros, -as		damos	vamos
vosotros, -as		dais	vais
Uds., ellos, ellas		dan	van

NOTE: A conjugated form of the verb *ir* followed by the preposition *a* and an infinitive is used to express a future action.

Voy a estudiar.   *I am going to study.*

¿Qué vas a hacer?   *What are you going to do?*

[4] IRREGULAR VERBS *SER* AND *ESTAR*

		ser *to be*	**estar** *to be*
yo		soy	estoy
tú		eres	estás
Ud., él, ella		es	está
nosotros, -as		somos	estamos
vosotros, -as		sois	estáis
Uds., ellos, ellas		son	están

EXERCISE J

Tell where each member of your family goes every day.

EXAMPLE: mi padre / a la oficina
            Mi padre **va** a la oficina.

1. mis hermanos / a la universidad

_____

2. mi hermana / a la escuela de enseñanza secundaria

_____

3. mamá / al supermercado

_____

4. yo / a la biblioteca

_____

5. el abuelo y yo / al parque

_____

EXERCISE K

What do each of these people give?

EXAMPLE: Carlos / dinero a los pobres
            Carlos **da** dinero a los pobres.

1. yo / regalos a mis amigos

_____

2. Phil y Juan / problemas a sus padres

_____

3. tú / flores a tu mamá

_____

4. el señor Díaz / dulces a su esposa

_____

5. Carmen y yo / pan a los pájaros

_____

6. el profesor / mucha tarea

_____

EXERCISE L

Gloria and her friends are discussing the nationality of people they know. Write what they say about each person.

EXAMPLE: Lourdes / España
            Lourdes **es** de España.

1. el profesor de español / Colombia

_____

2. mis primas / Venezuela

_____

3. Raquel / Costa Rica

_____

4. Gladys / Honduras

_____

5. Murray y yo / los Estados Unidos

_____

6. tú / Puerto Rico

_____

7. yo / Perú

_____

8. ustedes / Panamá

_____

EXERCISE M

When Mr. Lara calls home, only Tomás is there. Tell where everyone else is.

EXAMPLE: Mamá **está en el supermercado.**

1. Gilberto _____.

2. Bernardo y Felipe _____.

3. Yolanda _____.

4. Tú _____ .

5. Los abuelos _____ .

6. El perro _____ .

EXERCISE N

Complete this note that Ramón left for his parents by filling in the missing verbs. Use an appropriate form of *dar, ir, ser,* or *estar*.

Queridos padres:

Yo _____ a casa de mi amigo Marcos. Él _____ de México.
       1.   *2.*

Nosotros _____ a jugar al tenis. Yo _____ a estar en el parque que
            3.   *4.*

_____ cerca de la escuela. Yo _____ de comer a Fido después.
    5.   *6.*

Marcos _____ a cenar con nosotros porque sus padres _____
          7.   *8.*

en el centro. Hasta luego.

Ramón

EXERCISE O

Answer the questions that your inquisitive grandmother asks you when some friends come to visit. Use in your responses the cues in parentheses.

1. ¿Quiénes son estos jóvenes? *(mis amigos)*

_____

2. ¿Qué das a tus amigos? *(palomitas)*

_____

3. ¿Dónde está tu hermana? *(en su dormitorio)*

_____

4. ¿Qué van a hacer Uds. ahora? *(jugar a las damas)*

_____

5. ¿De dónde es ese chico? *(Argentina)*

_____

6. ¿Adónde vas tú esta noche? *(al cine)*

_____

MASTERY EXERCISES

EXERCISE P

Ricardo describes his neighbors to a friend. Fill in the appropriate form of the missing verbs.

Todos los días yo _____ a mi vecino, el señor Robles, cuando mi hermana y yo
  1. (ver)

_____ a la escuela. Él _____ en la calle con su perro Campeón.
  2. (ir)   *3.* (estar)

Campeón _____ muy fuerte y el señor Robles _____ al suelo a
  4. (ser)   *5.* (caer)

menudo. Nosotros _____ «Buenos días». Cuando yo _____ de la
  6. (decir)   *7.* (venir)

escuela yo _____ los ladridos de Campeón que _____ en el jardín.
  8. (oír)   *9.* (estar)

Campeón y yo _____ buenos amigos y a veces yo _____ que cuidarlo
  10. (ser)   *11.* (tener)

cuando los señores Robles no _____ en casa. Los Robles _____
  12. (estar)   *13.* (ser)

buenos vecinos y muchas veces Campeón _____ regalos a nuestra casa. Cuando mi
  14. (traer)

mamá _____ esto, mi hermana y yo _____ que devolver los regalos
  15. (ver)   *16.* (tener)

de Campeón.

EXERCISE Q

A classmate is conducting a survey to find out if people think alike. For each situation select the appropriate reaction from those given and write it, using the appropriate verb form in the space provided.

caer en la misma fecha	decir «Buenos días»	traer mi estéreo
dar la cuenta al cliente	ir a la fiesta	ver el programa
dar un regalo a mi hermana	oír las noticias en la radio	

1. Tú trabajas de mesero en un restaurante.

Yo _____ .

2. Hay una fiesta en casa de tu amigo Ricardo.

Yo _____ .

3. Tú y tu hermano encuentran a un vecino en la calle.

Nosotros _____ .

4. El tocadiscos de Ricardo no funciona.

Yo _____ .

5. Tú y un amigo celebran sus cumpleaños el 2 de enero.

Nuestros cumpleaños _____ .

6. Hay un programa bueno en la televisión.

Yo _____ .

7. Es el cumpleaños de tu hermana.

Yo _____ .

8. Estás en el auto y quieres saber qué pasa actualmente.

Yo _____ .

EXERCISE R

Answer these questions that a cousin asks you about school.

1. ¿A quién ves en la escuela todos los días?

_____

2. ¿Oyes las respuestas de los otros alumnos?

_____

3. ¿Traes tus libros a casa cada día?

_____

4. ¿Tienes mucha tarea por lo general?

_____

5. ¿De dónde es tu profesor de español?

_____

6. ¿Vienen Uds. a casa después de las clases?

_____

7. ¿Qué dice el maestro cuando contestas bien?

_____

8. ¿Caen muchos exámenes en el mismo día?

_____

9. ¿Vas al estadio para ver los partidos?

_____

10. ¿Estás en tus clases a tiempo?

_____

11. ¿Dan tus maestros notas altas?

_____

EXERCISE S

Express in Spanish what the teacher tells the students on the first day of classes.

1. I'm never absent.

_____

2. You *(pl.)* come to class on time.

_____

3. I see everything, and I hear everything.

_____

4. You *(pl.)* bring your books to class every day.

_____

5. The books don't fall to the floor.

_____

6. We're going to work a lot in this class.

_____

7. Every student is important.

_____

8. You _(pl.)_ always tell the truth when you don't have the assignment.

_____

9. I give many tests.

_____

10. You _(pl.)_ are going to learn a great deal in this class.

_____

Chapter 7
Verbs with Spelling Changes in the Present Tense

[1] VERBS ENDING IN -CER AND -CIR

a. Most verbs whose infinitives end in *-cer* or *-cir* have the ending *-zco* in the first-person singular of the present tense. This pattern occurs only if a vowel precedes the *c* in the infinitive.

	ofrecer *to offer*	**conducir** *to drive*
yo	ofrez**co**	conduz**co**
tú	ofreces	conduces
Ud., él, ella	ofrece	conduce
nosotros, -as	ofrecemos	conducimos
vosotros, -as	ofrecéis	conducís
Uds., ellos, ellas	ofrecen	conducen

b. Common *-cer* verbs

aparecer *to appear*   ofrecer *to offer*

conocer *to know; to meet*   parecer *to seem*

desaparecer *to disappear*   reconocer *to recognize*

obedecer *to obey*

c. Common *-cir* verbs

conducir *to drive; to lead*   traducir *to translate*

producir *to produce*

NOTE: The verbs *hacer* and *decir* are exceptions. (See Chapter 6.)

EXERCISE A

In an orientation session on community service, the students in your global studies class offer to perform service in various settings.

EXAMPLE: Gerardo / en el hospital
             Gerardo **ofrece servicio** en el hospital.

1. Rosita / en la escuela de párvulos

_____

2. yo / en la oficina de un veterinario

_____

3. Clara y Luz / en la biblioteca

_____

4. tú / en la corte

_____

5. Rogelio y yo / en la jefatura de la policía

_____

6. Elena / en la enfermería

_____

EXERCISE B

Gloria found in the attic an old box with a variety of documents written in English. You and other friends offer to help her translate them. Tell what each one translates.

EXAMPLE: Victoria / las cartas
Victoria **traduce** las cartas.

1. Ana y yo / los poemas

_____

2. Mariah / la canción

_____

3. yo / el artículo del periódico

_____

4. Kim y Adriana / las tarjetas

_____

5. tú / este párrafo corto

_____

EXERCISE C

Hugo is spending the summer on a farm. He quotes some of the farmer's comments in a letter to you. Fill in the missing verbs.

El sol _____ con el gallo pero _____ cuando hace mal tiempo. Yo
    1. (aparecer)   2. (desaparecer)

no _____ otra vida que la vida del campo. ¿ _____ tú esos animales?
    3. (conocer)   4. (reconocer)

Los caballos siempre _____ a los campesinos. ¿Y esas flores? _____
                5. (obedecer)   6. (parecer)

muy bonitas, ¿verdad? Nosotros _____ toda la comida que comemos en esta granja.
                        7. (producir)

Además, los viernes yo _____ mi camión a un mercado en el pueblo. Muchos turistas
                    8. (conducir)

visitan ese pueblo y _____ que vienen solamente para comprar las legumbres. Dicen que
                              9. (parecer)

nosotros _____ legumbres a precios bajos. ¿ _____ tú una vida mejor?
              10. (ofrecer)   11. (conocer)

EXERCISE D

Answer the questions your younger brother asks you as you walk on the beach at night. In your answers, use the cues in parentheses.

1. ¿Dónde aparece el sol? *(en el este)*

_____

2. ¿Cuándo desaparece la luna esta semana? *(por la mañana)*

_____

3. ¿Cómo parecen las estrellas? *(muy pequeñas)*

_____

4. ¿Reconoces esa estrella? *(no)*

_____

5. ¿Dónde ofrecen cursos sobre las estrellas? *(en la escuela)*

_____

6. ¿Conoces tú mucho del universo? *(un poco)*

_____

[2] *SABER* AND *CONOCER*

a. The verbs *saber* and *conocer* both mean "to know." All of the present-tense forms of these two verbs are regular except the *yo* form.

saber   *sé, sabes, sabe, sabemos, sabéis, saben*

conocer   *conozco, conoces, conoce, conocemos, conocéis, conocen*

b. *Saber* means "to know a fact, to have information about something, to know how to do something." *Saber* can be followed by a noun, a clause, or an infinitive.

Yo sé tu nombre.	*I know your name.*
María sabe dónde vivo.	*María knows where I live.*
Ellos no saben esquiar.	*They don't know how to ski.*

c. *Conocer* means "to know personally, to be acquainted with, to be familiar with." *Conocer* can be followed by names of people, places, or things.

Conozco a Juan y María.	*I know Juan and María.*
Ella conoce Bogotá.	*She knows Bogotá.*
Él conoce un restaurante bueno.	*He's familiar with a good restaurant.*

d. Note the difference in meaning between the following sentences:

Él **sabe** el nombre del alcalde.   *He knows the mayor's name.*

Él **conoce** al alcalde.   *He knows the mayor.*

EXERCISE E

Mr. Moreno is proud of his family's many talents. Based on the drawings below, tell what he says they know how to do.

EXAMPLE: Alberto **sabe tocar el violín.**

1. Mi esposa y yo _____.

2. Xavier _____.

3. Mónica y Beatriz _____.

4. Mis padres _____ .

5. Yo _____ .

EXERCISE F

Margarita has just moved to your city. She tells you the things with which she and her family are already acquainted.

EXAMPLE: mi mamá / el supermercado
            Mi mamá **ya conoce** el supermercado.

1. yo / el parque

_____

2. mis hermanos / el cine

_____

3. mi papá / a tu papá

_____

4. mi hermana y yo / todas las tiendas

_____

5. el perro / a nuestros vecinos

_____

6. mi familia / a toda tu familia

_____

EXERCISE G

As a party game, Dolores has prepared slips of paper with cues and the names of party guests. Whoever picks the slip must ask a question using *conocer* or *saber,* and the person(s) called upon must respond.

EXAMPLE: Rafael / jugar al boliche
Rafael, ¿**sabes tú** jugar al boliche?
Sí, **sé** jugar al boliche pero no muy bien.

1. Silvia y César / bailar el tango

_____

_____

2. Estela / el Parque Nacional

_____

_____

3. Isaac y Pedro / cocinar

_____

_____

4. Erika y Elena / la música del grupo «Los Amigos»

_____

_____

5. Ching / el presidente del país

_____

_____

6. Mirta / el número de teléfono de César

_____

_____

EXERCISE H

Pilar and her friend Rocío plan a shopping trip. Complete the dialogue below with the appropriate forms of *saber* or *conocer.*

ROCÍO: Yo ya _____ lo que quieres hacer hoy. Ir de compras, ¿verdad?
_1._

PILAR: Sí, tienes razón. Tú me _____ muy bien. ¿Vienes conmigo?
_2._

ROCÍO: ¡Cómo no!

PILAR: Yo _____ una tienda que acaba de abrir en el centro. Tienen ropa bonita.
                                3.

ROCÍO: ¿ _____ si es cara? No tengo mucho dinero.
              4.

PILAR: Yo no _____ pero vamos. Mi mamá _____ la dirección
                  5.   *6.*

de la tienda. También ella _____ a una señora que trabaja ahí. Si la tienda es
                                    7.

cara, solamente vamos a ver los diseños. Mi mamá y yo _____ coser.
                                                              8.

ROCÍO: Bueno, vamos. Quiero _____ la tienda.
                                    9.

EXERCISE I

You're visiting a school while you are in Madrid. Answer the questions the students ask you.

1. ¿Conoces la ciudad de Madrid?

_____

2. ¿Sabes conducir?

_____

3. ¿Conoces a otros chicos españoles?

_____

4. ¿Sabes tocar la guitarra?

_____

5. ¿Conoces la música española?

_____

6. ¿Sabes el nombre de un cantante español?

_____

7. ¿Conoces la comida española?

_____

8. ¿Sabes preparar un plato español?

_____

9. ¿Sabes cómo se llama el Rey de España?

_____

10. ¿Conoces la historia de España?

_____

M A S T E R Y   E X E R C I S E S

EXERCISE J

Raúl and Jaime talk about a concert. Fill in the missing verbs to complete the dialogue.

RAÚL: ¿ _____ tú que hay un concierto en el parque esta noche?
              1. (saber)

JAIME: Sí, lo _____ . _____ que todo el mundo va a asistir.
                    2. (saber)   *3. (parecer)*

RAÚL: ¿Qué grupos van a cantar y tocar?

JAIME: Yo _____ el nombre de uno de los grupos que anuncian, «The Zeros».
                4. (reconocer)

        ¿ _____ tú su música?
              5. (conocer)

RAÚL: Sí, yo _____ su música y me gusta mucho, pero cantan en inglés.
                  6. (conocer)

        Ellos _____ muchos discos.
                    7. (producir)

JAIME: ¿En inglés? Yo no _____ inglés. Si vamos al concierto,
                              8. (saber)

        ¿ _____ tú las canciones al español?
              9. (traducir)

RAÚL: Claro, pero hay un problema. Tengo que estar en casa a las once. Si yo no

        _____ a mis padres, no voy a poder salir por un mes. Tú ya
              10. (obedecer)

        _____ a mis padres.
              11. (conocer)

JAIME: ¿De veras? ¿Dices que si tú no les _____ , tú _____ de
                                              12. (obedecer)   *13. (desaparecer)*

        nuestra vida social?

RAÚL: Bueno. Yo pido permiso a mis padres, y si yo no _____ , vas solo.
                                                              14. (aparecer)

JAIME: Está bien.

EXERCISE K

As an exchange student in Caracas, you're being interviewed for the school newspaper. Answer the reporter's questions.

1. ¿Ya conoces bien la ciudad de Caracas?

_____

2. ¿Qué lugares conoces?

_____

3. ¿Qué deportes sabes jugar?

_____

4. ¿Qué clase de auto conduces?

_____

5. ¿Obedeces a los maestros venezolanos?

_____

6. ¿Sabes cuándo aparece esta entrevista en el periódico?

_____

7. ¿Qué comentario ofreces a los estudiantes venezolanos?

_____

8. ¿Qué proyecto produces durante este año?

_____

EXERCISE L

Your friend is writing to her Spanish pen pal about the summer camp you're both attending. Help her express the sentences in Spanish.

1. The days seem long here.

_____

2. I still don't know many of the boys.

_____

3. I know where the cafeteria and the pool are.

_____

4. Many boys don't obey the camp's rules.

_____

5. The counselor appears and disappears without making noise.

_____

6. I still don't know his name.

_____

7. We're producing a short skit.

_____

8. The camp offers many activities.

_____

9. We disappear when the counselor isn't here.

_____

10. I know how to play tennis better.

_____

Chapter 8
Ser and *Estar*

Spanish has two different verbs, *ser* and *estar,* that both correspond to the English verb "to be." Which one you should use depends on the context.

[1] USES OF *SER*

Ser is used:

a. to express a characteristic, a description, or an identification.

   (1) Characteristics

La sopa **es buena.**	*The soup is good.*
El profesor **es estricto.**	*The teacher is strict.*

   (2) Description

Martha **es alta.**	*Martha is tall.*
El señor Salas **es rico.**	*Mr. Salas is rich.*

   (3) Identification

¿Quién **es?**	*Who is it?*
Soy yo.	*It's me.*

b. to express occupation or nationality.

   (1) Occupation

Mi primo **es abogado.**	*My cousin is a lawyer.*
Ellos **son contadores.**	*They are accountants.*

   (2) Nationality

Pedro y Elenita **son españoles.**	*Pedro and Elenita are Spanish.*
Victoria **es peruana.**	*Victoria is Peruvian.*

c. to express time and dates.

   (1) Time

Son las dos.	*It's two o'clock.*
Es medianoche.	*It's midnight.*

   (2) Dates

Es el tres de mayo.	*It's May 3.*
Es el primero de abril.	*It's April 1.*

d. with *de,* to express origin, possession, or material.

   (1) Origin

El muchacho **es de México.**	*The boy is from Mexico.*
Las naranjas **son de Valencia.**	*The oranges are from Valencia.*

(2) **Possession**

Ese reloj **es de** Carmen.	*That watch is Carmen's.*
La casa **es de** mi tío.	*The house is my uncle's.*

(3) **Material**

La blusa **es de** seda.	*The blouse is made of silk.*
El reloj **es de** oro.	*The watch is made of gold.*

NOTE:

1. Adjectives used with *ser* must agree with the subject in number and gender.

Miguel y Adalberto **son mexicanos.**	*Miguel and Adalberto are Mexican.*
Tía Clara **es puertorriqueña** también.	*Aunt Clara is Puerto Rican too.*

2. In questions, the adjective usually follows the verb.

¿**Son viejos** los edificios?	*Are the buildings old?*

3. The adjective *feliz* is generally used with *ser.*

Ella **es feliz.**	*She is happy.*

4. The forms of *ser* are summarized in the section on irregular verbs in the Appendix, page 454.

EXERCISE A

After a party at your home, your mother asks you about the friends who attended. Tell her about them using the correct forms of *ser* and the suggested adjectives below.

aburrido	bonito	guapo	responsable
amable	celoso	independiente	simpático
antipático	divertido	inteligente	tacaño

EXAMPLE: Adela es **amable y divertida.**

1. Stephen _Stephen es intelliente, responsible._

2. Alicia y Sofía _Alicia y sofia son intelijente y responsible_

3. Gerardo y Raúl _Gerardo y Raul son inteligente y responsible_

4. Diana _Diana es divertida._

5. Hank _Hanke es bonita_

6. Marcos y Elsa _Marco y Elsa sympatico_

EXERCISE B

After introducing himself and some friends, Lorenzo tells their nationalities. Using the appropriate form of *ser,* tell what Lorenzo says.

EXAMPLE: Raquel / Chile
Raquel **es de** Chile. Ella **es chilena.**

1. yo / México

I am from Mexico

Yo es de Mexico

2. Beatriz / Argentina

Beatriz is from Argentina

Beatriz es de Argentina

3. Homero y Hugo / España

Homero and Hugo are from ~~Spain~~ Spain

Homero y Hugo son España

4. Gloria / Colombia

Gloria is from Colombia

Gloria es de Colombia

5. Inés y yo / México

Ines and I are from Mexico

Ines y yo son de Mexico

6. tú (Juan) / Puerto Rico

You are from Puerto Rico

Tú des de Puerto Rico

7. ellas / Perú

They are from Peru.

Ellas son de Peru

EXERCISE C

You are helping a teacher clean out the school's lost and found at the end of the year. You identify the owners of many of the lost objects.

EXAMPLE: el suéter / Belinda
             El suéter **es de** Belinda

1. los anteojos / Enrique

_____

2. el reloj / Berta

_____

3. las llaves / la señora Pérez

_____

4. el diccionario / Roberto

_____

5. los guantes de béisbol / Arturo y Víctor

_____

6. las fotos / Pilar

_____

EXERCISE D

Every student was asked to bring in an object or a picture of an object from another country.
Write the question and the answer for each item listed.

EXAMPLE: estas monedas / Rusia
¿**De dónde son** estas monedas?
Son de Rusia.

6:10

1. estas castañuelas / España

¿De dónde son estas castañuelas

Son de España

2. estas maracas / Puerto Rico

3. esta cámara / Japón

4. estas galletas / Inglaterra

5. esta tortilla / México

EXERCISE E

Enrique goes to a watch repair shop. All the watches there show a different time. Tell what time
it is on each clock.

EXAMPLE: **Son las cuatro y once.**

6:10

1. Son las seis y diez

2. Son las ocho y veinte y siete

3. Son las tres y treinta
   Son las tres y media

4:40

4. Son las cuatro y cuarenta
   Son las cinco menos veinte

5. Son las diez y cincuenta y tres
   Son las once menos siete

12

6. Es la medianoche
   Son las doce

6:00

7. Es la una

12:45
Es las unos menos cuarto
Es la uno menos quince

8. Son las doce y cuarenta y cinco

9. Son las dos y doce

9:00

10. Son las nueve

Son las once menos
veinte y cuatro

11. Son las diez y treinta y
    ses

12. Son las siete y diez y ses

EXERCISE F

Answer your new friend's questions.

1. ¿Quién es Ud.?

   _____

2. ¿De dónde es Ud.?

   _____

3. ¿Cuál es su nacionalidad?

_____

4. ¿Cómo es Ud.?

_____

5. ¿De qué color es su casa?

_____

6. ¿De qué material es su casa?

_____

7. ¿Es Ud. un(a) alumno(a) diligente?

_____

8. ¿Cómo son sus hermanos?

_____

9. ¿Qué es su padre?

_____

10. ¿Cómo son sus amigos?

_____

11. ¿Quién es su mejor amigo(a)?

_____

12. ¿De quién es esta cámara?

_____

13. ¿Qué día es hoy?

_____

14. ¿Cuál es la fecha de hoy?

_____

15. ¿Qué hora es?

_____

EXERCISE G

Complete this letter that Carmen received from a new pen pal, using the appropriate forms of the verb _ser_.

Querida Carmen:

Yo _____ Amelia Mariscal. _____ de un pueblo cerca de Buenos
　　　　　1.　　　　　　　　　　　　　　2.

Aires. _____ argentina. Mi padre _____ ingeniero. Nuestra
　　　　　3.　　　　　　　　　　　　　　　　　　　4.

casa _____ muy bonita. _____ nueva y _____
　　　　5.　　　　　　　　　　　　　6.　　　　　　　　　　　　7.

de ladrillo. Mi dormitorio _____ muy grande porque yo _____ la
　　　　　　　　　　　　　　8.　　　　　　　　　　　　　　　　9.

hija mayor de la familia. _____ de color rosado y _____ muy
　　　　　　　　　　　　　10.　　　　　　　　　　　　　　11.

lindo. Los dormitorios de mis hermanos (tengo tres) _____ más pequeños.
　　　　　　　　　　　　　　　　　　　　　　　　12.

La comida argentina _____ muy sabrosa. Comemos mucha carne. Yo sé cocinar y a
　　　　　　　　　　13.

veces yo _____ la cocinera y mis hermanos _____ los meseros.
　　　　14.　　　　　　　　　　　　　　　　　　　15.

_____ muy cómico cuando hacemos esto. Yo creo que mis hermanos
　　16.

_____ guapos. También ellos _____ fuertes y
　　17.　　　　　　　　　　　　　　18.

_____ buenos futbolistas. Ya sabes que en mi país nosotros _____
　　19.　　　　　　　　　　　　　　　　　　　　　　　　　　　　20.

aficionados al fútbol. Mis hermanos _____ miembros de un equipo y juegan bien.
　　　　　　　　　　　　　　　　21.

Ya _____ las cinco de la tarde y _____ la hora de mi clase de baile.
　　22.　　　　　　　　　　　　　　23.

Escríbeme pronto y cuéntame cómo tú _____ y cuáles _____ tus
　　　　　　　　　　　　　　　　　24.　　　　　　　　　　25.

pasatiempos favoritos. Hasta pronto.

　　　　　　　　　　　　　　　　　　　　　　　Amelia

[2]　USES OF *ESTAR*

Estar is used:

a. to express location or position.

Madrid **está** en España.	*Madrid is in Spain.*
Mi tío **está** en México.	*My uncle is in Mexico.*
El libro **está** en la mesa.	*The book is on the table.*
¿Dónde **están** los niños?	*Where are the children?*

b. to express a condition or state.

La sopa **está** caliente.   *The soup is hot.*

María **está** sentada.   *María is seated.*

El señor Salas **está** triste.   *Mr. Salas is sad.*

¿Cómo **está** Ud.? **Estoy** muy bien.   *How are you? I'm very well.*

La ventana **está** abierta.   *The window is open.*

NOTE:

1. Adjectives used with *estar* agree with the subject in number and gender.

Ana **está** ocupada.   *Ana is busy.*

Los jóvenes **están** ocupados.   *The young people are busy.*

2. In questions, the adjective usually follows the verb.

¿**Está** ocupada Ana?   *Is Ana busy?*

¿**Están** ocupados los jóvenes?   *Are the young people busy?*

3. The forms of *estar* are summarized in the section on irregular verbs in the Appendix, page 453.

EXERCISE H

When Luisa comes home from school, she asks her mother where everyone and everything is. Write Luisa's questions and her mother's responses.

EXAMPLE: los refrescos / el refrigerador
            ¿Dónde están los refrescos?
            Están en el refrigerador.

1. el pastel / el horno   where is the cake

¿Dónde está el pastel?

Está en el horno   It's in the oven

2. el correo / la mesa del comedor   where is the mail?

¿Dónde está el correo?   It's on the diningroom table

Está en la mesa del comedor

3. mis hermanos / el parque   where are your brothers?

¿Dónde están tis hermanos?

Están en el parque.   They are in the park

4. mi blusa roja / el armario

Dónde están mi blusa roja. Where is my red blouse.

Están en el armario. It is in your closet

5. la revista «Tú» / el sofá

Donde estan la revista, Where
Estan en la csofa   It is in the sofa

6. tú / la cocina

Donde estan mi diario, where is my diary,
Estan en la coma, It is your bed.

7. mi diario / la cama

Donde estan Papa. Where is father
Estan en la oficina He is in the office

8. papá / la oficina

Donde esta mis zapatos Where are my shoes
Estan en el cuarto They are in your room

9. mis zapatos / el cuarto

Estan en la cocina You are in the kitchen
Donde estan tu where am I?

EXERCISE I

The mathematics teacher is giving back a test. Tell how the students feel.

EXAMPLE: Marta / nervioso
Marta **está nerviosa.**

1. Gabriel / desilusionado   Gabriel is delusional
Gabriel este desilusionado

2. Rita y Linda / contento   Rita and Linda are content
Rita y Linda estan continto

3. yo / triste   I am sad.
Yo estoy trista

4. Sergei y José / preocupado   Sergei and Jose are preoccupied
Sergei y Jose estan preocupedo

5. Inés y Luigi / nervioso   Ines and Luigi are nervous
Ines y Luigi estan nervioso,

6. Sofía / sorprendido   Sofia is
Sofia esta soprandido

EXERCISE J

Alicia is working as a waitress. Write the complaints that she gets about what she serves. Use the suggestions below.

el café	agrio
la ensalada	caliente
la hamburguesa	crudo
el helado	derretido
la leche	duro
el pan	frío
las papas fritas	horrible
el refresco	seco
la sopa	viejo

EXAMPLE: La ensalada **está vieja.**

1. _____

2. _____

3. _____

4. _____

5. _____

6. _____

7. _____

8. _____

EXERCISE K

Your coach is upset and is delaying the start of practice because two teammates aren't there. Complete the dialogue with the appropriate forms of *estar.*

ENTRENADOR: ¿Quién _____ ausente hoy?
                          1.

TÚ: Creo que todos nosotros _____ presentes.
                                            2.

RAFAEL: No. José y Roberto no _____ aquí.
                                        3.

ENTRENADOR: ¿Y dónde _____ ellos? Yo _____ preocupado.
                        4.   5.

PABLO: Roberto y José _____ sentados debajo de un árbol.
                                6.

TÚ: ¿Por qué _____ ellos allí?
                        7.

PABLO: José _____ enfermo y Roberto _____ con él.
                      8.   9.

(Roberto llega.)

ENTRENADOR: Roberto, ¿cómo _____ José?

                                          10.

ROBERTO: Él _____ enfermo.

                        11.

(José llega.)

ENTRENADOR: ¿Cómo _____ tú?

                            12.

JOSÉ: Ahora yo _____ bien. Vamos a jugar.

                              13.

TÚ: Ahora nosotros _____ contentos porque podemos jugar.

                                       14.

EXERCISE L

Susana is trying to understand how people feel in different circumstances. Answer her questions using the cues provided.

1. ¿Cómo estás cuando recibes una buena nota en un examen? *(contento)*

    _____

2. ¿Cómo estás cuando no puedes contestar la pregunta del profesor? *(preocupado)*

    _____

3. ¿Cómo estás cuando estás solo(a) en la casa? *(nervioso)*

    _____

4. ¿Cómo estás cuando el profesor da un examen de sorpresa? *(enojado)*

    _____

5. ¿Cómo estás cuando ganas un partido? *(emocionado)*

    _____

6. ¿Cómo estás cuando ves una telenovela? *(triste)*

    _____

7. ¿Cómo estás cuando comes demasiado chocolate? *(enfermo)*

    _____

8. ¿Cómo estás cuando tus padres te dan un coche nuevo? *(sorprendido)*

    _____

9. ¿Cómo estás cuando tu novio(a) sale con otra(o) chica(o)? *(celoso)*

    _____

10. ¿Cómo estás después de ayudar en casa? *(cansado)*

    _____

MASTERY EXERCISES

EXERCISE M

While standing in line for the movies, you hear these statements. Complete them with the appropriate form of *ser* or *estar*.

1. Guillermo _____ sentado porque _____ cansado.

2. En ese cuarto hace calor porque las ventanas _____ cerradas.

3. No comprendo. ¿Dices que Julio _____ peruano pero

    no _____ de Perú?

4. La madre de Elena _____ enfermera pero ella _____ en el

    hospital porque _____ enferma.

5. Los señores Arvida _____ ricos. Sus hijos siempre _____ en
    otras ciudades.

6. En el verano su ropa _____ de algodón, y en el invierno sus pantalones

    _____ de lana.

7. Tú _____ pálida hoy. ¿Cómo _____ tú?

8. El señor Pardos trabaja mucho. Siempre _____ muy cansado.

9. Los niños _____ preocupados porque no saben dónde _____
    su perro.

10. ¿ _____ lunes hoy? ¿Y cuál _____ la fecha?

11. No traigo reloj. ¿Qué hora _____ ?

12. La motocicleta _____ nueva. _____ de mi hermana.

13. Mañana _____ día de fiesta. Yo _____ feliz.

14. Los colores vivos _____ más bonitos que los colores claros.

15. La película _____ aburrida. Nosotros _____ desilusionados.

EXERCISE N

Express in Spanish Amalia's description of an evening at home.

1. Today is Tuesday. It's October fifth.

_____

2. It's eight o'clock.

_____

3. It's a pleasant evening.

_____

4. My father is very tired.

_____

5. John is seated on the sofa.

_____

6. The dog is near him on the floor.

_____

7. My mother is in the kitchen.

_____

8. She's worried because my grandmother is ill.

_____

9. I'm a good student, but tonight I'm nervous.

_____

10. The math assignment is very difficult.

_____

11. My younger sister is unhappy.

_____

12. Her favorite television program is not tonight.

_____

13. The hot chocolate is delicious, but it's not very hot.

_____

14. This pen is my sister's.

_____

15. She's angry because I'm using her pen.

_____

Chapter 9
Commands

[1] FORMAL COMMANDS OF REGULAR VERBS

a. Formal or polite commands are formed by droppng the final *-o* from the first-person singular of the present tense and adding:

1. *–e* for *Ud.* (singular) and *–en* for *Uds.* (plural) in the case of *–ar* verbs.

2. *-a* for *Ud.* and *-an* for *Uds.* in the case of *-er* or *-ir* verbs.

	PRESENT TENSE	COMMAND FORMS		
INFINITIVE	FIRST PERSON SINGULAR	SINGULAR	PLURAL	MEANING
abrir	abro	abra	abran	open
cerrar	cierro	cierre	cierren	close
decir	digo	diga	digan	say, tell
hablar	hablo	hable	hablen	speak
hacer	hago	haga	hagan	do, make
leer	leo	lea	lean	read
perder	pierdo	pierda	pierdan	lose
servir	sirvo	sirva	sirvan	serve
tener	tengo	tenga	tengan	have
traducir	traduzco	traduzca	traduzcan	translate
venir	vengo	venga	vengan	come
ver	veo	vea	vean	see
volver	vuelvo	vuelva	vuelvan	return

NOTE:

1. The vowel of the endings of the command forms is the "opposite" of the vowel endings of the third-person singular form of the present tense: *-e* for *-ar* verbs, and *-a* for *-er* and *-ir* verbs.

2. The subject pronoun *(Ud., Uds.)* follows the verb.

3. In Spanish America, *Uds.* can be either formal or informal.

b. To form the negative command, place *no* before the verb.

No hablen inglés.   *Don't speak English.*
No pierda las llaves.   *Don't lose the keys.*

c. Verbs that end in *-zar*, *-car*, and *-gar* have spelling changes in the command forms. The spelling change in *-zar* verbs occurs because in Spanish, *z* is rarely followed by *e* or *i*. The spelling change in *-car* and *-gar* verbs occurs to keep the original sounds of *c* and *g*.

Study the following examples:

	PRESENT TENSE	COMMAND FORMS		
INFINITIVE	FIRST PERSON SINGULAR	SINGULAR	PLURAL	MEANING
empezar	empiezo	empiece	empiecen	begin
buscar	busco	busque	busquen	seek
jugar	juego	juegue	jueguen	play

EXERCISE A

The Santiago family just moved into a new house. Their neighbor invites Mrs. Santiago to her home. Write what she tells Mrs. Santiago to do.

EXAMPLE: venir a mi casa
           Venga a mi casa.

1. entrar en la casa

   _____

2. cerrar la puerta

   _____

3. pasar a la cocina

   _____

4. tomar un café

   _____

5. aprender a conducir

   _____

6. asistir a la reunión de la comunidad conmigo

   _____

7. subir al segundo piso

   _____

8. leer el periódico del barrio

   _____

9. pedir instrucciones a la policía

   _____

10. recordar nuestra cita mañana

    _____

EXERCISE B

Mrs. Ortega's grandchildren are leaving for camp. Write what she tells them to do.

EXAMPLE: prestar atención al consejero
           Presten atención al consejero.

1. no pelear con los otros chicos

   _____

2. decir la verdad siempre

_____

3. llamar a casa los domingos

_____

4. no perder sus cosas

_____

5. tener paciencia

_____

6. leer muchos libros

_____

7. escribir cada semana

_____

8. comer bien

_____

9. no correr mucho

_____

10. no beber muchos refrescos

_____

EXERCISE C

You have been hired as a waiter (waitress). Write the instructions that the restaurant manager gives you.

EXAMPLE: saludar a los clientes
             Salude a los clientes.

1. ofrecer los platos especiales del día

_____

2. describir los platos si los clientes preguntan

_____

3. contestar sus preguntas

_____

4. preguntar qué van a tomar

_____

5. poner pan y mantequilla en la mesa en seguida

_____

6. traer la comida rápidamente

_____

7. servir la ensalada primero

_____

8. recordar los postres y el café

_____

9. quitar los platos sucios de la mesa

_____

10. dejar la cuenta en la mesa

_____

11. volver a poner la mesa

_____

EXERCISE D

You are moving into a new house, and the moving van has arrived. Tell the movers where to put your things.

1. Señor, *(subir)* _____ estos cartones al segundo piso.

2. Señores, *(colocar)* _____ el sofá contra esta pared.

3. Señor, *(sacar)* _____ las lámparas de la caja.

4. Señores, no *(maltratar)* _____ los cuadros.

5. Señores, *(poner)* _____ esa caja en la cocina.

6. Señor, no *(dejar)* _____ este sillón aquí.

7. Señores, *(leer)* _____ las etiquetas de las cajas.

8. Señor, *(cerrar)* _____ la puerta.

9. Señor, *(tener)* _____ mucho cuidado con esa mesa.

10. Señores, *(volver)* _____ a colocar el sofá contra la otra pared.

[2] FORMAL COMMANDS OF IRREGULAR VERBS

The following verbs have irregular formal command forms:

INFINITIVE	PRESENT TENSE FIRST PERSON SINGULAR	COMMAND FORMS SINGULAR	PLURAL	MEANING
dar	doy	dé	den	*give*
estar	estoy	esté	estén	*be*
ir	voy	vaya	vayan	*go*
ser	soy	sea	sean	*be*

NOTE:

1. *Dé* has an accent mark to distinguish it from *de* (of).

2. *Esté* and *estén* have accent marks to indicate that the stress falls on the last syllable.

EXERCISE E

Write the instructions your mother gave you when you and your brother stayed at a friend's house.

1. *(ser)* ¡ ———————————— corteses!

2. *(hacer)* ¡ ———————————— la cama por la mañana!

3. *(poner)* ¡ ———————————— la ropa en el armario!

4. *(ir)* ¡ ———————————— despacio!

5. *(dar)* ¡ ———————————— las gracias después de comer!

6. *(tener)* ¡ ———————————— mucho cuidado en la casa!

EXERCISE F

You and some friends are in Sevilla for Carnaval. Write the advice the hotel manager gives you as you tell him your plans.

EXAMPLE: Yo traigo mucho dinero. *(no)*
           ¡**No traiga** mucho dinero!

1. Nosotros buscamos un guía. *(sí)*

   ———————————————————————————

2. Llevamos máscaras en Carnaval. *(sí)*

   ———————————————————————————

3. Vamos despacio por las calles. *(sí)*

   ———————————————————————————

4. Estamos listos para salir del hotel a las diez. *(sí)*

   ———————————————————————————

5. Volvemos muy tarde. *(no)*

_____

6. Conduzco mi coche. *(no)*

_____

7. Hacemos caso de los anuncios. *(sí)*

_____

8. Olvido la dirección del hotel. *(no)*

_____

9. Doy una propina al guía. *(sí)*

_____

10. Somos impacientes. *(no)*

_____

[3] AFFIRMATIVE FAMILIAR COMMANDS (SINGULAR)

a. The affirmative *tú* command of regular verbs and stem-changing verbs is the same as the *Ud.* form of the present tense.

INFINITIVE	PRESENT TENSE *UD.* FORM	MEANING
abrir	abre	*open*
cerrar	cierra	*close*
dar	da	*give*
hablar	habla	*speak*
leer	lee	*read*
perder	pierde	*lose*
servir	sirve	*serve*
ver	ve	*see*
volver	vuelve	*return*

b. The following verbs have irregular affirmative *tú* commands:

INFINITIVE	COMMANDS *TÚ* FORM	MEANING
decir	di	*say, tell*
hacer	haz	*do, make*
ir	ve	*go*
poner	pon	*put*
salir	sal	*leave, go out*
ser	sé	*be*
tener	ten	*have*
venir	ven	*come*

NOTE:

1. Subject pronouns are usually omitted.

2. The familiar commands are used: (1) between friends and classmates; (2) by parents and other adults when speaking to young children; (3) in other cases where there is a familiar (not a formal) relationship.

EXERCISE G

Write in Spanish the advice your father gave you on your first day of school.

EXAMPLE: llegar temprano a la escuela
             ¡**Llega** temprano a la escuela!

1. prestar atención en las clases

_____

2. escuchar al maestro

_____

3. preparar la tarea cada noche

_____

4. comenzar la tarea al llegar a casa

_____

5. asistir a la escuela todos los días

_____

6. leer la tarea

_____

7. pedir ayuda al maestro

_____

8. escribir la tarea con cuidado

_____

9. pensar antes de hablar

_____

10. recibir buenas notas

_____

EXERCISE H

You are in the kitchen while your mother hurries to finish preparing a special family meal. Write what she tells you to do.

EXAMPLE: tener paciencia conmigo
             ¡**Ten** paciencia conmigo!

1. ser bueno

_____

2. hacer la ensalada

_____

3. ir a la tienda

_____

4. poner la mesa

_____

5. salir de la cocina

_____

6. venir acá

_____

7. decir «buenas tardes» a los invitados

_____

8. tener la bondad de ayudarme

_____

EXERCISE I

Your friends always ask you for advice. What do you tell them to do in these circumstances?

EXAMPLE: La bicicleta de Roberto no funciona. *(pedir prestada la bicicleta de tu hermano)*
　　　　　　 ¡**Pide** prestada la bicicleta de tu hermano!

1. Gloria quiere resolver los problemas de la atmósfera. *(conservar energía, caminar más)*

_____

2. La novia de Jorge no quiere ir al baile de la escuela. *(ir solo)*

_____

3. Roberto pierde muchas cosas. *(tener más cuidado)*

_____

4. Alicia no va a patinar porque sus amigos no quieren ir. *(ser más independiente)*

_____

5. Sarita trabaja y acaba de recibir su primer cheque. *(poner el dinero en el banco)*

_____

6. Felipe necesita un nuevo guante de béisbol. *(ahorrar el dinero)*

_____

[4] NEGATIVE FAMILIAR COMMANDS (SINGULAR)

a. To form a negative *tú* command, use the stem of the *yo* form of the present tense and add *-es* for *-ar* verbs and *-as* for *-er* and *-ir* verbs.

INFINITIVE	PRESENT TENSE FIRST PERSON SINGULAR	NEGATIVE FAMILIAR COMMAND	MEANING
mirar	miro	no mir**es**	*don't look*
cerrar	cierro	no cierr**es**	*don't close*
decir	digo	no dig**as**	*don't say, tell*
leer	leo	no le**as**	*don't read*
perder	pierdo	no pierd**as**	*don't lose*
servir	sirvo	no sirv**as**	*don't serve*
tener	tengo	no teng**as**	*don't have*
ver	veo	no ve**as**	*don't see*

b. The following verbs have irregular *tú* commands:

dar	no des	*don't give*
estar	no estés	*don't be*
ir	no vayas	*don't go*
ser	no seas	*don't be*

c. Verbs that end in *-zar*, *-car*, and *-gar* have spelling changes in the negative familiar command forms. The spelling change in *-zar* verbs occurs because in Spanish, *z* is rarely followed by *e* or *i*. The spelling change in *-car* and *-gar* verbs occurs to keep the original sounds of *c* and *g*.

INFINITIVE	PRESENT TENSE FIRST PERSON SINGULAR	NEGATIVE FAMILIAR COMMAND	MEANING
almorzar	almuerzo	no almuerces	*don't have lunch*
buscar	busco	no busques	*don't look for*
llegar	llego	no llegues	*don't arrive*

EXERCISE J

While you're at the beach, you overhear a parent tell her small child not to do the following things. Write what she says.

EXAMPLE: no tomar el agua del mar
            ¡**No tomes** el agua del mar!

1. no poner arena en los zapatos

_____

2. no comer arena

_____

3. no estar en el mar solo

_____

4. no caminar lejos

_____

5. no perder los juguetes

_____

6. no tener miedo del agua

_____

7. no tirar arena

_____

8. no me quitar el dinero

_____

9. no molestar a las personas

_____

10. no dejar la cubeta ahí

_____

EXERCISE K

You are sitting in the dentist's waiting room with your younger brother. What do you tell him to do?

EXAMPLE: no gritar
             ¡No grites!

1. no romper la revista

_____

2. no poner los pies en la silla

_____

3. no ir ahí

_____

4. no decir eso

_____

5. no cerrar esa puerta

_____

6. no salir de la oficina

_____

7. no ser malo

_____

M A S T E R Y   E X E R C I S E S

EXERCISE L

You're visiting a botanical garden. As you enter the gate, you read the sign. Fill in the missing verbs.

1. *(pagar)* ¡ _____ la entrada en la caja!

2. *(entrar)* ¡No _____ sin pagar!

3. *(mirar)* ¡ _____ las flores!

4. *(tocar)* ¡No _____ las flores!

5. *(andar)* ¡ _____ en los caminos!

6. *(correr)* ¡No _____ en la hierba!

7. *(jugar)* ¡No _____ a la pelota en el jardín!

8. *(respetar)* ¡ _____ a las otras personas!

9. *(gritar)* ¡No _____ en el jardín!

10. *(comer)* ¡ _____ solamente en las mesas!

11. *(almorzar)* ¡No _____ en la hierba!

12. *(poner)* ¡ _____ los papeles en la basura!

13. *(tirar)* ¡No _____ papeles en el jardín!

14. *(gozar)* ¡ _____ de la naturaleza!

15. *(salir)* ¡Por favor, no _____ sin visitar nuestra tienda!

16. *(volver)* ¡Por favor, _____ al jardín pronto!

EXERCISE M

Several friends are helping you set up for a party. Tell them what to do.

1. *(colgar)* ¡Ricardo, _____ los globos ahí!

2. *(poner)* ¡Gladys, _____ los refrescos en esa mesa!

3. *(colocar)* ¡Arturo, no _____ las decoraciones en la puerta!

4. *(traer)* ¡Estela, no _____ el pastel ahora!

5. *(preparar)* ¡Mirta, _____ la limonada ahora!

6. *(sacar)* ¡Ricardo, no ＿＿＿＿＿＿＿＿ los discos todavía!

7. *(dejar)* ¡John, no ＿＿＿＿＿＿＿＿ los platos ahí!

8. *(ir)* ¡Estela, ＿＿＿＿＿＿＿＿ a la tienda para comprar hielo!

9. *(ayudar)* ¡Mirta, ＿＿＿＿＿＿＿＿ a Arturo con las decoraciones!

10. *(abrir)* ¡Gladys, no ＿＿＿＿＿＿＿＿ los regalos!

EXERCISE N

You're on a school trip, and the counselor gives the group the following instructions before leaving the airport in Caracas.

EXAMPLE: venir acá
       ¡**Vengan** acá!

1. poner las maletas en el autobús

＿＿＿＿＿＿＿＿＿＿＿＿＿＿＿＿＿＿＿＿＿＿

2. subir al autobús rápidamente

＿＿＿＿＿＿＿＿＿＿＿＿＿＿＿＿＿＿＿＿＿＿

3. no gritar en el autobús

＿＿＿＿＿＿＿＿＿＿＿＿＿＿＿＿＿＿＿＿＿＿

4. respetar al chófer

＿＿＿＿＿＿＿＿＿＿＿＿＿＿＿＿＿＿＿＿＿＿

5. bajar el equipaje del autobús

＿＿＿＿＿＿＿＿＿＿＿＿＿＿＿＿＿＿＿＿＿＿

6. no perder el pasaporte

＿＿＿＿＿＿＿＿＿＿＿＿＿＿＿＿＿＿＿＿＿＿

7. subir al cuarto en seguida

＿＿＿＿＿＿＿＿＿＿＿＿＿＿＿＿＿＿＿＿＿＿

8. volver en quince minutos

＿＿＿＿＿＿＿＿＿＿＿＿＿＿＿＿＿＿＿＿＿＿

9. no dejar nada de valor en el cuarto

＿＿＿＿＿＿＿＿＿＿＿＿＿＿＿＿＿＿＿＿＿＿

10. no dar la llave a extraños

＿＿＿＿＿＿＿＿＿＿＿＿＿＿＿＿＿＿＿＿＿＿

11. no perder la llave

＿＿＿＿＿＿＿＿＿＿＿＿＿＿＿＿＿＿＿＿＿＿

12. cerrar bien la puerta del cuarto

_____

13. recordar el número del cuarto

_____

14. no olvidar el nombre del hotel

_____

15. no pedir vino en el restaurante

_____

16. no ser irresponsables

_____

17. obedecer todas las reglas

_____

18. no gastar todo el dinero

_____

19. leer bien el itinerario

_____

20. traer la cámara

_____

EXERCISE O

You are directing a school play and are giving the actors instructions. Express the following in Spanish.

1. Everyone, pay attention now.

_____

2. Gloria, speak louder.

_____

3. Rafael, don't lose the ball.

_____

4. Alicia, come closer.

_____

5. John, don't make noises.

_____

6. Everyone, practice the dance.

_____

7. Everyone, listen to the music.

_____

8. Sergio, don't bring food here.

_____

9. Alfredo, wait a minute.

_____

10. Mrs. Beltrán, play the song again, please.

_____

11. Everyone, rest for ten minutes.

_____

12. José, don't put the chairs there.

_____

13. Francisco, repeat that phrase.

_____

14. Jorge, ask the question again.

_____

15. Everyone, don't be so disagreeable.

_____

FRANCIA
PORTUGAL ESPAÑA Barcelona
○ Madrid ITALIA
Islas Baleares
• Sevilla

[1] REGULAR -*AR* VERBS

a. The preterite tense of regular -*ar* verbs is formed by dropping the infinitive ending -*ar* and adding the personal endings -*é, -aste, -ó, -amos, -asteis, -aron.*

	hablar *to speak*	**cerrar** *to close*
yo	habl**é**	cerr**é**
tú	habl**aste**	cerr**aste**
Ud., él, ella	habl**ó**	cerr**ó**
nosotros, -as	habl**amos**	cerr**amos**
vosotros, -as	habl**asteis**	cerr**asteis**
Uds., ellos, ellas	habl**aron**	cerr**aron**

b. The first-person plural ending *(-amos)* is the same as in the present tense: *tomamos* (*we take, we took*).

c. Most verbs that are stem-changing (*o* to *ue*; *e* to *ie*) do not change the stem in the preterite tense: (*cerrar*) Present—*cierro*; Preterite—*cerré*.

d. The preterite tense has the following meanings in English:

Ud. habló	*you spoke, you did speak*
yo cerré	*I closed, I did close*

e. Verbs that end in -*car*, -*gar*, and -*zar* have a spelling change in the *yo* form. In -*car* and -*gar* verbs, this change occurs to keep the original sound of the *c* and *g*. The change occurs in -*zar* verbs because *z* rarely precedes *e* or *i* in Spanish.

sacar	yo saqué
jugar	yo jugué
empezar	yo empecé

Other verbs that have these changes are:

–car	practicar, tocar, buscar
–gar	llegar, pagar
–zar	comenzar, almorzar

[2] USES OF THE PRETERITE

a. The preterite tense is used to narrate an action or event in the past. It may indicate the beginning or end of the action, or the complete action or event begun and finished in the past.

(1) Beginning or End

Joe comenzó a trabajar.	*Joe began to work.*
Cerraron la tienda.	*They closed the store.*

(2) Complete Action

Visité a mi tía ayer.   *I visited my aunt yesterday.* (I went and returned.)

b. Some expressions that are often used with the preterite are:

anoche   *last night*   la semana pasada   *last week*

ayer   *yesterday*   el año pasado   *last year*

anteayer   *the day before yesterday*   el mes pasado   *last month*

EXERCISE A

Alejandro describes what he and his family did last night. Tell what he says.

EXAMPLE: mi padre / jugar al tenis
               Mi padre **jugó** al tenis.

1. yo / estudiar para un examen

     Yo estudié para un examen.

2. mi mamá / preparar un pastel

     Mi mama peparó un pastel.

3. mi hermana / limpiar su cuarto

     Mi nermana limpió su cuarto

4. Roberto y yo / mirar un programa de televisión

     Roberto y yo miramos un progama de televisión

5. Marta y tú / trabajar en la tienda

     Marta y tú trabajaron en la tienda.

6. mis hermanos / patinar

     Mis hermanos patinaron.

EXERCISE B

Laura spent last summer with her family on a farm. What does she say they did there?

EXAMPLE: mi tío / plantar maíz
               Mi tío **plantó** maíz.

1. yo / caminar en el bosque

     Yo caminé en el bosgue.

2. Carlos / ayudar a mi tío

     Carlos ayudó a mi tío.

3. mi mamá y mi tía / cocinar mucho

     Mi mamá y mi tía cocinaron mucho.

4. mi papá / cortar la hierba

Mi papá cortó la hierba

5. mi abuela / cuidar los pollos

Mi abuela cuidó los pollos.

6. Ernesto y yo / nadar en un lago

Ernesto y yo nadamos en un lago.

EXERCISE C

Alfonso has just returned from a trip to Spain. Using the words in parentheses, answer the questions Rafael asks him.

1. ¿Qué país visitaste? *(España)*

País visité es España.

2. ¿Con quién viajaste? *(mi familia)*

Yo viajé con mi familia.

3. ¿Cuánto tiempo pasaron Uds. allí? *(quince días)*

Nosotros pasamos quince días.

4. ¿Quién pagó el viaje? *(mi padre)*

Mi padre pagué viaje.

5. ¿Cómo viajaron Uds.? *(en avión y en autobús)*

Nosotros viajamos en avión y en autobús.

6. ¿Alquilaron Uds. un coche allí? *(no)*

No, no alquilé un coche.

7. ¿A qué ciudad llegaron Uds.? *(Madrid)*

Nosotros llegamos Madrid.

8. ¿En qué ciudad terminaste el viaje? *(Málaga)*

Yo terminé Málaga.

9. ¿Entraste en muchos museos? *(sí)*

Si, entré en muchos museos.

10. ¿Sacó tu hermano muchas fotos? *(sí)*

Si, mi hermano sacó mucho fotos

EXERCISE D

Complete this letter that Teresa writes to a friend by filling in the appropriate preterite form of the verbs indicated.

Querida Alicia:

Ayer yo _____ pensé _____ en ti varias veces. Yo _____ comencé _____ a escribir esta carta en
        1. (pensar)   *2. (comenzar)*

muchas ocasiones pero nunca _____ llegué _____ a terminar la carta. Anoche la orquesta de la
                          3. (llegar)

escuela _____ tocó _____ en una competencia. Yo _____ toqué _____ el violín y nosotros✗
        4. (tocar)   *5. (tocar)*

_____ ganamos _____ el premio de segundo lugar. El coro _____ cantó _____ también pero
        6. (ganar)   *7. (cantar)*

no _____ ganó _____ ningún premio. Todavía me fascina la música y el mes pasado yo
        8. (ganar)

_____ empecé _____ a estudiar la guitarra. Como ves, _____ cambié _____ el violín por un
        9. (empezar)   *10. (cambiar)*

instrumento «menos serio».

La semana pasada yo _____ celebré _____ mi cumpleaños. Mis padres me _____ regalaron _____
                    11. (celebrar)   *12. (regalar)*

muchos regalos bonitos. Mi familia me _____ llevaron _____ a cenar en un restaurante elegante.
                                  13. (llevar)

Nosotros _____ pasamos _____ un buen rato allí. Después, dos amigos me _____ invitaron _____ a
        14. (pasar)   *15. (invitar)*

una discoteca y nosotros _____ bailamos _____ hasta la medianoche. Yo _____ llegué _____ a
                      16. (bailar)   *17. (llegar)*

casa cansada pero contenta. Al día siguiente yo _____ jugué _____ al tenis con mis hermanos pero
                                          18. (jugar)

ellos _____ ganaron _____ .
        19. (ganar)

¿Cómo _____ pasaste _____ tú tu cumpleaños? ¿ _____ visitaste _____ tú algún lugar divertido?
        20. (pasar)   *21. (visitar)*

¿A quién _____ invitaste _____ ? Yo _____ busqué _____ la foto que tu padre
        22. (invitar)   *23. (buscar)*

_____ saqué _____ de nosotras en la fiesta, pero no la _____ encontramos _____ .
        24. (sacar)   *25. (encontrar)*

Hasta pronto.

Teresa

EXERCISE E

Tell whether or not you and your friends did these things yesterday.

EXAMPLE: escuchar discos
            Mi amigo Pedro **escuchó** discos ayer.
    OR: Yo **no escuché** discos ayer.

1. practicar un deporte
   Mi amigo Pedro practco un deporte ayer.

2. trabajar mucho
   Mi amigo Pedro trabajó mucho ayer.

3. descansar por la tarde
   Mi amigo Pedro descansó por la tarde ayer.

4. lavar el carro
   Mi amigo Pedro lavó el carro ayer.

5. usar la aspiradora
   Mi amigo Pedro usar la aspiradó ayer.

6. sacar fotografías
   Mi amigo Pedro sacó fotografías ayer

7. buscar un disco nuevo
   Mi amigo Pedro buscó un disco nuevo ayer.

8. almorzar en el centro
   Mi amigo Pedro almuerzó en el centro ayer.

EXERCISE F

Answer these questions that a friend asks while you're riding the school bus together one morning.

1. ¿Qué programa de televisión miraste anoche?
   Yo miré deportes en la televisión anoche.

2. ¿Hablaste con tus amigos por teléfono anoche?
   Sí yo hablé con mi amigas por teléfono anoche

3. ¿Qué música tocaste?
   Yo toqué país música.

4. ¿Estudiaron juntos tú y Alicia para el examen?
   Sí nosotros estudiamos para el examen

5. ¿Prepararon Uds. la escena para la clase de español?

Si, prepararon la escena para la clase de español.

6. ¿Terminaste la carta a tu amigo por correspondencia?

Si mi amigo terminé la carta por correspondencia.

7. ¿Preguntaste a tus padres si puedes cenar conmigo esta noche?

Yo pregunto mi padres para dinero.

8. ¿Qué desayunaste hoy?

huevos es para desayuno

EXERCISE G

Gloria is showing her yearbook to a cousin. Write what the person in each picture did.

EXAMPLE: Lorenzo sacó fotografías.

1. Yo _____.

2. Gilberto y Anita _____.

3. Ricardo _____.

4. Juan y yo  _____.

5. Sarita _____.

[3] REGULAR -ER AND -IR VERBS

a. The preterite tense of regular -er and -ir verbs is formed by dropping the infinitive ending -er or -ir and adding the personal endings -í, -iste, -ió, -imos, -isteis, -ieron.

	perder *to lose*	**abrir** *to open*
yo	perd**í**	abr**í**
tú	perd**iste**	abr**iste**
Ud., él, ella	perd**ió**	abr**ió**
nosotros, -as	perd**imos**	abr**imos**
vosotros, -as	perd**isteis**	abr**isteis**
Uds., ellos, ellas	perd**ieron**	abr**ieron**

b. The preterite endings are the same for -er and -ir verbs.

c. In -ir verbs, the first-person plural ending (-imos) is the same as in the present tense. In -er verbs, however, the endings are different.

viv**imos** *we live*   viv**imos** *we lived*
beb**emos** *we drink*   beb**imos** *we drank*

d. The accent mark is omitted over the following forms of *ver: vi, vio.*

e. Stem-changing verbs ending in -er do not change the stem vowel in the preterite tense. Stem-changing verbs ending in -ir have special stem changes in the preterite and are discussed in Chapter 11.

EXERCISE H

Raúl and some friends are telling what they had for dinner last night. Write what they say.

EXAMPLE: Rosa / arroz con frijoles
Rosa **comió** arroz con frijoles.

1. Luis y Daniel / pescado

Luis y Daniel comieron pescado.

2. yo / arroz con pollo

Yo comí arroz con pollo

3. Alicia / una ensalada

Aicia comió una ensalada.

4. Bobby y yo / hamburguesas

Bobby y yo comimos hamburguesas

5. tú / chuletas de cerdo

Tú comiste chuletas de cerdo

6. ellos / paella

Ello comieron paella

EXERCISE I

The students are selecting their courses for the following year. What did they decide to study?

EXAMPLE: Tomás / francés
            Tomás **decidió estudiar** francés.

1. Lola / literatura

Lola estudió literatura.

2. Carmen y Mary / baile

estudieron

3. yo / biología

estudí

4. José y yo / música

estudimos

5. tú / química

estudiste

6. Jane / geografía

estudió

EXERCISE J

You're talking to a new friend who spent part of her life in the Dominican Republic. Write the questions you ask her about her background.

EXAMPLE: dónde / aprender el español
¿Dónde **aprendiste** el español?

1. cuándo / vivir en Santo Domingo

<u>Cuándo viviste en Santo Domingo</u>

2. a qué escuela / asistir

<u>A que escuela asiste</u>

3. cuándo / volver a los Estados Unidos

<u>Cuándo volviste a los Estados Unidos.</u>

4. cuándo / decidir volver aquí

<u>Cuándo decidiste volver aquí.</u>

5. por qué / salir de Santo Domingo

<u>Por que saliste de Santo Domingo.</u>

EXERCISE K

Complete this letter that Ramona, who is visiting acquaintances in Mexico, writes to a friend back in her hometown.

Querida Gabriela:

Anoche yo ___asiti___ a una fiesta en casa de mi amiga Lourdes. Ellos ___celebrieron___
1. (asistir)   2. (celebrar)

el cumpleaños de su hermana menor. Muchas personas ___asistieron___ a la fiesta y la
3 (asistir)

hermana de Lourdes ___recibó___ muchos regalos.
4. (recibir)

La fiesta ___comenzi___ a las nueve de la noche. Muchas personas no ___llegieron___
5. (comenzar)   6. (llegar)

hasta las diez. Un grupo de mariachis ___cantieron___ «Las mañanitas» a la hermana de
7. (cantar)

Lourdes. Yo no ___entendí___ todas las palabras, pero me ___gusti___ mucho y
8. (entender)   9. (gustar)

___aprendi___ dos canciones más. Cuando ___termini___ los mariachis, el padre
10. (aprender)   11. (terminar)

de Lourdes _____colgió_____ una piñata y todos nosotros _____tratimos_____ de romperla.
12. (colgar)   13. (tratar)

Un joven guapo _____rompió_____ la piñata.
14. (romper)

Nosotros _____comimos_____ y _____bebimos_____ muy bien. La mamá de Lourdes y sus
15. (comer)   16. (beber)

tías _____prepararon_____ unos platillos muy sabrosos. Yo _____comí_____ tacos de pollo y
17. (preparar)   18. (comer)

tamales. La mamá de Lourdes _____prometió_____ enseñarme a preparar los tamales. Yo
19. (prometer)

_____volví_____ a casa a las doce y media de la noche.
20. (volver)

Hasta pronto.
Ramona

EXERCISE L

Answer these questions from your older sister. Use the cues provided.

1. ¿A qué hora saliste de la casa anoche? *(7:00)*
   Yo salí de la casa siete anoche.

2. ¿Con quién asististe al concierto? *(Manuela)*
   Yo asití con Manuela al concierto.

3. ¿Qué decidieron Uds. hacer después del concierto? *(ir a un restaurante)*
   Decidieron ir a un restaurante después del concierto

4. ¿Dónde comieron Uds.? *(el Café Colón)*
   Nosotros comimos en el Café Colón.

5. ¿Qué comiste? *(una hamburguesa)*
   Yo comí una hamburguesa.

6. ¿A qué hora prometiste estar en la casa? *(11:00)*
   Yo prometí estar en la casa once.

7. ¿Cómo volviste a casa? *(en taxi)*
   Yo volví en taxi a casa.

8. ¿A qué hora abriste la puerta de la casa? *(11:30)*
   Yo abrí la puerta de la casa once y media.

MASTERY EXERCISES

EXERCISE M

Describe what you and a friend did during a weekend trip to another city. Use the suggestions below.

asistir a un concierto
caminar por la ciudad
comer en un restaurante español
comprar unos discos
correr en una carrera

gastar mucho dinero
jugar al tenis (boliche ...)
perder la cartera
ver a unos amigos
visitar el museo

1. Nosotros asistimos a un concierto

2. Nosotros caminimos por la ciudad.

3. Nosotros comimos en un restaurante español

4. Nosotros comprimos unos discos

5. Nosotros corrimos una carrera

6. Nosotros gastimos mucho dinero.

7. Nosotros jugimos al tenis (boliche...)

8. Nosotros perdimos la cartero

9. Nosotros vimos a unos amigos

10. Nosotros visitimos el museo.

EXERCISE N

While visiting Costa Rica, you meet a girl who used to be an exchange student at your school. Tell her about yourself and the other people you both knew there.

EXAMPLE: el señor Álvarez / dejar de enseñar
El señor Álvarez **dejó** de enseñar.

1. Miriam / volver a vivir en Puerto Rico
Miriam volvó a vivir en Puerto Rico

2. Jorge y Pedro / asistir a la misma universidad
asistieron

3. Eddy / abrir una tienda de juguetes
abrió

4. tu professor de inglés / escribir un libro de poemas
escribó

5. yo / ver a Daniel en España

Vi

6. Malika y yo / viajar a Europa

viajimos

7. las hermanas Silva / correr en muchas carreras

corrieron

8. Janet / recibir una beca

recibó

9. Alicia y Berta / aprender el japonés

aprendieron

10. la señora Oyama / salir de la escuela

salió

EXERCISE O

You have to give an oral report about your trip abroad last summer. Express in Spanish what you plan to say.

1. Last summer I spent one month in Europe.

pasar *el verano pasado yo gastado una mes en Europa.*

2. My friends and I visited three countries.

visitar *Mi amigas y yo visitimos tres países.*

3. We flew to Madrid.

volver *Nosotros voló a Madrid*

4. We decided to travel by bus and bicycle in each country.

decidir *Nosotros decidimos viaje de autobus y bicicle en países.* *cada uno*

5. I learned to ride a bicycle very well.

aprender *Yo doeto para montar a bicicleta muy bueno.*

6. I saw many interesting monuments.

Yo miro mucho interesante monumentos

7. I met young people in each city.

conocer *Yo encontradi gente en cada uno países*

8. Many times they invited us to eat dinner in their homes.

cenar *Muchas veces invitieron uds. para comer cena en sus casas.*

9. Pablo lost his passport in Paris.

Pablo perdidi su pasaporte en Paris.

dejar cambio

10. He left his passport at the bank when he changed a traveler's check.

El se fue su pasaporte @ el banco quer su - cambiado un viajo cheque

11. The police found his passport.

La policia encontró su pasaporte

12. They returned the passport to Pablo.

Volvieron el   pasaporte a Pablo

13. In Madrid, I understood the people when they spoke Spanish, but I answered in English.

En Madrid, entendía la gente cuando hablaron español, solamente, me conteste en ingles.

14. I looked for a Spanish dictionary.

Busqué un diccionario español

olvidar traer

15. I forgot to bring my dictionary with me.

Olvidar traer mi diccionario conmigo

16. I paid five thousand pesetas for the dictionary.

Pague circo mil pesetas el diccionario

tomar

17. I also took many pictures in each city.

Tambrén tomé cuadros del hombre en cada ciudad

18. We returned home tired but happy.

Volvimos cansado pero feliz caseros

19. We learned a great deal during the trip.

aprendimos mucho durante el viaje

20. We became acquainted with many nice young people.

Hicimos conocidas con mucha gente joven agradable

Chapter 11
Verbs Irregular in the Preterite Tense

[1]   PRETERITE TENSE OF *-IR* STEM-CHANGING VERBS

a. Stem-changing verbs ending in *-ir* change the stem vowel *e* to *i* and *o* to *u* in the third-person singular and plural of the preterite tense.

	servir *to serve*	**dormir** *to sleep*
yo	serví	dormí
tú	serviste	dormiste
Ud., él, ella	sirvió	durmió
nosotros, -as	servimos	dormimos
vosotros, -as	servisteis	dormisteis
Uds., ellos, ellas	sirvieron	durmieron

b. Other verbs that change *e* to *i* are:

medir *to measure*	referir *to tell*	sentir *to feel*
pedir *to ask for*	reñir *to argue*	vestir *to dress*
preferir *to prefer*	repetir *to repeat*	

Other verbs that change *o* to *u* are:

morir *to die*   podrir *to rot*

c. Verbs ending in *-ar* or *-er* that are stem-changing don't change the stem vowel in the preterite tense.

pensar *to think:*   pensé, pensaste, pensó, pensamos, pensasteis, pensaron
volver *to return:*   volví, volviste, volvió, volvimos, volvisteis, volvieron

EXERCISE A

Luis tells what he and his friends preferred to do yesterday. Write what he says.

EXAMPLE: Paul y yo / ir al cine
             Paul y yo **preferimos** ir al cine.

1. Enrique / ir a la piscina

_____

2. tú / ver a tus amigos

_____

3. Abdul y Mateo / montar en bicicleta

_____

4. Jean y yo / ir a la playa

_____

5. mi hermano / ver una película

_____

6. Marta / mirar la televisión

_____

7. ellos / jugar al fútbol

_____

EXERCISE B

You overhear your mother on the phone telling a friend how late everyone slept. Write in Spanish what she says.

EXAMPLE: mi esposo y yo / 7:30
            Mi esposo y yo **dormimos hasta** las siete y media

1. Alejandro / 12:00

_____

2. María y Elena / 10:30

_____

3. tú / 8:15

_____

4. Gregorio y Felipe / 11:00

_____

5. yo / 7:00

_____

6. mi padre / 5:00

_____

EXERCISE C

Carmen is writing in her diary about the night she stayed at Raquel's house. Fill in the appropriate preterite forms of the verbs given.

Yo ___dicide___ pasar la noche en casa de Raquel porque nosotras ___volvimos___
  1. (decidir)   2. (volver)

tarde del teatro. Antes de ir al teatro, nosotras ___comimos___ en un restaurante francés. Yo
                                                     3. (comer)

___pide___ sopa de cebollas y me ___gusto___ mucho. Raquel
  4. (pedir)   5. (gustar)

___pidó___ caracoles pero no le ___gusto___ . Ella ___resolver___
  6. (pedir)   7. (gustar)   8. (resolver)

no volver a ese restaurante. A veces Raquel es antipática. Ella ___riñó___ al mesero una vez
<u>9. (reñir)</u>

y luego le ___repitiera___ su orden. Yo no ___dormí___ bien en su casa pero
<u>10. (repetir)</u>   <u>11. (dormir)</u>

Raquel ___durmió___ profundamente toda la noche.
<u>12. (dormir)</u>

[2] VERBS THAT CHANGE *I* TO *Y* IN THE PRETERITE

a. *-er* and *-ir* verbs whose stems end in a vowel change the endings of the preterite tense from *-ió* to *-yó* in the third-person singular and from *-ieron* to *-yeron* in the third-person plural. The endings for all other persons take an accent on the *-i.*

caer *to fall*			
yo	caí	nosotros, -as	caímos
tú	caíste	vosotros, -as	caísteis
Ud., él, ella	cayó	Uds., ellos, ellas	cayeron

b. Verbs like *caer:*

construir   *to build*   leer   *to read*

creer   *to believe*   oír   *to hear*

distribuir   *to distribute*   poseer   *to possess; to own*

incluir   *to include*

EXERCISE D

Some friends are telling what they heard on the radio last night. Write what they say.

EXAMPLE: nosotros / las noticias
Nosotros **oímos** las noticias.

1. tú / el tiempo

_____

2. Tiffany / un debate

_____

3. Felipe y Nicolás / un partido de fútbol

_____

4. yo / música

_____

5. ellos / un concierto

_____

6. Beverly y yo / un concurso

_____

EXERCISE E

The students in the woodworking class tell what they built. Write what they say.

EXAMPLE: Esteban / una mesa
Esteban **construyó** una mesa.

1. yo / una lámpara

_____

2. ellos / un librero

_____

3. Sarita / un marco

_____

4. tú / un banco

_____

5. Chun y Susan / una caja

_____

6. Juan y yo / una silla

_____

EXERCISE F

Some neighbors are discussing an incident that took place nearby. Write what they say.

EXAMPLE: yo / creer que mi hijo / cerrar la puerta
Yo **creí** que mi hijo **cerró** la puerta.

1. mi esposo / oír las noticias en el radio del carro
Mi esposo oír las noticias en la radio de carro.

2. los señores Delgado / construir esa casa el año pasado
Los señores Delgado construir esa casa el año pasado

3. yo / leer las noticias en el periódico
Yo leer las noticias en el periódico

4. la policía / incluir a mi hermano en la investigación
La policía incluir a mi hermano en la investigación

5. nosotros / creer / que un meteoro / caer en la casa
Nosotros creer que un meteoro caer en la casa.

6. La explosión / destruir toda la casa de los señores Delgado y / romper las ventanas de mi casa
La explosión destruir toda la casa de los señores Delgado y romper las ventanas de mi casa.

[3] *I*-STEM VERBS IN THE PRETERITE

The following verbs have irregular stems and endings in the preterite:

	hacer *to do;* *to make*	**querer** *to want;* *to love*	**venir** *to come*
yo	hice	quise	vine
tú	hiciste	quisiste	viniste
Ud., él, ella	hizo	quiso	vino
nosotros, -as	hicimos	quisimos	vinimos
vosotros, -as	hicisteis	quisisteis	vinisteis
Uds., ellos, ellas	hicieron	quisieron	vinieron

NOTE: The preterite endings of *i*-stem verbs do not have accent marks.

EXERCISE G

Mrs. Montes organized a potluck dinner. She tells who made each dish. Write what she says.

EXAMPLE: Silvia / el pastel de chocolate
Silvia **hizo** el pastel de chocolate.

1. yo / la ensalada

_____

2. los señores Rivas / la paella

_____

3. Carmen / las legumbres

_____

4. tú / el té helado

_____

5. Rosa y yo / el arroz con pollo

_____

6. Uds. / el flan

_____

EXERCISE H

Roberto is not speaking to any of his friends because they didn't want to do what he wanted to do. Tell what his friends wanted to do.

EXAMPLE: Jaime / montar en bicicleta
Jaime **quiso** montar en bicicleta.

1. Yolanda / ir al cine

_____

2. Kenji / estudiar

_____

3. tú / sacar fotografías

_____

4. Eduardo y Patricia / mirar la televisión

_____

5. Gabriel y yo / jugar al voleibol

_____

6. Tony / descansar

_____

EXERCISE I

Caterina tells her cousin how the members of her family came to her grandparents' anniversary party. Write what she says.

EXAMPLE: mi hermana / en taxi
            Mi hermana **vino** en taxi.

1. mis tíos / en autobús

_____

2. el hermano de mi abuela / en tren

_____

3. mis hermanos y yo / en coche

_____

4. mi tía / en avión

_____

5. mis padres / en coche

_____

6. tú / a pie

_____

7. mi madrina / en motocicleta

_____

EXERCISE J

Answer these questions that a friend asks you. Use the words in parentheses.

1. ¿Hiciste la tarea anoche? *(sí)*

_____

2. ¿Vinieron Carlos y Juanita a la escuela hoy? *(no)*

_____

3. ¿Qué quiso hacer Alfredo el sábado pasado? *(ir de compras)*

_____

4. ¿Cuándo vinieron tus primos a verte? *(el agosto pasado)*

_____

5. ¿Cómo vino Berta a la escuela hoy? *(en taxi)*

_____

6. ¿Por qué vino ella en taxi? *(perder el autobús)*

_____

7. ¿Qué hizo tu mamá para cenar anoche? *(pollo)*

_____

[4]   *U*-STEM VERBS IN THE PRETERITE

The following verbs have irregular stems and endings in the preterite:

INFINITIVE	STEM	PRETERITE FORMS
andar	anduv	anduv*e*, anduv*iste*, anduv*o* anduv*imos*, anduv*isteis*, anduv*ieron*
estar	estuv	estuv*e*, estuv*iste*, estuv*o* estuv*imos*, estuv*isteis*, estuv*ieron*
poder	pud	pud*e*, pud*iste*, pud*o* pud*imos*, pud*isteis*, pud*ieron*
poner	pus	pus*e*, pus*iste*, pus*o* pus*imos*, pus*isteis*, pus*ieron*
saber	sup	sup*e*, sup*iste*, sup*o* sup*imos*, sup*isteis*, sup*ieron*
tener	tuv	tuv*e*, tuv*iste*, tuv*o* tuv*imos*, tuv*isteis*, tuv*ieron*

NOTE: The preterite endings of *u*-stem verbs do not have accent marks.

[5]   THE VERBS *DAR, SER,* AND *IR*

The verbs *dar, ser,* and *ir* are also irregular in the preterite. *Dar* takes the endings of regular *-er, -ir* verbs, but without a written accent in the first- and third-person singular forms. *Ser* and *ir* have the same forms in the preterite.

dar   *to give*   di, diste, dio, dimos, disteis, dieron

ser   *to be*
ir   *to go*   } fui, fuiste, fue, fuimos, fuisteis, fueron

EXERCISE K

Gerardo describes what he and a friend did last Saturday. Complete the statements with the correct forms of the preterite tense.

El sábado pasado Enrique y yo ___fuimos___ al centro. Nosotros ___estuvimos___ allí
                                    1. (ir)   *2. (estar)*

porque yo ___tuve___ que comprar una nueva raqueta de tenis. Nosotros no
              3. (tener)

___pudimos___ encontrar la tienda que recomendó un amigo de Enrique. Este amigo le
   4. (poder)

___dar___ un papel con el nombre y la dirección de la tienda a Enrique, pero él no
   5. (dar)

___pudo___ recordar dónde ___pone___ ese papel. Enrique
   6. (poder)   *7. (poner)*

___tuvo___ que llamar por teléfono a su amigo y luego nosotros ___fuimos___
   8. (tener)   *9 (ir)*

a la tienda. Yo le ___dar___ las gracias a Enrique por su ayuda.
                      10. (dar)

EXERCISE L

Conchita and some friends are talking about what they did during the spring vacation. Tell what they say, using the preterite tense.

EXAMPLE: yo / hacer un viaje en autobús
            Yo **hice** un viaje en autobús.

1. Bonnie / andar en la playa

_____

2. Paul y Eduardo / ir a Puerto Rico

_____

3. nosotros / dar muchos paseos en el parque

_____

4. tú / tener que trabajar

_____

5. yo / estar en casa de una prima

_____

6. Uds. / poder divertirse en casa

_____

EXERCISE M

Answer the questions that a friend asks you about a party he didn't attend at Lorenzo's home.

1. ¿Con quién fuiste a la fiesta?

_____

2. ¿Quiénes estuvieron allí?

_____

3. ¿Supo Lorenzo por qué yo no fui a la fiesta?

_____

4. ¿Cómo fuiste a casa de Lorenzo?

_____

5. ¿Cómo fue la música?

_____

6. ¿Pudiste bailar con Estela?

_____

7. ¿Fueron Uds. al jardín de la casa?

_____

8. ¿Tuviste que volver a casa temprano?

_____

9. ¿Estuviste en casa a esa hora?

_____

10. ¿Quién puso las decoraciones?

_____

EXERCISE N

Your sister has just returned from an exchange program in Colombia. Answer the questions a friend asks you about her trip.

1. ¿Cuánto tiempo estuvo ella en Colombia?

   _____

2. ¿A quién pidió ella permiso para ir?

   _____

3. ¿Hizo ella el viaje sola?

   _____

4. ¿Con quién fue a Colombia?

   _____

5. ¿Cómo fue la familia con que vivió?

   _____

6. ¿Pudiste pedirle muchos regalos?

   _____

7. ¿Pudo ella traer muchas cosas?

   _____

8. ¿Qué quiso ella hacer allí?

   _____

9. ¿Tuviste que ir al aeropuerto cuando llegó?

   _____

10. ¿Quién más fue a recibirla al aeropuerto?

    _____

11. ¿Cómo supiste la hora de su llegada?

    _____

12. ¿Durmió ella en el avión?

    _____

13. ¿Quién vino con ella?

    _____

14. ¿Tuvo ella alguna dificultad en Colombia?

_____

15. ¿Qué ciudad de Colombia prefirió ella?

_____

EXERCISE O

Complete the latest entry in Laura's diary, using the correct forms of the preterite tense.

Hoy por la mañana yo ___estuve___ en casa de mi amiga Gloria. Su padre
 1. (estar)

___→ construir___ una casita de muñecas para su hermana menor, Teresa.
 2. (construir)

___→ ser___ una sorpresa para la niña. Teresa y yo ___ponemos___ los muebles en
 3. (ser)   4. (poner)

la casa. Después nosotras ___fuimos___ al centro para comprar otros muebles. Nosotras
 5. (ir)

___andamos___ por muchas tiendas hasta que nosotras ___damos___ con unos
 6. (andar)   7. (dar)

muebles bonitos. Teresa ___prefiere___ comprar todos los muebles pero nosotras no
 8. (preferir)

___pudimos___ encontrar una mesita para el comedor. Ella ___leemos___ un
 9. (poder)   10. (leer)

catálogo de muebles y ___pedimos___ una mesita bonita. Antes de salir de la casa, Teresa y
 11. (pedir)

Gloria ___medimos___ las ventanitas de la casita. Ellas ___compramos___ tela
 12. (medir)   13. (comprar)

e ___hago___ cortinas para todos los cuartos de la casita. Yo quería comprar un regalito para
 14. (hacer)

Teresa pero no ___pudo___ encontrar nada. Cuando regresamos a casa, Teresa
 15. (poder)

___ponerse___ a llorar. La casita de muñecas ___caer___ de la mesa al suelo. Yo
 16. (ponerse)   17. (caer)

___sentir___ mucho lo que pasó. El perro ___destruir___ la casa al correr a la
 18. (sentir)   19. (destruir)

puerta. La madre de Teresa ___reñir___ al perro y el perro ___tener___ que
 20. (reñir)   21. (tener)

estar en el jardín. Yo ___venir___ a casa a las ocho de la noche.
 22. (venir)

EXERCISE P

Express in Spanish what Elisa tells a friend about her date with Jamal.

1. I wasn't nervous.

   _____

2. The weather was bad.

   _____

3. Jamal and I went to the movies.

   _____

4. I put my wallet in my purse.

   _____

5. I couldn't find my keys.

   _____

6. We walked to the movie theater.

   _____

7. We had to wait in line.

   _____

8. I read the posters about the film.

   _____

9. Jamal preferred to see another film.

   _____

10. We quarreled.

   _____

11. We had to sit in the second row of the theater.

   _____

12. The ticket included a box of popcorn.

   _____

13. I gave Jamal some popcorn.

   _____

14. He asked for more popcorn.

   _____

15. He slept in the theater.

_____

16. It was a terrible movie.

_____

17. After the movie, I went home.

_____

18. Jamal wanted to go with me.

_____

19. I preferred to return alone.

_____

20. He went to a party.

_____

Chapter 12
Imperfect Tense

[1] REGULAR VERBS

a. The imperfect tense of regular verbs is formed by dropping the infinitive ending *(-ar, -er, -ir)*, and adding the following endings:

INFINITIVE	STEM	IMPERFECT ENDINGS
mostrar	mostr	-aba, -abas, -aba, -ábamos, -abais, -aban
volver	volv	-ía, -ías, -ía, -íamos, -íais, -ían
abrir	abr	-ía, -ías, -ía, -íamos, -íais, -ían

b. Verbs that are stem-changing in the present tense do not change the stem vowel in the imperfect.

c. The first- and third-person singular forms are the same. Subject pronouns are used if necessary to clarify the meaning of the verb.

EXERCISE A

At a high-school reunion, some friends are remembering where they used to eat lunch when they were students. Write what they say.

EXAMPLE: Shaquille / la cafetería / siempre
Shaquille **almorzaba en** la cafetería siempre.

1. Luis y Yoko / el parque / a veces

_____

2. tú / el restaurante / de vez en cuando

_____

3. Jack y yo / casa / siempre

_____

4. yo / la clase de arte / todos los días

_____

5. ellos / el gimnasio / con frecuencia

_____

6. nosotros / el patio de la escuela / a veces

_____

7. mis primos / mi casa

_____

EXERCISE B

David and some friends have given up eating sweets. What did they used to eat?

EXAMPLE: Pedro / helado todos los días
Pedro **comía** helado todos los días.

1. Pascal / muchos chocolates

_____

2. Yolanda / pastel en cada comida

_____

3. Carol y yo / dulces todos los días

_____

4. Arturo y Nick / flan con frecuencia

_____

5. tú / helado después de las clases

_____

6. María / jalea de guayaba

_____

EXERCISE C

A group of friends are telling where they used to live. Write what they say.

EXAMPLE: Juan / Nevada
Juan **vivía en** Nevada.

1. yo / Tejas

_____

2. Ana / California

_____

3. los hermanos Casero / Honduras

_____

4. tú / la Florida

_____

5. Fabiana y yo / San Juan

_____

6. Uds. / Nueva York

_____

EXERCISE D

Javier describes what life was like when he was younger. Write what he says.

EXAMPLE: nosotros / vivir en una casa grande
           Nosotros **vivíamos** en una casa grande.

1. yo / tener un perro

   _____

2. mis hermanos / jugar al fútbol conmigo

   _____

3. mi mamá / no trabajar

   _____

4. toda la familia / visitar a los abuelos los domingos

   _____

5. mi abuela / preparar comidas deliciosas

   _____

6. mis amigos y yo / correr en la calle

   _____

7. tú / hacer muchas bromas

   _____

8. mi papá / tener un automóvil convertible

   _____

9. mi hermano mayor / querer aprender a conducir

   _____

10. nosotros / salir de la ciudad con frecuencia

   _____

EXERCISE E

Your little brother asks your grandfather questions about his life. Answer his questions in the imperfect, using the cues provided.

1. ¿Dónde vivías cuando tenías mi edad? *(en un pueblo)*

   _____

2. ¿Con quién vivías? *(mis padres y hermanos)*

   _____

3. ¿Jugabas al béisbol a veces? *(sí)*

_____

4. ¿Conocías a mi abuela cuando Uds. estaban en la escuela? *(no)*

_____

5. ¿Asistían Uds. a la misma escuela? *(no)*

_____

6. ¿Tenías una bicicleta? *(sí)*

_____

7. ¿Cómo celebrabas tu cumpleaños? *(una fiesta)*

_____

8. ¿Te daban muchos regalos? *(sí)*

_____

9. ¿Nadaban tú y tus amigos en una piscina? *(un lago)*

_____

10. ¿De qué tenías miedo? *(nada)*

_____

[2] VERBS IRREGULAR IN THE IMPERFECT TENSE

There are three irregular verbs in the imperfect tense: *ir*, *ser*, and *ver*.

INFINITIVE	IMPERFECT ENDINGS
ir	iba, ibas, iba, íbamos, ibais, iban
ser	era, eras, era, éramos, erais, eran
ver	veía, veías, veía, veíamos, veíais, veían

EXERCISE F

Write where these people used to go in the summer.

EXAMPLE: José / a la playa
José **iba** a la playa.

1. tú / a las montañas

_____

2. mi hermana y yo / al campamento

_____

3. Hugo / a casa de sus abuelos

_____

4. yo / al campo

_____

5. Rodolfo y César / a la escuela

_____

6. Ud. / al extranjero

_____

EXERCISE G

Write what these people were like when they were younger.

EXAMPLE: Gladys / muy alta
          Gladys **era** muy alta.

1. yo / tímido

_____

2. Patricia / bonita

_____

3. los niños / traviesos

_____

4. tú / cariñoso

_____

5. Nilda y Victoria / muy enérgicas

_____

6. Esteban y yo / consentidos

_____

EXERCISE H

Write the types of programs these people used to watch.

EXAMPLE: mi mamá / telenovelas todos los días
          Mi mamá **veía** telenovelas todos los días.

1. Enrique / las películas policíacas los sábados

_____

2. tú / los deportes los lunes

_____

3. mi papá y yo / el reportaje deportivo cada noche

_____

4. Kyoko y Pilar / las comedias

_____

5. Pat y Mike / las noticias cada noche

_____

6. Uds. / los programas de ciencia ficción cada semana

_____

EXERCISE I

Tell who used to do these things. Write about each activity using the imperfect tense.

ayudar a mi madre siempre   practicar con el equipo por la tarde
ir al circo en la primavera   vender limonada en el verano
ir de compras con sus amigas los sábados   ver los concursos cada noche
jugar al tenis cada sábado

1. Mi abuela _____ .

2. Yo _____ .

3. Mis hermanos y yo _____ .

4. Mis amigos _____ .

5. Tú _____ .

6. Mi hermana _____ .

7. Mi prima _____ .

[3] USES OF THE IMPERFECT TENSE

The imperfect tense is used:

a. to express what used to happen.

Íbamos a México todos los veranos.   *We would go (used to go) to Mexico every summer.*
Yo tocaba la guitarra.   *I played (used to play) the guitar.*

b. to express what happened repeatedly in the past.

Yo trabajaba a menudo durante las vacaciones.   *I often worked (used to work) during vacation.*

Pablo **me llamaba** mucho.   *Pablo called (used to call) me a lot.*

c. to describe what was going on at a particular time.

Leía el periódico durante el concierto.   *I read (was reading) the newspaper during the concert.*

d. to describe simultaneous actions in the past. *Mientras* is usually used to connect the two actions.

Yo **escribía** una carta **mientras**   *I wrote a letter while I listened to the radio.*
escuchaba la radio.

e. to describe what was going on in the past (imperfect) when something else began or ended (preterite). *Cuando* usually links the two actions.

Yo **escribía** una carta **cuando** Carlos   *I was writing a letter when Carlos entered.*
entró.

f. to describe persons or things in the past.

Jane **era** alta y bonita.   *Jane was tall and pretty.*
Los aviones **eran** muy grandes.   *The planes were very large.*

g. to express the time of day (hour) in the past.

Eran las once.   *It was eleven o'clock.*

EXERCISE J

The weather often affects what people do. Felipe's talking about the things he and his friends used to do in different kinds of weather. Write what he says, using the imperfect tense.

EXAMPLE: Yo **iba a la playa cuando hacía sol.**

1. Alicia y Melique _____.

2. Federico, John y yo _____ .

3. Tú _____ .

4. Yo _____ .

5. El equipo _____ .

EXERCISE K

Answer the questions that a new friend asks you about your childhood. Use the imperfect tense and the cues provided.

1. ¿Acompañabas a tu mamá a las tiendas? *(a veces)*

   _____

2. ¿Obedecías a tus padres? *(siempre)*

   _____

3. ¿Buscabas a tu mamá todos los días? *(sí)*

   _____

4. ¿Llorabas a menudo? *(sí)*

   _____

5. ¿Eras un niño (una niña) exigente? *(sí)*

   _____

6. ¿Poseían tú y tus hermanos muchos juguetes? *(no)*

   _____

7. ¿Gritabas mucho? *(no)*

   _____

8. ¿Dividían tus hermanos su dinero contigo? *(no)*

   _____

9. ¿Quitabas sus juguetes a los otros niños? *(sí)*

   _____

10. ¿Caías enfermo(a) a menudo? *(no)*

   _____

EXERCISE L

Someone played a prank in school, and the principal wants to know what everyone was doing at that time. Use the suggestions below to tell what these people were doing.

comer en la cafetería	hacer gimnasia
estar en la clase de biología	ir a la oficina
estudiar con Beto	leer en la biblioteca
hablar con el profesor de español	ver una película en la clase de historia

1. Juan _____.

2. Peggy y yo _____ .

3. Eduardo y Mai-Li _____ .

4. Tú _____ .

5. Ellas _____ .

6. Yo _____ .

7. Adela _____ .

8. Tú y Yolanda _____ .

EXERCISE M

Something interrupted what various people were doing. Relate each pair of events in a complete sentence.

EXAMPLE: yo / hablar por teléfono / mi padre / llegar
Yo **hablaba** por teléfono **cuando** mi padre **llegó**.

1. Elena / bañarse / el teléfono / sonar

_____

2. mi madre / cocinar / ella ver un ratoncito

_____

3. yo / mirar la televisión / yo / oír un ruido

_____

4. Gordon y yo / correr en el parque / empezar a llover

_____

5. Ellos / dormir / el perro / ladrar

_____

6. tú / leer un libro / la alarma / sonar

_____

7. Janice y José / subir al árbol / una rama / caer

_____

8. mi hermano / dormir profundamente / el despertador / sonar

_____

EXERCISE N

Who was your hero (heroine) when you were younger? Use the imperfect tense in a series of sentences describing this person.

_____

_____

_____

_____

_____

_____

_____

MASTERY EXERCISES

EXERCISE O

Rewrite this story in the imperfect tense.

Es la una de la mañana y todo el mundo duerme profundamente menos yo. Yo no puedo dormirme. No sé por qué. No estoy preocupado. No estoy enfermo.

Estoy ansioso porque pasado mañana voy a esquiar con mis amigos. Nosotros tenemos todo preparado y no me falta nada. Me gusta salir con ellos. Ya son las dos y media. Continúo despierto. Quiero tomar un vaso de leche caliente pero no tengo ganas de salir de la cama. Voy a contar ovejas—mi abuela dice que eso siempre le ayuda a dormir. Cuento ovejas pero después de quince minutos pierdo la cuenta.

Quiero gritar y llorar de la frustración. Ya son las cuatro. Trato de leer pero no puedo fijarme en el cuento. Siempre soy así la noche antes de mi cumpleaños.

_____

_____

_____

_____

_____

_____

_____

_____

_____

_____

_____

_____

_____

EXERCISE P

Answer the questions that you are asked when you return from summer camp.

1. ¿Tenías muchos amigos en el campamento?

_____

2. ¿Qué hacían durante el día?

_____

3. ¿Cuándo nadaban Uds.?

_____

4. ¿Cómo se llamaba tu consejero?

_____

5. ¿Cómo era?

_____

6. ¿Qué deportes practicabas?

_____

7. ¿Adónde ibas después de cenar?

_____

8. ¿Con quién pasabas mucho tiempo?

_____

9. ¿Gastabas mucho dinero en los videojuegos?

_____

10. ¿Qué hacían Uds. cuando llovía?

_____

EXERCISE Q

Express in Spanish what Diego's father tells him about his youth.

1. When I was your age I was very responsible.

   _____

2. I used to study and work.

   _____

3. I wanted to buy a car.

   _____

4. I had to save my money.

   _____

5. I had a girlfriend.

   _____

6. Her name was Diana.

   _____

7. She was sixteen years old when I met her.

   _____

8. She was very pretty, and she liked to dance.

   _____

9. I preferred to play football.

   _____

10. We used to go to a lot of parties and football games.

    _____

11. I used to see Diana on Saturdays.

    _____

12. We couldn't go out alone.

    _____

13. Diana's younger sister used to go with us.

    _____

14. She was very spoiled and cried a lot when I didn't pay attention to her.

    _____

15. Diana's parents were very strict.

_____

16. I couldn't save any money for my car because I was always paying for Diana and her sister.

_____

17. I was unhappy, but I liked Diana a lot.

_____

18. We were very good friends, and I used to write to her when she was away at college.

_____

19. Those were the good days.

_____

Chapter 13
Future Tense

[1] IR A + INFINITIVE

An action in the future can be expressed in Spanish by the present tense of *ir* followed by the preposition *a* and the infinitive of the verb that indicates the future action.

Voy a estudiar más tarde.　　*I'm going to study later.*

¿Qué vas a hacer?　　*What are you going to do?*

EXERCISE A

Jorge can never guess what his friends are going to do. Write what Jorge guesses and what his friends are actually going to do.

EXAMPLE:　Luis / jugar al tenis / trabajar
　　　　　Luis **va a** jugar al tenis.
　　　　　No, Luis **va a** trabajar.

1. Sergei / descansar / escuchar música

_____

_____

2. tú y Antonio / jugar al boliche / jugar al tenis

_____

_____

3. María / cocinar / tocar el piano

_____

_____

4. tú / ayudar a Felipe / leer un libro

_____

_____

5. Uds. / ver televisión / lavar los platos

_____

_____

6. Paco / dormir / estudiar

_____

_____

EXERCISE B

It's the end of the school year. Write six sentences in which you tell what you, your family, and your friends are going to do during the summer vacation.

_____

_____

_____

_____

_____

_____

EXERCISE C

The weather often affects our plans. Tell what you and your friends are going to do under these weather conditions.

EXAMPLE: si hace fresco
Si hace fresco, **vamos a montar** en bicicleta.

1. Si hace sol _____ .

2. Si hace frío _____ .

3. Si llueve _____ .

4. Si hace calor _____ .

5. Si nieva _____ .

[2] FUTURE TENSE OF REGULAR VERBS

a. The future tense of regular verbs is formed by adding the following personal endings to the infinitive form of the verb.

	hablar	comer	vivir
yo	hablaré	comeré	viviré
tú	hablarás	comerás	vivirás
Ud., él, ella	hablará	comerá	vivirá
nosotros, -as	hablaremos	comeremos	viviremos
vosotros, -as	hablaréis	comeréis	viviréis
Uds., ellos, ellas	hablarán	comerán	vivirán

b. In English, the future tense is expressed by means of the helping verb *will* or *shall*.

Visitaré a mis primos el domingo.   *I shall visit my cousins on Sunday.*

¿Viajarás a México pronto?   *Will you visit Mexico soon?*

c. All the endings have an accent mark except *-emos.*

EXERCISE D

Write what these people will do next summer.

EXAMPLE: Bernardo / trabajar en una oficina
Bernardo **trabajará** en una oficina.

1. Eva / visitar a sus primos en el campo

_____

2. mi hermana y yo / aprender a conducir

_____

3. Fumi y Mario / jugar al tenis

_____

4. mis padres / ir a Santo Domingo

_____

5. yo / tomar una clase de baile

_____

6. Elena y Teodoro / viajar a Costa Rica

_____

7. tú / asistir a la universidad

_____

8. Kim / ayudar a su padre en la tienda

_____

9. Rosalía / participar en un concurso

_____

10. nosotros / vivir cerca de la playa

_____

EXERCISE E

Write when these people will do these things.

EXAMPLE: Elisa / volver a las montañas / el próximo invierno
Elisa **volverá** a las montañas el próximo invierno.

1. Alicia y yo / preparar la cena / esta noche

_____

2. Simon / lavar el coche / pasado mañana

_____

3. yo / ir a la biblioteca / mañana

_____

4. los niños / jugar en un partido / el sábado que viene

_____

5. tú / dar un paseo en el parque / por la tarde

_____

6. Silvia y Amalia / correr en una carrera / en septiembre

_____

7. el maestro / escribir una carta de recomendación / más tarde

_____

EXERCISE F

You're saying good-bye to your best friend before going on vacation with your family to Mexico. Answer your friend's questions.

1. ¿Cuánto tiempo estarán Uds. en México? (*un mes*)

_____

2. ¿Cuántas ciudades visitarás? (*tres*)

_____

3. ¿Quién conducirá el coche? (*mis padres*)

_____

4. ¿Qué cosas verás allí? (*monumentos y playas*)

_____

5. ¿Me escribirás? (*sí*)

_____

6. ¿Conocerán Uds. las playas de Acapulco también? (*sí*)

_____

7. ¿Dormirás la siesta todos los días? (*sí*)

_____

8. ¿Cuándo volverán Uds.? (*en agosto*)

_____

[3] VERBS IRREGULAR IN THE FUTURE TENSE

Some verbs form the future tense by adding the future personal endings (*-é, -ás, -á, -emos, -éis, -án*) to an irregular stem.

a. Verbs like *poder* drop the *e* of the infinitive and then add the endings of the future tense.

poder: podr -é, -ás, -á, -emos, -éis, -án
Like **poder:**   haber, querer, saber

b. In verbs like *poner*, the *e* (or *i*) of the infinitive is replaced by a *d*, and the endings of the future tense are added.

poner: pondr -é, -ás, -á, -emos, -éis, -án
Like **poner:**   salir, tener, venir

c. The verbs *decir* and *hacer* drop two letters to form an irregular future stem.

decir: dir -é, -ás, -á, -emos, -éis, -án
hacer: har -é, -ás, -á, -emos, -éis, -án

EXERCISE G

Upon arrival in Buenos Aires, a group of students take a bus to their hotel. They're excited about what they'll be able to do in Argentina. Write what they say.

EXAMPLE: nosotros / poder conocer el barrio italiano
            Nosotros **podremos** conocer el barrio italiano.

1. yo / poder conocer muchos lugares

_____

2. Elena / poder ir de compras

_____

3. Spiros y Estela / poder aprender a bailar el tango

_____

4. tú / poder asistir a la ópera

_____

5. Raúl / poder conocer las pampas argentinas

_____

6. Diana y yo / poder ver a muchos gauchos

_____

7. Uds. / poder tomar fotografías

_____

EXERCISE H

Raquel writes to a friend and tells her about her plans. Complete her note with the appropriate forms of the future tense of the verbs indicated.

Querida Elena:

¡Buenas noticias! Mi familia _____ un viaje a tu ciudad el mes que viene. Yo
                                        1. (hacer)

_____ el viaje con ellos. Yo no _____ la fecha exacta en que
        2. (hacer)   *3.* (saber)

nosotros _____ hasta la próxima semana, pero yo _____ verte
                4. (salir)   *5.* (querer)

durante mi visita. ¿ _____ tú ir a verme al hotel? Creo que Gloria y María
                            6. (poder)

_____ también. Nosotras _____ mucho que contar. Yo
        7. (venir)   *8.* (tener)

_____ el placer de invitarte a almorzar. Al saber la fecha de mi llegada yo te la
        9. (tener)

_____ en otra carta o te la _____ por teléfono.
        10. (poner)   *11.* (decir)

Hasta pronto,

Raquel

EXERCISE I

You and some friends are talking about the future. Where will you be in twenty years? Answer these questions.

1. ¿Tendrás un trabajo bueno?

_____

2. ¿Ganarás mucho dinero?

_____

3. ¿Saldrás todavía con tus amigos?

_____

4. ¿Vendrás a ver a tus amigos de la juventud?

_____

5. ¿Sabrás hablar español?

_____

6. ¿Querrás vivir en otra ciudad?

_____

7. ¿Harás muchos viajes a Europa?

_____

8. ¿Pondrás mucho dinero en el banco?

_____

9. ¿Qué dirás de tus amigos?

_____

EXERCISE J

You're the stage manager for a school play. Using the verbs indicated, write what each of your crew members will do.

EXAMPLE: Yo no **podré** hacer todas las cosas.

1. Claude _____ la mesa al lado del sofá.
               (poner)

2. Miguel y Luz _____ que ayudar a Gerardo.
                    (tener)

3. El director _____ todo listo a las seis.
                  (querer)

4. Todos nosotros _____ los adornos.
                     (hacer)

5. Elena _____ dónde poner las flores.
             (saber)

6. Tú _____ a buscar una lámpara.
          (salir)

7. Los actores _____ aquí a las seis y cuarto.
                   (venir)

8. Nosotros no _____ descansar hasta más tarde.
                   (poder)

MASTERY EXERCISES

EXERCISE K

José is the youngest child in the family, and he loves to reaffirm what his parents say his brothers and sisters will do. Write what his parents say and then what José says.

EXAMPLE: Marcos / sacar la basura
            Marcos **va a sacar** la basura.
            Marcos s**acará** la basura.

  1. Pablo / lavar el coche

_____

_____

2. Anita / hacer la ensalada

_____

_____

3. Gregory / vender su bicicleta

_____

_____

4. Susan / poner la mesa

_____

_____

5. José, tú / ayudar a Susana

_____

_____

6. Gregory y Pablo / venir a casa temprano

_____

_____

7. Paul y yo / descansar

_____

_____

EXERCISE L

On New Year's Eve, Mr. Moore is talking with you about what will happen during the coming year. Write what he says.

EXAMPLE: Gabriel / terminar sus estudios
Gabriel **terminará** sus estudios.

1. Lorenzo / poder comprar un coche

_____

2. Lorenzo y Gabriel / tener que buscar un trabajo

_____

3. tú / hacer un viaje a Puerto Rico

_____

4. Alicia y yo / salir a menudo

_____

5. yo / venir a casa temprano

_____

6. mis padres / vivir en otro estado

_____

EXERCISE M

Help an American exchange student in Caracas to communicate with his host family. Express what he wants to say in Spanish.

1. I'll leave Atlanta on Saturday morning.

_____

2. I'll make the trip by plane.

_____

3. I'm going to bring two suitcases.

_____

4. Will you meet me at the airport?

_____

5. How will I know you?

_____

6. Will we take a taxi to your house?

_____

7. Are we going to go directly to your house?

_____

8. I'll have to exchange money.

_____

9. I'll have to call my parents upon arriving.

_____

10. We'll spend six weeks together.

_____

11. My friends will want your address.

_____

12. It will be fun.

_____

Chapter 14
Reflexive Verbs

FRANCIA

PORTUGAL   ESPAÑA

○ Madrid   Barcelona ●

ITALIA

Islas Baleares

● Sevilla

[1] REFLEXIVE VERBS IN SIMPLE TENSES

a. A reflexive verb requires a reflexive pronoun (*me, te, se, nos, os, se*) that refers the action of the verb back to the subject.

Yo me lavo.	*I wash myself.*
Ellos se visten.	*They dress themselves. (They get dressed.)*

b. Reflexive pronouns generally precede the verb in the simple tenses.

PRESENT TENSE	
yo me lavo	nosotros (-as) nos lavamos
tú te lavas	vosotros (-as) os laváis
Ud., él, ella se lava	Uds., ellos, ellas se lavan

PRETERITE TENSE	
yo me lavé	nosotros (-as) nos lavamos
tú te lavaste	vosotros (-as) os lavasteis
Ud., él, ella se lavó	Uds., ellos, ellas se lavaron

IMPERFECT TENSE	
yo me lavaba	nosotros (-as) nos lavábamos
tú te lavabas	vosotros (-as) os lavasteis
Ud., él, ella se lavaba	Uds., ellos, ellas se lavaban

FUTURE TENSE	
yo me lavaré	nosotros (-as) nos lavaremos
tú te lavarás	vosotros (-as) os lavaréis
Ud., él, ella se lavará	Uds., ellos, ellas se lavarán

c. When a reflexive verb is used as an infinitive, the reflexive pronoun is attached to the end of the infinitive or placed before the conjugated verb. Both forms are accepted.

Voy a bañar**me**. **Me** voy a bañar.	*I'm going to take a bath.*
Queremos levantar**nos** ahora. **Nos** queremos levantar ahora.	*We want to get up now.*

d. Common reflexive verbs:

acostarse (ue) *to go to bed*	divertirse (ie) *to enjoy oneself, have a good time*
afeitarse *to shave*	dormirse (ue) *to fall asleep*
bañarse *to take a bath, bathe*	irse *to go away*
cepillarse *to brush* (one's teeth, hair, or clothes)	lavarse *to wash oneself*
	levantarse *to get up*
desayunarse *to have breakfast*	llamarse *to be named, be called*
despertarse (ie) *to wake up*	

peinarse *to comb one's hair*	quitarse *to take off* (clothing)
ponerse *to put on* (clothing)	sentarse (ie) *to sit down*
quedarse *to stay, remain*	vestirse (i) *to get dressed*

NOTE:

1. Some verbs that are reflexive in Spanish are translated nonreflexively in English.

   nos quedamos   *we remain*   él **se va**   *he goes away*

2. Some reflexive verbs are stem-changing. In the end vocabulary, the stem change is indicated after the verb.

   sentarse (ie)   me s**ie**nto   *I sit down*

   vestirse (i)   me v**i**sto   *I get dressed*

EXERCISE A

Lola thinks that her family has many idiosyncrasies. Write what she says.

EXAMPLE: mi hermano / peinarse sin peine
             Mi hermano **se peina** sin peine.

1. mi abuelo / lavarse las manos cincuenta veces al día

_____

2. mi papá / afeitarse mientras bañarse

_____

3. mis hermanas / bañarse por la mañana y por la noche

_____

4. yo / ponerse perfume cinco veces al día

_____

5. Berta y yo / ponerse la misma ropa

_____

6. tú / vestirse en la oscuridad

_____

EXERCISE B

Rita has been baby-sitting her neighbor's children. Answer the questions Rita is asked when the neighbor returns home.

EXAMPLE: ¿Se lavaron las manos? *(no)*
             No, **no se lavaron** las manos.

1. ¿Se puso Juan la pijama sin problema? *(sí)*

_____

2. ¿Se bañaron Angela y Elena? *(no)*

_____

3. ¿Se acostó Juan a las ocho? *(sí)*

_____

4. ¿Se durmió delante de la televisión? *(no)*

_____

5. ¿Se peinó Elena antes de acostarse? *(sí)*

_____

6. ¿Te lavaste las manos? *(sí)*

_____

7. ¿Se despertó Juan alguna vez? *(no)*

_____

8. ¿Te dormiste cuando los niños se acostaron? *(no)*

_____

EXERCISE C

Luis is at a camp reunion, reminiscing with his friends about the things they used to do. Write what he says, using the imperfect tense.

EXAMPLE: yo / levantarse temprano
           Yo **me levantaba** temprano.

1. Abraham y Sergio / despertarse a las seis

_____

2. tú / vestirse rápidamente

_____

3. el consejero / cepillarse los dientes después de cada comida

_____

4. Paco y yo / nunca desayunarse

_____

5. Alberto / dormirse en la cama y no quitarse la ropa

_____

6. nosotros / divertirse en el lago

_____

EXERCISE D

You are on vacation. Write five sentences in which you describe how you spend one day. Use the verbs suggested below.

acostarse	despertarse	dormirse	peinarse	quedarse
desayunarse	divertirse	lavarse	ponerse	vestirse

_____

_____

_____

_____

_____

_____

_____

_____

EXERCISE E

Using the cues provided, write what these people will do.

EXAMPLE: Esteban tiene hambre por la mañana. *(desayunarse)*
            Él **se desayunará.**

1. La señora Singh está cansada. *(acostarse)*

_____

2. Tú vas a ver un programa en la televisión. *(sentarse en el sillón)*

_____

3. Los niños van a comer ahora. *(lavarse las manos)*

_____

4. Richie acaba de jugar al béisbol. *(bañarse)*

_____

5. Marta va a salir con sus amigas. *(peinarse bien)*

_____

6. Yo tengo frío. *(ponerse un suéter)*

_____

7. Llueve mucho y no queremos salir. *(quedarse en casa)*

_____

8. Vemos un programa aburrido en la televisión. *(dormirse en el sofá)*

_____

9. Luz oye el despertador. *(levantarse rápidamente)*

_____

10. Tus tíos tienen un bebé recién nacido. *(llamarse Francisco)*

_____

[2] REFLEXIVE COMMANDS

In affirmative commands, reflexive pronouns follow the verb and are attached to it. In negative commands, reflexive pronouns precede the verb. Affirmative reflexive commands with more than two syllables have a written accent over the stressed vowel.

AFFIRMATIVE COMMANDS		NEGATIVE COMMANDS	
(tú) ¡**Lávate**!	(Uds.) ¡**Lávense**!	(tú) ¡**No te laves**!	(Uds.) ¡**No se laven**!
(Ud.) ¡**Lávese**!		(Ud.) ¡**No se lave**!	

EXERCISE F

Your parents are away, and your older sister is in charge. Write in Spanish the commands she gives you.

EXAMPLE: bañarse ahora
          ¡**Báñate** ahora!

1. cepillarse los dientes

_____

2. acostarse temprano

_____

3. quitarse los zapatos

_____

4. ponerse ropa limpia

_____

5. quedarse en la casa

_____

EXERCISE G

While you rehearse a school play, the teacher gives you directions. Write what she says you shouldn't do.

EXAMPLE: levantarse de la silla ahora
¡**No te levantes** de la silla ahora!

1. peinarse en este momento

_____

2. sentarse en el sofá

_____

3. ponerse el sombrero todavía

_____

4. quitarse el suéter hasta más tarde

_____

5. irse de la escena

_____

EXERCISE H

A teacher walking through the school cafeteria tells a group of students to do the following things. Write what she says.

EXAMPLE: quedarse en la cafetería
¡**Quédense** en la cafetería!

1. desayunarse en silencio

_____

2. quitarse los anteojos de sol

_____

3. sentarse en las sillas

_____

4. lavarse las manos

_____

5. quedarse donde están ahora

_____

EXERCISE I

What does she tell them they shouldn't do?

EXAMPLE: irse de la cafetería
          ¡No se vayan de la cafetería!

1. desayunarse en el piso

_____

2. ponerse los anteojos de sol

_____

3. peinarse aquí

_____

4. quedarse cerca de la ventana

_____

5. quitarse los zapatos

_____

6. sentarse en la mesa

_____

M A S T E R Y   E X E R C I S E S

EXERCISE J

Rosa, Annette, Theresa, and Mary are sharing a hotel room on an overnight school trip. Complete their dialogue using the appropriate form of the reflexive verbs.

ROSA: _____, muchachas. Ya son las siete de la mañana.
              1. (despertarse)

MARY: ¿Quién _____ primero?
                   2. (bañarse)

THERESA: La persona que _____ primero puede _____ primero.
                      3. (levantarse)   *4.* (bañarse)

ROSA: Bueno, mientras yo _____, Uds. _____ .
                        5. (bañarse)   *6.* (peinarse)

MARY: Buena idea. Annette, _____ . Vamos a llegar tarde.
                       7. (levantarse)

ANNETTE: Tengo mucho sueño. Vuelvo a _____ mientras Uds. _____ .
                            8. (dormirse)   *9.* (vestirse)

THERESA: ¡No _____ otra vez, Annette! Tenemos que _____
                   10. (dormirse)   **11.** (desayunarse)

a las ocho.

ANNETTE: Bueno, ahora yo _____ .
                          12. (levantarse)

MARY: Theresa, ¿qué _____ hoy?
                              13. (ponerse)

THERESA: Hace calor. Rosa y yo decidimos _____ pantalones cortos. ¿Y tú?
                                                      14. (ponerse)

MARY: Yo _____ lo mismo.
                  15. (ponerse)

ROSA: ¡Annette, no _____ aquí! _____ en el cuarto de baño,
                         16. (peinarse)   **17.** (peinarse)

por favor. Y mientras estás allí, _____ y _____ la cara.
                                           18. (bañarse)   **19.** (lavarse)

Después yo _____ la cara y _____ también.
                  20. (lavarse)   **21.** (peinarse)

THERESA: ¡Mary, _____ esa blusa! Es mía. ¡ _____ otra blusa!
                      22. (quitarse)   **23.** (ponerse)

MARY: Bueno, yo voy a _____ esta blusa blanca.
                              24. (ponerse)

ROSA: Annette, no _____ en esa silla, por favor. Mi ropa está allí.
                         25. (sentarse)

ANNETTE: Yo no quiero salir. Prefiero _____ aquí. Todavía tengo sueño y hay
                                             26. (quedarse)

buenos programas en la televisión por la mañana.

MARY: De ninguna manera, Annette. _____ ahora porque nosotras estamos listas
                                          27. (vestirse)

y _____ .
      28. (irse)

EXERCISE K

Express in Spanish Mirta's description of a new friend.

1. Her name is Susan.

_____

2. She likes to stay at home.

_____

3. She and her sisters enjoy themselves in the garden.

_____

4. Susan wakes up at seven o'clock.

_____

5. Her family has breakfast together every day.

_____

6. She bathes and dresses rapidly.

_____

7. She and I prefer to comb our hair after we get dressed.

_____

8. She and I fall asleep in history class sometimes.

_____

9. She sits at the first desk.

_____

10. The teacher tells her: "Wake up!"

_____

11. She tells me: "Don't fall asleep in this class again!"

_____

12. When we wake up, we leave the room to wash our faces.

_____

13. She wears pretty clothes.

_____

14. She always asks: "What are you going to wear tomorrow?"

_____

15. We have a good time together.

_____

16. Her mother always says: "Don't go to bed late!"

_____

17. She and her sisters are going away.

_____

Chapter 15
Common Idiomatic Expressions with Verbs

Many Spanish verbs are used in idiomatic expressions. A list of common expressions follows:

[1] EXPRESSIONS WITH *HACER*

¿Qué tiempo hace? *How's the weather?*
¿Qué tiempo hace en julio? *How's the weather in July?*

hacer buen / mal tiempo *to be good / bad weather*
Hace mal tiempo hoy. *Today the weather is bad.*

hacer (mucho) frío / calor / fresco *to be (very) cold / warm / cool* (weather)
Hizo mucho frío anoche. *It was very cold last night.*

hacer (mucho) sol *to be (very) sunny*
Hace mucho sol por la tarde. *It's very sunny in the afternoon.*

hacer (mucho) viento *to be (very) windy*
Hace viento. *It's windy.*

hacer el favor de + infinitive *please . . .*
Haga el favor de abrir la ventana. *Please open the window.*

hacer un viaje *to take a trip*
Hacen un viaje cada año. *They take a trip each year.*

hacer una pregunta *to ask a question*
El niño hace muchas preguntas. *The boy asks many questions.*

hacer una visita *to pay a visit*
Ella hizo una visita a su abuela. *She paid a visit to her grandmother.*

EXERCISE A

Tell what you like to do in different kinds of weather. Use the suggestions below.

andar en el parque	ir al cine	mirar la televisión
correr en el parque	jugar al tenis	nadar en la piscina
ir a las montañas	leer un libro	quedarse en casa

EXAMPLE: hacer buen tiempo
Cuando **hace** buen tiempo **me gusta andar en el parque.**

1. hacer sol

_____

2. hacer mucho viento

_____

3. hacer mal tiempo

_____

4. hacer mucho calor

_____

5. hacer fresco

_____

6. hacer mucho frío

_____

EXERCISE B

Describe the weather in each of the drawings below.

EXAMPLE: **Hace mucho viento.**

1. _____   **3.** _____

2. _____   **4.** _____

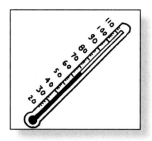

5. _____

EXERCISE C

Use an idiomatic expression with *hacer* to tell what these people do.

1. Moses no comprende un problema de la clase de matemáticas.

Él _____.

2. Alicia y Ramona se visten para ir a la escuela.

Ellas preguntan _____.

3. Los señores Ortiz quieren conocer Chile.

Ellos _____.

4. Yo estoy en la biblioteca y quiero estudiar, pero unos jóvenes hablan en voz alta.

Yo digo _____.

5. Tú tienes ganas de ver a tus primos.

Tú _____.

[2] EXPRESSIONS WITH *TENER*

¿Qué tiene Ud.?   *What's the matter with you?*
¿Qué tiene Ud. ahora?   *What's the matter with you now?*

tener... años   to be ... years old
¿Cuántos años tiene Juan?   *How old is Juan?*
Juan tiene diez años.   *Juan is ten years old.*

tener (mucho) calor   *to be (very) warm (persons)*
¿Tiene Ud. calor?   *Are you warm?*

tener cuidado   *to be careful*
¡Ten cuidado en la playa!   *Be careful at the beach!*

tener dolor de cabeza   *to have a headache*
Ella tiene dolor de cabeza.   *She has a headache.*

tener dolor de muelas   *to have a toothache*
Él tiene dolor de muelas.   *He has a toothache.*

tener (mucho) frío   *to be (very) cold* (persons)
Los niños tienen frío.   *The children are cold.*

tener ganas de   *to feel like, want to*
Tengo ganas de gritar.   *I feel like screaming.*

tener (mucha) hambre   *to be (very) hungry*
No tengo hambre.   *I'm not hungry.*

tener la bondad de + infinitive   *to be kind enough to*
Tenga la bondad de cerrar la puerta.   *Be kind enough to close the door.*

tener miedo de   *to be afraid of*
Tienen miedo del mar.   *They're afraid of the sea.*

tener (mucha) sed   *to be (very) thirsty*
Tenemos sed ahora.   *We're thirsty now.*

tener (mucho) sueño   *to be (very) sleepy*
¿Tienen Uds. sueño?   *Are you sleepy?*

tener prisa   *to be in a hurry*
¡No tengas prisa!   *Don't be in a hurry!*

tener que + infinitive   *to have to, must*
Mi padre tiene que trabajar.   *My father has to work.*

tener razón / no tener razón   *to be right / to be wrong*
Mary siempre tiene razón.   *Mary is always right.*
Jamal no tiene razón.   *Jamal is wrong.*

EXERCISE D

Using an expression with *tener,* tell why these people do what they do.

EXAMPLE: Llevo pantalones cortos hoy.
            Yo **tengo calor**.

1. Pilar va al dentista.

_____

2. Tú usas un suéter.

_____

3. Yo busco otra respuesta a la pregunta.

_____

4. Vamos a la playa.

_____

5. Ellos comen una manzana.

_____

6. Juan se acuesta.

_____

7. El niño grita.

_____

8. Ud. bebe una limonada.

_____

9. Estudio ocho horas para un examen.

_____

10. El señor corre.

_____

11. Al no ver autos, el niño cruza la calle.

_____

12. La madre toma dos aspirinas.

_____

EXERCISE E

Use the expressions with _tener_ in parentheses to complete Martín's dialogue with the school nurse.

ENFERMERA: Hola, Martín. ¿ _____ ?
               1. (qué tener)

MARTÍN: _____ .
               2. (tener dolor de cabeza)

ENFERMERA: ¿ _____ ?
               3. (tener fiebre)

MARTÍN: No creo. _____ y a veces _____ .
               4. (tener frío)   **5.** (tener calor)

ENFERMERA: ¿Quieres comer algo?

MARTÍN: No, gracias. _____ .
               6. (no tener hambre)

ENFERMERA: ¿ _____ beber algo?
               7. (tener ganas de)

MARTÍN: Sí, _____ .
               8. (tener sed)

ENFERMERA: Yo _____ llamar a tu mamá.
               9. (tener que)

MARTÍN: Ud. _____ . Yo _____ ir a casa.
               10. (tener razón)   **11.** (tener ganas de)

ENFERMERA: _____ darme tu número de teléfono.
                12. (tener la bondad de)

MARTÍN: Es el 555-0021.

ENFERMERA: Está bien. Tú _____ esperar a tu madre. Ella viene por ti.
                      13. (tener que)

MARTÍN: Muchas gracias. Ahora yo _____ .
                            14. (tener sueño)

[3] OTHER IDIOMATIC VERBAL EXPRESSIONS

acabar de + infinitive   *to have just*
Él acaba de llegar.   *He has just arrived.*

dar la hora   *to strike the hour*
El reloj da las tres.   *The clock strikes three.*

dar las gracias   *to thank*
Damos las gracias al profesor.   *We thank the teacher.*

dar un paseo   *to take a walk*
Doy un paseo en el parque cada día.   *I take a walk in the park every day.*

darse la mano   *to shake hands*
Nos damos la mano.   *We shake hands.*

dejar caer   *to drop*
El niño deja caer la leche.   *The child drops the milk.*

dejar de + infinitive   *to fail to; to stop; to neglect to*
John deja de estudiar.   *John stops studying.*

echar al correo   *to mail*
Echo la carta al correo.   *I mail the letter.*

echar de menos   *to miss* (a person or thing)
Echo de menos a mis primos.   *I miss my cousins.*

estar de acuerdo   *to agree*
Estamos de acuerdo.   *We agree.*

guardar cama   *to stay in bed*
Él guarda cama por dos días.   *He's staying in bed for two days.*

llegar a ser   *to become; to get to be*
Quiero llegar a ser médico.   *I want to become a doctor.*

pensar + infinitive   *to intend to*
Pienso hacer un viaje.   *I intend to take a trip.*

ponerse + adjective   *to become; to turn*
El niño se puso triste.   *The child became sad.*

querer decir
¿Qué quiere decir «dinero»?   *What does "dinero" mean?*

sacar una fotografía   *to take a picture*
Pedro saca muchas fotografías.   *Peter takes many pictures.*

EXERCISE F

Several friends are commenting on various topics. Select the expression from those listed below and write its appropriate form in the space provided.

dar	dejar caer	estar de acuerdo	ponerse
dar las gracias	dejar de	guardar cama	querer decir
darse la mano	echar de menos	llegar a ser	sacar fotografías
dar un paseo	echarla al correo	pensar	

1. Luis está enfermo. Él _____ por tres días.

2. Cuando mis padres no están en casa, mi hermana menor los _____ .

3. Estoy contento porque trabajo en un hospital. Quiero _____ médico.

4. Cuando conoces a una persona, es correcto _____ .

5. Escribí esta carta. Ahora voy a _____ .

6. Roy y yo tenemos las mismas ideas. Nosotros _____ .

7. Yo voy a jugar al tenis mañana. ¿Qué _____ tú hacer?

8. Jorge no quiere ponerse gordo. Él _____ comer dulces.

9. Mi tía me dio este reloj. Ahora tengo que _____ a ella.

10. Phyllis tiene una cámara nueva. Le fascina _____ .

11. Yo no pasé el examen de conducir y _____ furioso.

12. Felipe no comprende nada. Él siempre pregunta: «¿Qué _____ eso?»

13. Hace buen tiempo y necesito ejercicio. Voy a _____ en el parque.

14. ¡No le des ese vaso de cristal a Jaime! Él _____ todo.

15. ¿Qué hora es? El reloj _____ la una y media.

EXERCISE G

Answer these questions a friend asks you.

1. ¿Sacas muchas fotografías cuando haces un viaje?

_____

2. ¿Guardas cama cuando estás enfermo(a)?

_____

3. ¿Te pones nervioso(a) antes de un examen?

_____

4. ¿Echas de menos a tus amigo(a)s durante las vacaciones?

_____

5. ¿Acabas de comprar ese suéter?

_____

6. ¿Dejas de estudiar cuando tus amigo(a)s te llaman por teléfono?

_____

7. ¿Das un paseo cada noche?

_____

8. ¿Das las gracias a tu madre cuando ella sirve la cena?

_____

9. ¿Piensas trabajar durante el verano?

_____

10. ¿Qué haces cuando conoces a una persona?

_____

MASTERY EXERCISES

EXERCISE H

The teacher asks the class to rewrite these sentences using an expression with _dar, hacer, tener,_ **or** _querer._

EXAMPLE: **Le duele** el estómago.
Tiene dolor de estómago.

1. Desea ir al cine esta noche.

_____

2. Tú **debes** estudiar.

_____

3. Abra la puerta, **por favor**.

_____

4. ¿Qué **significa** esta palabra?

_____

5. Ellos **caminan** por el parque.

_____

6. ¿**Qué edad tienes**?

_____

7. Me duele la cabeza.

_____

EXERCISE I

Carmen is spending a few weeks at a nature camp. Complete this letter with the appropriate idiomatic expressions.

Querida Susana:

Yo _____ volver de un paseo formidable. Casi todos los días hacemos lo
       1. (to have just)

mismo. El grupo _____ en el bosque y vemos muchas cosas interesantes.
         2. (to take a walk)

Cuando _____ salimos muy temprano y no volvemos hasta muy tarde. Yo
       3. (the weather is good)

_____ usar un sombrero, especialmente cuando
    4. (to have to)

_____ . Tengo mi cámara conmigo y yo _____ .
   5. (it's very sunny)   **6.** (to take many pictures)

Un día una chica _____ mi cámara y yo _____
         7. (to drop)   **8.** (to become)

furiosa. La cámara está bien y ella y yo _____ en que fue un accidente.
        9. (to agree)

Nosotras _____ y ahora somos buenas amigas.
    10. (to shake hands)

Por lo general, _____ aquí. Por la mañana y por la tarde
     11. (the weather is good)

_____ . Nosotras _____ llevar un suéter con
  12. (it's cold)   **13.** (to have to)

nosotras cuando salimos. También cuando nosotras _____ a otro sitio
         14. (to take a trip)

llevamos comida y bebidas para no _____
      15. (to be hungry)

ni _____ .
  16. (to be thirsty)

Las actividades son fuertes y a las ocho de la noche yo ya _____ . Yo
           17. (to be sleepy)

_____ a mis amigas pero Uds. pueden _____ a
  18. (to miss)   **19.** (to pay a visit)

este campamento. Ahora yo _____ porque quiero
                        20. (to be in a hurry)

_____ esta carta. _____ contestar esta carta.
      21. (to mail)   **22.** (please)

Cariñosamente,

Carmen

EXERCISE J

A friend's helping you study for a Spanish test. He asks how you would say various things in Spanish. Tell him.

EXAMPLE: How would you ask someone if he's thirsty?
          ¿Tiene Ud. sed?

1. How would you ask someone how the weather is?

    _____

2. How would ask someone if she's cold?

    _____

3. How would you ask someone if he has a toothache?

    _____

4. How would you ask someone if it's windy today?

    _____

5. How would you ask someone if she's hungry?

    _____

6. How would you tell someone that he's wrong?

    _____

7. How would you ask someone how old she is?

    _____

8. How would you tell someone that today it's sunny?

    _____

9. How would you tell your mother that you're thirsty?

    _____

10. How would you tell someone that the weather's fine?

    _____

11. How would you ask a sick man what's the matter with him?

    _____

12. How would you ask someone what the word *algodón* means?

_____

13. How would you ask someone to please close the door?

_____

14. How would you ask your friends if they're planning to take a trip?

_____

15. How would you tell your father that your younger brother is sleepy?

_____

16. How would you tell a friend to be careful?

_____

17. How would you tell someone that you are in a hurry?

_____

18. How would you tell a friend that you feel like taking a walk?

_____

19. How would you tell a friend that he has to leave?

_____

20. How would you tell someone that you agree?

_____

21. How would you tell someone that you want to become a teacher?

_____

22. How would you tell someone that you have to stay in bed?

_____

23. How would you ask a friend if she misses her sister?

_____

24. How would you tell your mother that you have just eaten?

_____

25. How would you ask a friend why she becomes nervous?

_____

Chapter 16
Negation

[1] NEGATIVES

a. The most common negative is *no*, which always precedes the conjugated verb.

Yo **no** leo el libro.　　　*I don't read the book.*

¿**No** escribiste la carta?　　*Didn't you write the letter?*

EXERCISE A

Pablo is answering a friend's questions about where the students in his class are from. Write what he says.

EXAMPLE:　¿Es Marta de México? *(Venezuela)*
　　　　　No, Marta **no es** de México. Ella **es** de Venezuela.

1. ¿Son Juan y Xavier de Puerto Rico? *(España)*

_____

2. ¿Es Alberto de la República Dominicana? *(Colombia)*

_____

3. ¿Es Laura de Guatemala? *(Costa Rica)*

_____

4. ¿Son Rafael y Linda de la Argentina? *(Chile)*

_____

5. ¿Eres tú de los Estados Unidos? *(Nicaragua)*

_____

EXERCISE B

You and your friends are in your basement. Your mother wants to know what you're doing. Answer her questions.

EXAMPLE:　¿Miran Uds. la televisión?
　　　　　No, no miramos la televisión.

1. ¿Juegan Uds. al ajedrez?

_____

2. ¿Leen Uds. el periódico?

_____

3. ¿Come Enrique helado?

_____

4. ¿Hablas tú por teléfono?

_____

5. ¿Preparas tú la tarea para mañana?

_____

6. ¿Arreglan Uds. el cuarto?

_____

7. ¿Practicas tú el diálogo con Luis?

_____

EXERCISE C

From the list below, tell five things you are not going to do this weekend.

caminar en el parque	jugar al fútbol	ver una película
estudiar en la biblioteca	lavar el coche	visitar a los abuelos
ir a la playa	nadar	

EXAMPLE: **No voy a ir a la playa.**

1. _____

2. _____

3. _____

4. _____

5. _____

b. Other negatives are:

nada   *nothing, (not) anything*

nadie   *no one, nobody, (not) anyone*

ni... ni   *neither... nor; not . . . either . . . or . . .*

ninguno (-a)   *no, none, (not) any*

no   *no, not*

nunca   *never, (not) ever*

tampoco   *neither, not either*

c. A double negative is acceptable in Spanish. In fact, this construction occurs frequently. If one of the negatives is *no*, it precedes the verb. If *no* is omitted, the other negative must precede the verb.

No veo **nada**
Nada veo.   } *I don't see anything.*

Él no juega **nunca**.
El **nunca** juega.   } *He never plays.*

d. *Nadie* can be used as the subject or the object of the verb. When it is the object of the verb, it is preceded by the preposition *a*.

Nadie entra. ⎫
No entra **nadie**. ⎭   *No one enters.*

BUT

No veo **a nadie**.   *I don't see anyone (anybody).*

A nadie veo.   *I see no one (nobody).*

e. *Ninguno* drops the final *-o* and takes a written accent over the *u* if it comes immediately before a masculine singular noun. If a preposition comes between *ninguno* and the noun, the full form is used.

Ning**ún** alumno está ausente.   *No pupil is absent.*

Ninguno de los alumnos está ausente.   *None of the pupils is absent.*

Ninguna casa tiene ascensor.   *No house has an elevator.*

EXERCISE D

Sarita's telling her mother the chores that her friends never do. Tell what she says.

EXAMPLE: ayudar en casa *(Juanita)*
               Juanita nunca ayuda en casa.

1. sacar la basura *(Raquel)*

_____

2. ir de compras *(Jorge y Pedro)*

_____

3. lavar el coche *(Alejandro)*

_____

4. preparar la ensalada *(Beatriz y Alex)*

_____

5. pasar la aspiradora *(Tomás y Víctor)*

_____

6. sacar al perro *(Oyuki)*

_____

7. poner la mesa *(Esteban)*

_____

8. secar los platos *(Lola y Emilio)*

_____

EXERCISE E

During a camping trip, your friend tries your patience with her questions. Answer them in Spanish, using a form of *ninguno*, **if possible, or** *nada*.

EXAMPLE: ¿Cuántos videojuegos tienes?
            No tengo **ninguno**.

1. ¿Ves los pájaros?

_____

2. ¿Tienes una lamparita?

_____

3. ¿Lees el mapa?

_____

4. ¿Llevas la mochila?

_____

5. ¿Preparas la cena?

_____

6. ¿Necesitas mi ayuda?

_____

EXERCISE F

Mr. Perales is complaining to his wife about his day at work. Tell what he says.

EXAMPLE: saludar a los jefes
            Nadie saluda a los jefes.

1. contestar el teléfono

_____

2. ayudar a la secretaria

_____

3. llegar a tiempo

_____

4. tomar una hora de almuerzo

_____

5. arreglar su escritorio

_____

6. recibir a los clientes

_____

7. hablar en voz baja

_____

EXERCISE G

During a date, Theresa finds Juan very distracted. Give Juan's answers to her questions.

EXAMPLE: ¿A quién miras?
  No miro a nadie.

1. ¿A quién hablas?

_____

2. ¿A quiénes buscas?

_____

3. ¿A quién esperas?

_____

4. ¿A quién admiras?

_____

5. ¿A quiénes respondes?

_____

EXERCISE H

Maria's helping her mother prepare a shopping list. Tell what she says to her mother.

EXAMPLE: pan
  No tenemos ningún pan.

1. fruta

_____

2. chocolate

_____

3. helado

_____

4. queso

_____

5. cebolla

_____

6. mantequilla

_____

7. pastel

_____

EXERCISE I

Lupe is comparing herself to a popular actress she just saw on a talk show. Tell what she says.

EXAMPLE: No le gusta el color rojo.
             No me gusta el color rojo **tampoco**.

1. Nunca se levanta temprano.

_____

2. No come carne.

_____

3. No le gusta decir adiós.

_____

4. Nunca usa paraguas.

_____

5. No fuma.

_____

EXERCISE J

César is describing a new neighbor. Tell what he says about him.

EXAMPLE: jugar al béisbol o al fútbol
             Él **no juega ni** al béisbol **ni** al fútbol.

1. leer periódicos o revistas

_____

2. jugar a las damas o al ajedrez

_____

3. ver películas o documentales

_____

4. correr o caminar a la escuela

_____

5. coleccionar estampillas o monedas

_____

6. dibujar o pintar

_____

EXERCISE K

Pedro describes a dream he had. Complete his description with the appropriate negative expressions.

Roberto y yo estamos en una fiesta. Estamos sentados en el sofá porque _____
                                                                           1.

conocemos _____ . _____ nos habla. La fiesta es muy aburrida.
                2.   **3.**

Tenemos hambre pero _____ hay _____ de comer. Por fin una
                         4.   **5.**

chica sale de la cocina con unos platos en la mano pero ella _____ nos ofrece
                                                                  6.

_____ . Roberto y yo vamos a la mesa y vemos que _____
       7.   **8.**

hay _____ plato bueno. A nosotros _____ nos gustan
        9.   **10.**

_____ los tacos _____ los frijoles. Queremos salir pero
     11.   **12.**

_____ encontramos _____ puerta. _____
     13.   **14.**   **15.**

contesta nuestras preguntas. _____ chico quiere ayudarnos.
                                   16.

Yo _____ puedo salir de allí y Roberto _____ puede salir
       17.   **18.**

_____ . Le digo a Roberto que _____ voy a aceptar una
     19.   **20.**

invitación a una fiesta donde _____ conozco _____ . En ese
                                   21.   **22.**

momento oigo una voz que me pregunta: —Pedro, ¿ _____ vas a comer con tus
                                                      23.

compañeros en la cafetería? Entonces me despierto y digo: —_____ vuelvo a
                                                                    24.

dormirme en la clase otra vez.

[2]   NEGATIVE EXPRESSIONS

Some useful negative expressions are:

Creo que no.   *I don't think so.*

De nada.   *You're welcome.*

en ningún lado
en ninguna parte   } *nowhere*

Mejor no.   *Better not.*

Ni yo tampoco.   *Me neither.*

No es así.   *It's not so.*

No es para tanto.   *It's not such a big deal.*

No hay más remedio   *It can't be helped.*

No importa.   *It doesn't matter.*

No lo creo.   *I don't believe it.*

¡No me digas!   *Don't tell me! (You don't say!)*

No me gusta nada.   *I don't like it at all.*

No puede ser.   *It can't be.*

No puedo más.   *I can't take it anymore.*

¿No te parece?   *Don't you think so?*

¿Por qué no?   *Why not?*

EXERCISE L

Several friends are sitting around and making plans. Using the following expressions, react to their statements.

De nada.	No lo creo.	No puede ser.
Ni yo tampoco.	No me gusta nada.	¿Por qué no?
No es para tanto.		

EXAMPLE: Juan dice: —Cuando mis primos dicen «gracias» yo nunca sé qué contestar.
Tú dices: **—Debes decir «de nada».**

1. Roberto dice: —Yo no tengo clases mañana.

Tú dices: _____

2. Luis dice: —Después de estos días de lluvia, dicen que va a hacer buen tiempo mañana.

Tú dices: _____

3. Laura dice: —Si vamos a la playa podemos practicar el esquí acuático.

Tú dices: _____

4. Esteban dice: —Mañana es el cumpleaños de Lázaro.

Tú dices: _____

5. Anita dice: —Lázaro tiene un coche de último modelo.

Tú dices: _____

6. Tomás dice: Vamos a llamar a Lázaro por teléfono.

Tú dices: _____

EXERCISE M

Poor Enrique spent the summer working while his friends went to Mexico. Using the expressions given, write appropriate responses that Enrique would make as his friends tell him about their trip.

Creo que no.	No hay más remedio.	No me gusta nada.
En ningún lado.	No lo creo.	No puedo más.
No es para tanto.	No me digas.	

EXAMPLE: Raúl dice: —¡En el avión nos sentamos en primera clase!
Enrique dice: **—No es para tanto.**

1. Joaquín dice: —Encontramos a tu maestra de español en un restaurante.

Enrique dice: _____

2. Felipe dice: —Cuando fuimos a pescar, yo pesqué un pez de cien libras.

Enrique dice: _____

3. Laura dice: —Visitamos muchos museos.

Enrique dice: _____

4. Alfredo dice: —Vamos a volver a México el verano que viene. ¿Vas con nosotros?

Enrique dice: _____

5. Héctor dice: —¿Vas a trabajar otra vez durante el verano?

Enrique dice: _____

6. Alicia dice: —Me encanta la música de los mariachis. ¿Sabes dónde venden discos de esta música?

Enrique dice: _____

7. Ofelia dice: —Tienes que ver las fotos que sacamos durante el viaje.

Enrique dice: _____

MASTERY EXERCISES

EXERCISE N

An exchange student asks you some questions in Spanish. Answer using a negative word or expression.

1. ¿Están cerradas las tiendas hoy?

No, _____ de las tiendas está cerrada hoy.

2. ¿Visitaste el museo de arte?

No visité _____ museo de arte.

3. ¿Vas al concierto o al cine?

No voy _____ al concierto _____ al cine.

4. ¿Cuándo juegas al tenis?

_____ juego al tenis.

5. ¿Quién habla español en tu casa?

_____ habla español en mi casa.

6. ¿A quién acompañas después de las clases?

No acompaño _____ después de las clases.

7. ¿Qué haces por la noche?

No hago _____ por la noche.

8. ¿Lees algún libro interesante?

No leo _____ libro interesante.

9. ¿Te gustan las películas de ciencia ficción?

No, _____ veo esas películas.

EXERCISE O

You're telling a friend about your school and classes. Express the following in Spanish.

1. No school is open today.

_____

2. We never have tests on Mondays.

_____

3. I never ask questions in any of my classes.

_____

4. No one goes to Spanish class without the homework.

_____

5. You can't speak to anyone in class.

_____

6. None of the tests are very difficult.

_____

7. We don't have a football team or a baseball team.

_____

8. The other teams never win.

_____

9. I'm not a member of any team.

_____

10. We never see any movies in school.

_____

11. No one likes to eat in the school cafeteria.

_____

12. The teachers are never absent.

_____

Part two

Noun and pronoun structures

ESPAÑA

Islas Baleares

Islas Canarias

MÉXICO

REPÚBLICA
DOMINICANA

PUERTO RICO

CUBA

HONDURAS

NICARAGUA

GUATEMALA

EL SALVADOR

COSTA RICA

PANAMÁ

VENEZUELA

COLOMBIA

ECUADOR

PERÚ

BOLIVIA

PARAGUAY

CHILE

URUGUAY

ARGENTINA

4. Kyung Mi y Mi Soo / Corea

_____

5. Arturo / Chile

_____

6. Arturo y Miriam / Colombia

_____

7. Pietro / Italia

_____

EXERCISE B

A new student asks you the following questions. Use the correct subject pronouns in your answers.

1. ¿Cómo te llamas?

_____

2. ¿Dónde vives?

_____

3. ¿Quién es ese chico?

_____

4. ¿Adónde van tú y tus amigos por la tarde?

_____

5. ¿Qué hacen Uds. allí?

_____

6. ¿Quiénes son esos señores?

_____

7. ¿Podemos tú y yo estudiar juntos?

_____

8. ¿Dónde juegan al tenis tus amigos?

_____

9. ¿Quieres ver una película esta noche?

_____

10. ¿Qué clases vas a tomar el año próximo?

_____

[2] PREPOSITIONAL PRONOUNS

Prepositions, which will be more fully explained in the next chapter, are words that define a relationship to a person, place, or thing. When a personal pronoun follows a preposition, it takes the following forms:

SINGULAR	PLURAL
mí *me*	**nosotros, -as** *us*
ti *you* (familiar)	**vosotros, -as** *you* (familiar)
usted (Ud.) *you*	**ustedes (Uds.)** *you*
él *him, it*	**ellos** *them* (masculine)
ella *her, it*	**ellas** *them* (feminine)

a. Prepositional pronouns are used as the objects of a preposition and always follow the preposition.

No es para **mí**; es para **ella**.   *It's not for me; it's for her.*

b. The pronouns *mí* and *ti* combine with the preposition *con* as follows:

conmigo   *with me*   contigo   *with you*

NOTE:

1. Prepositional pronouns are identical to subject pronouns, except for *mí* and *ti*.

2. The forms *conmigo* and *contigo* do not change in gender and number.

3. The familiar plural form *vosotros, -as* is used in Spain but rarely in Spanish America, where the form *ustedes (Uds.)* is preferred.

c. Common prepositions

a *to, at*	**entre** *between, among*
cerca de *near*	**hacia** *toward*
con *with*	**para** *for*
contra *against*	**por** *for*
de *of, from*	**sin** *without*
en *in, on*	**sobre** *on top of, over*

EXERCISE C

While visiting Mexico, you and a friend are in a department store. Your friend wants to know for whom you're buying gifts. Answer her questions, using prepositional pronouns in your responses.

EXAMPLE: ¿Es el cinturón para tu papá?
             Sí, el cinturón **es** para **él**.

1. ¿Es la bolsa para tu mamá?

_____

2. ¿Son los guantes para tus tías?

_____

3. Los zapatos son para ti, ¿verdad?

_____

4. ¿Son las botas para tu hermano?

_____

5. ¿Es la estatua para Jaime?

_____

6. ¿Son los libros para César y Arturo?

_____

7. Los aretes son para mí, ¿verdad?

_____

8. ¿Son los discos para nosotros?

_____

EXERCISE D

Before Alfredo goes to the movies, he wants to know what his younger brother is going to do. Answer Alfredo's questions, using the appropriate prepositional pronoun and the cue provided.

EXAMPLE: ¿Vas al parque con Luis? *(no)*
            No, no voy al parque con **él.**

1. ¿Vas al centro con mamá? *(no)*

_____

2. ¿Vas a la piscina con Beto y Anita? *(no)*

_____

3. ¿Vas al estadio con Víctor? *(no)*

_____

4. ¿Vas al museo con Gloria y Antonia? *(no)*

_____

5. ¿Vas al supermercado con papá? *(no)*

_____

6. ¿Vas a la biblioteca con tus amigos? *(no)*

_____

7. ¿Vas al cine conmigo? *(sí)*

_____

EXERCISE E

Your little cousin is asking you a lot of questions while you're baby-sitting her in the park. Answer her questions, using the correct pronoun.

EXAMPLE: ¿Viven muchos animales en el parque?
Sí, muchos animales viven en **él**.

  OR: **No**, muchos animales **no** viven en **él**.

1. ¿Reman muchas personas en el lago?

_____

2. ¿Juegan muchos niños cerca de la piscina?

_____

3. ¿Andan tus amigos por el parque?

_____

4. ¿Estamos lejos del carrusel ahora?

_____

5. ¿Te gusta sentarte en los bancos?

_____

6. ¿Te subes a las atracciones conmigo?

_____

7. ¿Venden globos en la entrada?

_____

8. ¿Crecen flores debajo de las piedras?

_____

9. ¿Mueren las plantas sin agua?

_____

10. ¿Vuelan los pájaros sobre las nubes?

_____

11. ¿Viven muchas personas en el edificio?

_____

[3] DIRECT OBJECT PRONOUNS

a. Direct object pronouns tell who or what receives the action of the verb. Direct object pronouns replace direct objects and agree with them in gender and number.

SINGULAR	PLURAL
me *me*	**nos** *us*
te *you* (fam.)	**os** *you* (fam.)
le *him, you*	**los** *them, you* (m.)
lo *him, you* (formal, m.); *it* (m.)	
la *her, you* (formal, f.); *it* (f.)	**las** *them, you* (f.)

NOTE:

1. Either *le* or *lo* may be used to express *him*.

2. The plural form of both *le* and *lo* is *los*.

b. The direct object pronoun is usually placed directly before the verb.

¿Quién pronuncia **las palabras**?   *Who pronounces the words?*

El profesor **las** pronuncia.   *The teacher pronounces them.*

¿Tiene **el libro** Albert?   *Does Albert have the book?*

Albert no **lo** tiene.   *Albert doesn't have it.*

c. The direct object pronoun precedes the main verb or is attached to an infinitive.

Nos van a visitar.
Van a visitar**nos**.   }   *They're going to visit us.*

Ella no **la** desea ver.
Ella no desea ver**la**.   }   *She doesn't want to see it/her/you (formal).*

d. Direct object pronouns follow the affirmative command, but they come immediately before the verb in the negative command.

Bórre**la**.   *Erase it.*

BUT

No **la** borre.   *Don't erase it.*

NOTE: When the direct object pronoun follows the affirmative command, an accent mark is normally required on the stressed vowel of the verb in order to keep the original stress. If the affirmative command has only one syllable *(pon)*, no accent mark is required *(ponlo)*.

EXERCISE F

Julio describes to his mother what happens in his Spanish class. His little brother repeats everything he says, with a slight variation. Tell what his brother says.

EXAMPLE: La maestra enseña la lección.
               La maestra **la** enseña.

1. La clase saluda a la profesora.

2. Ella tiene un periódico español.

_____

3. La maestra muestra los anuncios a la clase.

_____

4. Teresa lee un anuncio en voz alta.

_____

5. Roberto mira las fotos.

_____

6. La profesora ayuda a Ahmed.

_____

7. Beatriz y Lorenzo no comprenden un párrafo.

_____

8. Fernando explica unas palabras.

_____

EXERCISE G

Answer your friend's questions in Spanish, using the correct direct object pronoun.

EXAMPLE: ¿Lees el periódico todos los días?
          Sí, **lo leo** todos los días.
   OR: **No, no lo leo** todos los días.

1. ¿Vas a ayudar a Peter?

_____

2. ¿Quieres esta hamburguesa?

_____

3. ¿Compró las flores Sarita?

_____

4. ¿Van a vender la casa tus abuelos?

_____

5. ¿Lavas tu ropa los sábados?

_____

6. ¿Escribes tus cartas en español?

_____

EXERCISE H

The Spanish Club is planning a party. Tell what one of the co-presidents tells the members to do.

EXAMPLE: Jorge / poner las banderas allí.
Jorge, **ponlas** allí.

1. Sarita / preparar la limonada

_____

2. Rafael y Emma / comprar los refrescos

_____

3. Gabriel / quitar las sillas

_____

4. Simón e Hilda / traer los vasos

_____

5. Estela / invitar a los profesores

_____

6. Gustavo / mandar las invitaciones

_____

7. Alejandro / revisar la música

_____

EXERCISE I

Using the statements in Exercise H, tell what the other co-president tells the members not to do.

EXAMPLE: Jorge, ponlas allí.
Jorge, **no las pongas** allí.

1. _____

2. _____

3. _____

4. _____

5. _____

6. _____

7. _____

EXERCISE J

Answer the questions that a new friend asks you. Use a direct object pronoun in your responses.

EXAMPLE: ¿Usas un diccionario en tu clase?
             Sí, **lo uso** en mi clase.
   OR: No, **no lo uso** en mi clase.

1. ¿Tienes el dinero?

   _____

2. ¿Contestas las preguntas correctamente?

   _____

3. ¿Me comprendes cuando hablo rápidamente?

   _____

4. ¿Esperas recibir regalos para la Navidad?

   _____

5. ¿Recibes buenas notas en todas tus clases?

   _____

6. ¿Piensas celebrar tu cumpleaños este mes?

   _____

7. ¿Lees el periódico todos los días?

   _____

8. ¿Perdiste tu cartera recientemente?

   _____

9. ¿Llevas un abrigo en el invierno?

   _____

10. ¿Aprendes a bailar el tango?

    _____

11. ¿Vas a comer la hamburguesa?

    _____

12. ¿Preparas las tareas por la noche?

    _____

13. ¿Estudias la química este año?

    _____

14. ¿Ayudan los profesores a los alumnos?

_____

15. ¿Escuchas a la profesora?

_____

[4] INDIRECT OBJECT PRONOUNS

a. Indirect objects tell to whom or for whom the action of the verb is performed. Indirect object pronouns replace indirect objects and agree with them in gender and number.

SINGULAR	PLURAL
me *to me* **te** *to you* (fam.) **le** *to you* (formal) *to him, to her*	**nos** *to us* **os** *to you* (fam.) **les** *to you* (formal) *to them* (m. and f.)

NOTE:

1. The forms *le* and *les* are used as both masculine and feminine indirect object pronouns.

2. If the meaning is not clear or if we wish to add emphasis, a phrase with *a + a prepositional* pronoun may be used in addition to the indirect object pronouns.

   (Clarity)   Yo les hablo **a ellos**.   *I speak to them.*

   (Emphasis)   **A mí** me gusta comer.   *I like to eat.*

   Sentences with both indirect object and indirect object pronoun are very common in Spanish.

3. The forms *me, te, nos,* and *os* are also used for direct object pronouns and for reflexive pronouns.

4. The indirect object pronoun may be identified in English by the preposition *to + a person.* The *to* may be expressed or implied.

   Les da el dinero.   *He gives the money to them.*

   (He gives them the money.)

b. The indirect object pronoun is usually placed before the verb.

   Ana **le** habla.   *Ana speaks to him/her/you* (formal).

   Ella **me** escribe una carta.   *She writes a letter to me.*

   (She writes me a letter.)

c. When a verb is followed by an infinitive, indirect object pronouns precede the verb or are attached to the infinitive.

   ¿**Me** quieres decir la verdad?   }   *Do you want to tell me the truth?*

   ¿Quieres decir**me** la verdad?

d. The indirect object pronoun is attached to the end of an affirmative command, but is placed before a negative command.

Escríbeme una carta.   *Write a letter to me. (Write me a letter.)*

BUT

No **me** escribas una carta.   *Don't write a letter to me. (Don't write me a letter.)*

NOTE: When the indirect object pronoun follows and is attached to the affirmative command, an accent mark is normally required on the stressed vowel of the verb in order to keep the original stress.

EXERCISE K

Rogelio is telling a friend what gifts he is giving to various people. Tell what he says.

EXAMPLE: a mi abuela / flores
Le doy flores a mi abuela.

1. a mis tíos / dulces

_____

2. a Luisa / un pañuelo

_____

3. a Pablo / un disco

_____

4. a mis primas / una muñeca

_____

5. a Martín / un juego electrónico

_____

6. a ti / un cartel

_____

EXERCISE L

Tomás's father is very proud of the trophy his son won and wants to show it to everyone, but Tomás already did that. Tell what Tomás tells his father.

EXAMPLE: Quiero mostrarle el trofeo a tu abuelo.
Ya le mostré el trofeo a **mi** abuelo.

1. Quiero mostrarles el trofeo a tus hermanos.

_____

2. Quiero mostrarle el trofeo a tu tío.

_____

3. Quiero mostrarles el trofeo a tus padrinos.

_____

4. Quiero mostrarle el trofeo al profesor.

_____

5. Quiero mostrarle el trofeo a tu mamá.

_____

6. Quiero mostrarles el trofeo a todos mis amigos.

_____

EXERCISE M

Phil is telling a friend what to do for various people before leaving for camp.

EXAMPLE: a Alejandro / devolver la raqueta de tenis
   Debes devolverle la raqueta de tenis a Alejandro.

1. a mí / comprar otro disco

_____

2. a Billy / prestar los patines

_____

3. a Sarita y a Pilar / pedir una disculpa

_____

4. a la profesora / escribir una carta

_____

5. a Miguel y a mí / invitar a comer

_____

6. a tu hermana / pagar los diez dólares

_____

7. a Vicente y a Dan / hablar

_____

8. a tus padres / pedir dinero

_____

EXERCISE N

Using an indirect object pronoun, express your boss's instructions to you on your first day of work as a waiter.

EXAMPLE: dar el menú a los clientes
¡**Dales** el menú!

1. llevar agua a la señora

_____

2. dar otra cuchara al niño

_____

3. pedir la orden a los jóvenes

_____

4. quitar el menú a los niños

_____

5. llevar la hamburguesa al señor

_____

6. servir el postre a las señoras

_____

7. ofrecer más café a esa señorita

_____

8. dar la cuenta a los hombres

_____

9. traer el dinero a mí

_____

EXERCISE O

Sarita and her sister are preparing to leave for a study-abroad program. Write what their father tells them.

EXAMPLES: a mí / llamar cada domingo
Llámenme cada domingo.

a sus amigas / no hablar por teléfono
No les hablen a sus amigas por teléfono.

1. a mí / escribir todos los días

_____

2. a nosotros / no comprar regalos

_____

3. a Gloria / no buscar revistas de telenovelas

_____

4. a su profesora / mandar una tarjeta

_____

5. a Arturo y a Felipe / no traer recuerdos

_____

6. a mí / no llamar todos los días

_____

7. a tus hermanos / no prometer nada

_____

8. a su abuela / comprar un regalo

_____

EXERCISE P

Answer the questions that an exchange student asks you. Use the appropriate indirect object pronoun in each of your answers.

1. ¿Pides dinero a tu abuelo?

_____

2. ¿Quién te presta dinero?

_____

3. ¿Quién enseña a los alumnos?

_____

4. ¿Haces tú muchas preguntas al profesor?

_____

5. ¿Escribes a tus primos que viven lejos?

_____

6. ¿Haces favores a tus compañeros?

_____

7. ¿Prometen Uds. a sus padres estudiar diligentemente?

_____

8. ¿Contestas tú al maestro correctamente?

_____

9. ¿Pides muchos regalos a tu tío?

_____

10. ¿Ofreces tu ayuda a tu papá cuando él conduce el carro?

_____

11. ¿Das regalos a tu mamá con frecuencia?

_____

12. ¿Te hablan tus amigos por la mañana?

_____

13. ¿Muestras tus buenas notas a tus amigos?

_____

14. ¿El maestro les da a Uds. muchos exámenes?

_____

15. ¿Siempre dices la verdad a tus padres?

_____

[5] THE VERB *GUSTAR*

a. *Gustar* (to please) is used to express "to like."

Me gusta la comida.	*I like the food.* (Literally: *The food pleases me.*)
Te gustan las manzanas.	*You like the apples.* (Literally: *The apples please you.*)
Nos gusta jugar a las damas.	*We like to play checkers.* (Literally: *To play checkers pleases us.*)

b. *Gustar* is preceded by an indirect object pronoun. The form of *gustar* agrees with the subject, which generally follows it.

Te **gusta** el libro.	*You like the book.*
Te **gustan** los libros.	*You like the books.*
Nos **gusta** la revista.	*We like the magazine.*
Nos **gustan** las revistas.	*We like the magazines.*
Les **gusta** leer.	*They like to read.*

NOTE: If the thing liked is not a noun but an action (expressed by a verb in the infinitive), *gustar* is used in the third person singular.

Me gusta leer y escribir.	*I like to read and write.*

c. To clarify the indirect object pronouns *le* and *les*, or to give emphasis, the indirect object normally precedes the indirect object pronoun.

A Josefa no le gusta cantar.	*Josefa doesn't like to sing.*
A los niños les gusta correr.	*The children like to run.*
A José le gusta el helado.	*Joseph likes the ice cream.*
A mí no me gusta saltar.	*I don't like to jump.*

[6] OTHER VERBS LIKE *GUSTAR*

encantar
fascinar } *to delight* (Used for things that someone likes a lot or loves.)

Me encantan las películas.   *I love movies.*

parecer *to seem*
La comida **me parece** buena.   *The food seems good to me.*

doler *to be painful, to cause sorrow*
faltar *to be lacking, to need*
tocar (a uno) *to be one's turn*

NOTE: Since *parecer* is usually followed by an adjective, the adjective must agree in number and gender with the item described.

La blusa me parece **bonita**.   *The blouse seems pretty to me.*
Las noches me parecen **largas**.   *The nights seem long to me.*

EXERCISE Q

Tell whether you like or dislike each of the following activities.

EXAMPLE: **Me gusta bailar.**
   OR: **No me gusta bailar.**

1. _____   2. _____

3. _____

4. _____

5. _____

6. _____

7. _____

8. _____

9. _____

10. _____

EXERCISE R

You've taken a young cousin to an amusement park, and it's now time to eat. Based on the illustrations, ask him what he likes and write his responses as indicated.

EXAMPLE: ¿Te gusta el helado?
Sí, me gusta el helado.

1. _____

No, _____ .

2. _____

No, _____ .

3. _____

Sí, _____ .

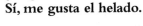

4. _____

Sí, _____ .

5. _____

Sí, _____ .

6. _____

Sí, _____ .

EXERCISE S

You and your friends are talking about your likes and dislikes. Tell what is said.

EXAMPLE: a Gloria / gustar / ir al cine
            A Gloria **le gusta** ir al cine.

1. a ti / no gustar / los dibujos animados

_____

2. a ustedes / gustar / las comedias

_____

3. a mí / no gustar / los documentales

_____

4. a Estela / gustar / comer en un restaurante

_____

5. a Felipe y a mí / encantar / los tacos de pollo

_____

6. a ellas / encantar / las telenovelas

_____

7. a Gonzalo / no gustar / las noticias

_____

8. a ellos / encantar / mirar los partidos de fútbol

_____

9. a nosotros / no gustar / las novelas largas

_____

10. a ella / encantar / cocinar

_____

EXERCISE T

After your school's varsity soccer practice, you and your friends are describing what hurts. Tell what you and they say.

EXAMPLE: a Ramón / las piernas
            A Ramón **le duelen** las piernas.

1. a mí / los ojos

_____

2. a Vinnie / la espalda

_____

3. a Juan y a mí / la cabeza

_____

4. a Gunther / los oídos

_____

5. a Clara y a Antonia / las manos

_____

6. a Esteban / la garganta

_____

EXERCISE U

As the Pérez family sits down to dinner with their guests, Mrs. Pérez notices that certain things are missing from the table. Tell what she says.

EXAMPLE: a tu papá / un cuchillo
A tu papá **le falta** un cuchillo.

1. a tus abuelos / la ensalada

_____

2. a mí / una cucharita

_____

3. a Eduardo y a Lourdes / un vaso

_____

4. a ti / un plato

_____

5. a nosotros / la sal y la pimienta

_____

6. a Carlos / un tenedor y una cuchara

_____

7. a Uds. / la servilleta

_____

EXERCISE V

Marisol is telling her mother what she and various classmates think of their math class. Tell what she says.

EXAMPLE: a mí / Beto / muy inteligente
A mí, Beto **me parece** muy inteligente.

1. al profesor / la clase / perezoso

_____

2. a Griselda y a Gladys / el maestro / estricto

_____

3. a Tomás / las tareas / difícil

_____

4. a Luz y a mí / los exámenes / justo

_____

5. a Angel / los alumnos / simpático

_____

6. a mí / la clase / aburrido

_____

MASTERY EXERCISES

EXERCISE W

Complete this letter that Roberto writes to a new pen pal, stating in Spanish the words or expressions given beneath the blanks.

Querido amigo:

_____ me llamo Roberto Casares. Mi familia y _____ vivimos en
　　1. (I)　　　　　　　　　　　　　　　　　　　　　　　2. (I)

Chicago, una ciudad grande de los Estados Unidos. _____ practicar los deportes,
　　　　　　　　　　　　　　　　　　　　　　　　3. (I like)

especialmente el béisbol. _____ practico casi todos los días. Soy miembro de un equipo
　　　　　　　　　　4. (it)

que se llama «Los cuervos». Tengo muchos amigos en el equipo y _____ ganar partidos.
　　　　　　　　　　　　　　　　　　　　　　　　　　5. (they like)

Mi familia no es grande. Mi hermano Alfredo comparte el cuarto _____ .
　　　　　　　　　　　　　　　　　　　　　　　　　6. (with me)

_____ es un chico bueno, pero nunca puedo estar en el cuarto
    7. (he)

_____ . Hay un televisor en nuestro cuarto, pero _____ los dibujos
    8. (without him)   9. (he loves)

animados. _____ muy cómicos y _____ mira todos los sábados por
        10. (they seem to him)   11. (them)

la mañana cuando _____ dormir. Muchas veces yo dejo de hablar
        12. (I like)

_____ porque él no _____ respeta. Él tiene once años y
    13. (with him)   14. (me)

_____ molestar _____ . Es difícil salir con mis amigos sin
    15. (he loves)   16. (me)

_____ . Siempre quiere acompañar _____ cuando salgo con
    17. (him)   18. (us)

_____ .
    19. (them)

Tengo una amiga especial. _____ se llama Connie. Yo _____
        20. (she)   21. (her)

admiro mucho. Pasamos mucho tiempo juntos: _____ caminar en el parque y sacar
        22. (we like)

fotografías. Ella _____ guarda en un álbum. Ella hizo copias para _____
    23. (them)   24. (me)

de todas las fotos que sacamos. Ella _____ en otro álbum y _____ el
    25. (put them)   26. (gave me)

álbum como regalo.

¡ _____ pronto! La foto del equipo es para _____ . ¡No
    27. (write to me)   28. (you)

_____ enseñes a tus amigos!
    29. (it)

Hasta pronto,

Roberto

EXERCISE X

José found an old board game. Express the following in Spanish.

1. José found it *(the game).*

_____

2. He showed the game to his friends.

_____

3. He invited them to play with him.

_____

4. He explained the rules to them.

_____

5. He told them: "Follow them *(the rules)*!"

_____

6. José loves to win.

_____

7. His friends don't like to lose.

_____

8. He told Carlos: "The red is for you; the black is for them."

_____

9. They told him: "It's not your turn now."

_____

10. Now it's our turn.

_____

11. The game seemed boring to Juan.

_____

12. Juan doesn't like this game a lot.

_____

13. Juan doesn't want to play with them.

_____

14. He told them: "You can play without me."

_____

15. They need (are lacking) three points to win.

_____

Chapter 19
Prepositions

Prepositions are words that relate a noun or pronoun to some other word in the sentence.

Yo voy **a** la tienda.	*I'm going to the store.*
Ella estudia **con** George.	*She studies with George.*
Trabajo **en** la biblioteca.	*I work in the library.*

[1] USES OF THE PREPOSITION A

a. The preposition *a* is used to indicate destination or direction.

Vamos **a** la fiesta.	*We're going to the party.*
Llegamos temprano **a** la escuela.	*We arrived at school early.*
El café está **a** la derecha.	*The café is to the right.*

NOTE:

1. The preposition *a* (to) combines with *el* (the) to form the contraction *al* (to the).

María va **al** mercado.	*María goes to the market.*
El profesor habla **al** alumno.	*The teacher speaks to the student.*

2. The preposition *a* never combines with the other articles *(la, los, las)* to form a single word.

Rosa va **a la** tienda.	*Rosa goes to the store.*
El profesor habla **a los** alumnos.	*The teacher speaks to the students.*

3. In some expressions, *a* plus the definite article is used where there's no equivalent in English.

Juegan **al** béisbol.	*They play baseball.*

EXERCISE A

Tell where you're going, based on the drawings below.

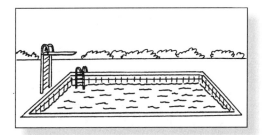

EXAMPLE: **Voy a la piscina.**

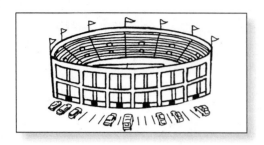

1. _____

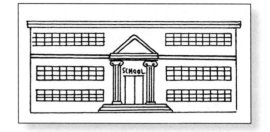

2. _____

3. _____

4. _____

5. _____

6. _____

7. _____

8. _____

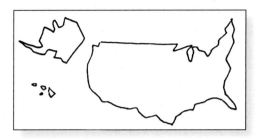   

9. _____   10. _____

b. The preposition *a* is required before the direct object of a verb if the direct object is a person, a personalized group, a pet, or something personified.

Ana visita **a** Peter.   *Ana visits Peter.*

El niño ve **al** hombre.   *The boy sees the man.*

Pablo invita **a** sus amigos.   *Pablo invites his friends.*

Lola saca **al** perro.   *Lola takes the dog out.*

BUT

Ana visita la escuela.   *Ana visits the school.*

El niño ve la pelota.   *The boy sees the ball.*

c. The preposition *a* is required before the pronouns *¿quién?, ¿quiénes?, nadie,* and *alguien,* when they refer to a person.

No conoce **a** nadie.   *He doesn't know anyone.*

Vio **a** alguien en la calle.   *He saw someone in the street.*

¿**A** quién defendemos?   *Whom do we defend?*

NOTE:

1. When used before a direct object, the preposition *a* (personal *a*) has no equivalent in English. When used before an indirect object, it is translated as "to."

Veo **a** mi prima.   *I see my cousin.*

Hablo a mi prima.   *I speak to my cousin.*

2. The personal *a* is not used after the verb *tener* (to have).

Tiene una hermana bonita.   *He has a pretty sister.*

Tengo muchos amigos.   *I have many friends.*

EXERCISE B

You and a friend are attending a civic function. Tell your friend who's talking to whom.

EXAMPLE: el alcalde / los ciudadanos
           El alcalde **habla a** los ciudadanos.

1. el médico / la enfermera

_____

2. el profesor / los alumnos

_____

3. el zapatero / el cliente

_____

4. la señorita Vargas / los señores Polaski

_____

5. Veronique / las amigas

_____

6. Luis y Fernando / la chica

_____

7. tú y yo / el alcalde

_____

8. mi madre / la profesora

_____

EXERCISE C

Complete this letter that Cristina writes to her friend while visiting Spain. Insert the personal _a_ or the contraction _al_ only when needed.

Querida Gloria:

Mientras espero _____ mozo para bajar la maleta, te escribo estas pocas palabras.
                        1.

Durante mi viaje vi _____ muchos lugares bonitos e interesantes. También tuve la
                         2.

oportunidad de conocer _____ muchos jóvenes españoles. Un día visité
                              3.

_____ mi familia en Sevilla. Mi prima invitó _____ otros
        4.   **5.**

parientes y _____ unos amigos a una cena en su casa. Me divertí mucho.
                 6.

Ahora salgo para Barcelona donde quiero ver _____ Enrique. Él estudió en mi escuela
                                                    7.

el año pasado. Tiene _____ muchos amigos. Pienso llamar _____
                           8.   **9.**

mis padres esta noche. Oigo _____ alguien en la puerta. Adiós por ahora.
                                 10.

Cristina

EXERCISE D

Tell your plans for this evening. Use *a* or *al* when needed.

EXAMPLE: ver la televisión
 Pienso ver la televisión.

1. escuchar / el grupo «Coquí»

_____

2. hablar / el vecino

_____

3. jugar / las damas

_____

4. llamar / Elsa

_____

5. esperar / mis padres

_____

6. oír / una cinta

_____

7. acompañar / mi madre

_____

EXERCISE E

Use complete sentences and the cues in parentheses to answer the questions that your new friend asks you.

1. ¿A quiénes saludas por la mañana? *(los vecinos)*

_____

2. ¿A quién ayudas tú? *(mis amigos)*

_____

3. ¿Respetan los jóvenes a sus padres? *(sí)*

_____

4. ¿A quién admiras más? *(el presidente)*

_____

5. ¿Tienes muchos primos y amigos? *(sí)*

_____

6. ¿A quién esperas tú al salir de la escuela? *(nadie)*

_____

7. ¿Cuándo visitas al dentista? *(cada año)*

_____

8. ¿Escuchas a los maestros en tu escuela? *(sí)*

_____

9. ¿A quién buscas cuando tienes un problema? *(mi hermana)*

_____

10. ¿Amas tú a toda tu familia? *(sí)*

_____

d. The preposition *a* is used in time expressions to indicate "at."

¿A qué hora es la fiesta?	*At what time is the party?*
Es **a** las ocho.	*It's at 8 o'clock.*
Llego **a** la una.	*I arrive at one o'clock.*

EXERCISE F

While vacationing in Puerto Rico, Javier wants to know at what time different activities will take place. Using the cues provided, answer his questions.

EXAMPLE: ¿A qué hora es la excursión en barco? *(2:00)*
          Es **a las dos.**

1. ¿A qué hora es el desayuno? *(7:30)*

_____

2. ¿A qué hora es la clase de natación? *(9:00)*

_____

3. ¿A qué hora vamos a comer el almuerzo? *(1:00)*

_____

4. ¿A qué hora vamos al Viejo San Juan? *(4:00)*

_____

5. ¿A qué hora quieres cenar? *(8:00)*

_____

6. ¿A qué hora comienza el baile? *(10:30)*

_____

[2] USES OF THE PREPOSITION *DE*

a. The preposition *de* corresponds to *of, from,* or *about* in English.

¿**De** qué hablas?	*What are you speaking about?*
Hablo **de** la fiesta.	*I'm speaking about the party.*
Recibo cartas **de** Juan.	*I receive letters from Juan.*
Sacan fotos **de** los niños.	*They take photos of the children.*

NOTE:

1. The preposition *de* (of, from) combines with *el* (the) to form *del* (of the, from the, about).

El Sr. Pérez es el presidente **del** país.	*Mr. Pérez is the president of the country.*
Ana recibe dinero **del** jefe.	*Ana receives money from the boss.*

2. The preposition *de* never combines with the other articles *(la, los, las)* to form a single word.

¿Recibe Ud. cartas **de las** muchachas?	*Do you receive letters from the girls?*

EXERCISE G

A group of friends went to see a movie. Say what they're talking about afterwards.

EXAMPLE: Alejandro / la película
Alejandro **habla de** la película.

1. Elena / los actores

_____

2. Esteban y Flor / el cuento

_____

3. Ernie / el reparto

_____

4. Beto y Antonio / los carros antiguos

_____

5. Aisha y Marcel / la ropa

_____

6. Alicia / el fin

_____

7. Hiroshi y Pedro / las escenas cómicas

_____

8. yo / la actriz principal

_____

EXERCISE H

You and a friend are visiting his grandmother. Say what she tells you to do.

EXAMPLE: cerrar las ventanas / el comedor
           ¡Cierren las ventanas **del** comedor!

1. traer flores / el jardín

_____

2. sacar las fotos / los nietos

_____

3. oír el ruido / la calle

_____

4. abrir la puerta / la sala

_____

5. salir / la casa

_____

b. In Spanish, possession is expressed as follows: *noun* (thing possessed) followed by *de* plus *noun* (possessor). This is equivalent to the English possessive expressed with *of*. In Spanish, there is no apostrophe to show possession.

el libro **de** Alberto $\begin{cases} the\ book\ of\ Alberto \\ Alberto's\ book \end{cases}$

la cámara **de** la muchacha $\begin{cases} the\ camera\ of\ the\ girl \\ the\ girl's\ camera \end{cases}$

los lápices **de** los alumnos $\begin{cases} the\ pencils\ of\ the\ students \\ the\ student's\ pencils \end{cases}$

c. *¿De quién?, ¿De quiénes?* (Whose?) are used to ask *to whom* something belongs.

¿**De quién** son las plumas?   *Whose (sing.) pens are they?*
¿**De quiénes** son las fotos?   *To whom (pl.) do the photos belong?*

EXERCISE I

Tell whom the following items belong to.

EXAMPLE: los anteojos / el maestro
           Son los anteojos **del** maestro.

1. la mochila / la alumna

_____

2. el diccionario / Isaac

_____

3. los tenis / los chicos

_____

4. el reloj / el director

_____

5. la cámara / mi hermano

_____

6. la bandera / la escuela

_____

7. las tarjetas / Beatriz y Charlotte

_____

8. la calculadora / el señor Rivas

_____

9. las fotos / Javier

_____

10. las estampillas / la secretaria

_____

EXERCISE J

A friend is helping you clean up the living room. Tell her who owns the various things she finds.

EXAMPLE: ¿De quién son las historietas? *(mi hermano menor)*
            Son de mi hermano menor.

1. ¿De quién son las llaves? *(mi mamá)*

_____

2. ¿De quién es el pasaporte? *(el novio de mi hermana)*

_____

3. ¿De quién son las revistas? *(la amiga de mi mamá)*

_____

4. ¿De quién es el suéter? *(el primo de Juan)*

_____

5. ¿De quién es la novela? *(el profesor de inglés)*

_____

6. ¿De quién es el bolígrafo? *(mi papa)*

_____

d. A *de* phrase may also function as an adjective.

la clase **de** biología   *the biology class*
un reloj **de** oro   *a gold watch*

EXERCISE K

Juanita is playing a game with her little cousin. He has to identify an object or person based on the clues Juanita gives him. Help him get the correct answers.

EXAMPLES: Juan Pardo / el padre
el padre **de** Juan

un examen / matemática
un examen **de** matemática

1. un reloj bueno y caro / oro

_____

2. un libro de palabras en inglés y español / diccionario

_____

3. una bandera roja, blanca y azul / los Estados Unidos

_____

4. julio y agosto / meses

_____

5. martes y jueves / días

_____

6. la primavera y el otoño / estaciones

_____

7. a, be, ce, de / letras

_____

8. Beto Suárez Olmeda / Tomás Ramos Olmeda *(primo)*

_____

e. The phrase *de + la mañana (la tarde, la noche)* is used following a specific hour to indicate A.M. or P.M.

Son las diez **de la mañana**.   *It's 10:00 A.M.*

Te veo a las dos **de la tarde**.   *I'll see you at 2:00 P.M.*

EXERCISE L

Tell at what time you usually do the following activities. Be sure to include the Spanish equivalent of A.M. or P.M. in your response.

EXAMPLE: desayunarte
           Me desayuno a las siete de la mañana.

1. despertarte

_____

2. almorzar

_____

3. entrar en la escuela

_____

4. salir del colegio

_____

5. cenar con tu familia

_____

6. lavar los platos

_____

7. jugar con tus amigos

_____

8. acostarte

_____

9. apagar la luz

_____

f. *De* is also used together with other prepositions to indicate location.

El jardín está **detrás de** la casa.   *The garden is behind the house.*

Las flores están **dentro del** florero.   *The flowers are in the vase.*

EXERCISE M

Use the expressions below to tell where the buildings in the pictures are located.

a la derecha de	dentro de	enfrente de
al lado de	detrás de	a la izquierda de
cerca de		

EXAMPLE: El teatro está **al lado de la iglesia.**

1. El museo está _____ .

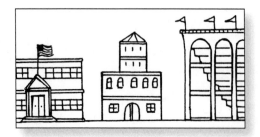

2. La escuela está _____ .

3. El supermercado está _____ .

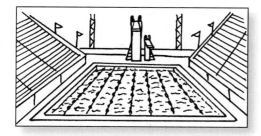

4. La piscina está _____ .

5. El hotel está _____ .

6. La estatua está _____ .

[3] PREPOSITIONS WITH INFINITIVES

a. In Spanish, the infinitive is the only verb form that may follow a preposition. The following prepositions and prepositional phrases are commonly used before an infinitive:

a *to, at*	después de *after*
al *upon, on*	en vez de *instead of*
antes de *before*	sin *without*
de *of, to*	

Al salir de la casa, él cerró la puerta.	*Upon leaving the house, he closed the door.*
Ella corrió **en vez de caminar.**	*She ran instead of walking.*
Pensó **antes de contestar.**	*She thought before answering.*

EXERCISE N

Combine a suggestion from each of the columns below and tell what you and your friends do in various situations.

al	cenar	mi amiga	contar el secreto
antes de	estudiar	mi amigo	decir gracias
después de	ir al cine	mis amigos	hablar por teléfono
en vez de	pedir permiso	mis amigos y yo	mirar la televisión
sin	pensar	yo	salir de la casa
	recibir un regalo		tomar un refresco

EXAMPLE: **Sin pensar, mi amigo contó el secreto.**

1. _____

2. _____

3. _____

4. _____

5. _____

b. The preposition *a* is required before any infinitive that follows a verb of (1) beginning, (2) movement, (3) teaching/learning, or (4) helping.

(1) Beginning

comenzar a + *infinitive*
empezar a + *infinitive* } *to begin to + verb*

Comienzan a cantar.	*They begin to sing.*
Empezamos a correr.	*We began to run.*

(2) Movement

ir a + *infinitive*   *to go to + verb*
Va a tocar el piano. *She's going to play the piano.*

correr a + *infinitive*   *to run to + verb*
Corren a cerrar las ventanas. *They run to close the windows.*

venir a + *infinitive*   *to come to + verb*
Vengo a verte. *I'm coming to see you.*

(3) Teaching/Learning

enseñar a + *infinitive*   *to teach to + verb*
El maestro nos **enseña a leer.** *The teacher teaches us to read.*

aprender a + *infinitive*   *to learn to + verb*
Aprendemos a hablar español. *We're learning to speak Spanish.*

(4) Helping

ayudar a + *infinitive*   *to help (to) + verb*
Ella me **ayuda a bailar.** *She helps me dance.*

EXERCISE O

Gladys describes an afternoon with some friends. Put what she says in complete sentences. Be sure to include the preposition.

EXAMPLE: dos jóvenes españoles / venir / almorzar conmigo
Dos jóvenes españoles **vienen a almorzar** conmigo.

1. yo / ir / esperarlos en el restaurante

_____

2. yo / correr / llegar temprano al restaurante

_____

3. el mesero / correr / poner la mesa

_____

4. nosotros / empezar / comer en seguida

_____

5. mis amigos / aprender / hablar inglés

_____

6. yo / ir / hacer un viaje a España

_____

7. ellos / ayudarme / pronunciar las palabras

_____

8. yo / enseñarles / cantar en inglés

_____

EXERCISE P

Using a verb from column A and an expression from column B, tell what these people are doing.

A	B
aprender	contar el dinero
ayudar	decirme las noticias
comenzar	lavar el carro
correr	limpiar la casa
empezar	patinar en hielo
enseñar	pronunciar bien
ir	trabajar por la tarde
venir	ver el accidente

EXAMPLE: Tú **comienzas** a **trabajar por la tarde.**

1. Yo _____ .

2. Mi hermano _____ .

3. Mis padres _____ .

4. Mi hermana _____ .

5. Mis amigos _____ .

6. Mi madre _____ .

7. Mi profesor _____ .

    c. The preposition *de* is required before any infinitive that comes after one of the following four verbs:

acabar de + *infinitive   to have just*
Acaban de cenar.   *They've just eaten dinner.*

cesar de + *infinitive   to stop*
Cesó de llover.   *It stopped raining.*

dejar de + *infinitive   to quit, stop*
Juan **dejó de darme** el dinero.   *Juan stopped giving me the money.*

tratar de + *infinitive   to try to*
Trataron de llamarme.   *They tried to call me.*

EXERCISE Q

Tell what these people have just done.

EXAMPLE: yo / ver un partido de fútbol
           Yo **acabo de ver** un partido de fútbol.

1. Gerardo / jugar al tenis

_____

2. mi mamá / ir de compras

_____

3. mis hermanas / salir con sus amigas

_____

4. Tommy y Enrique / lavar el carro

_____

5. Alicia y yo / hablar por teléfono

_____

EXERCISE R

You're working as a counselor in a day camp. Using the cues, tell the children to stop doing the following.

EXAMPLE: correr *(Uds.)*
            ¡Dejen de correr!

1. gritar *(tú)*

_____

2. pelear *(Ana y Kyoko)*

_____

3. hablar *(tú—Carlos)*

_____

4. tirar la pelota *(Bárbara y Juan)*

_____

5. silbar *(tú—Isabel)*

_____

EXERCISE S

Help Ricardo write a note to a friend in Venezuela.

EXAMPLE: las clases / acabar / terminar
            Las clases **acaban de** terminar.

1. yo / acabar / recibir mi licencia de conducir

_____

2. Jorge / dejar / tomar clases de conducir

_____

3. él / tratar / pasar el examen varias veces

_____

4. Jorge y yo / cesar / ser amigos

_____

5. Jorge / no tratar / llamarme

_____

d. The following verbs are used without a preposition before an infinitive:

deber *ought to, must*	pensar *to intend*
dejar *to let, allow*	poder *to be able, can*
desear *to wish, desire*	preferir *to prefer*
esperar *to hope, expect to*	prometer *to promise*
necesitar *to need*	querer *to want, wish to*
oír *to hear*	saber *to know how to*

Debo ir a la escuela hoy.	*I ought to go to school today.*
No **pueden salir** ahora.	*They can't go out now.*
Él **promete ser** bueno.	*He promises to be good.*
Ella **sabe jugar** al ajedrez.	*She knows how to play chess.*

NOTE: **Remember that the verb *dejar* changes meaning when it's followed by the preposition *de*.**

¡Déjenme entrar!	*Let me in!*
Ya **dejó de** llover.	*It already stopped raining.*

EXERCISE T

Answer these questions that a new friend asks you.

1. ¿Qué prefieres, caminar en el parque o ir de compras?

_____

2. ¿Qué debes hacer para mañana?

_____

3. ¿Necesitas pedirles permiso a tus padres antes de salir?

_____

4. ¿Qué esperas hacer este fin de semana?

_____

5. ¿Puedes acompañarme a un concierto el sábado?

_____

6. ¿Deseas comer en un restaurante argentino?

_____

7. ¿Sabes tocar la guitarra?

_____

8. ¿Prometes llamarme por teléfono mañana?

_____

9. ¿Piensas ir a la fiesta de Marisol?

_____

10. ¿Con quién esperas ir a la fiesta?

_____

EXERCISE U

Your teacher is telling your class what should happen when she's absent. Write what she says, using the suggestions provided in the three columns below.

EXAMPLE: **Yo debo dejar una lección interesante.**

la clase	deber	aprender la lección
todos	desear	cooperar con el maestro
Uds.	esperar	dejar una lección interesante
yo	necesitar	estudiar mucho
	pensar	prestar atención
	poder	repasar la lección
	preferir	sentarse en su propio asiento
	prometer	ser amables
	querer	trabajar en grupos
		traer los libros a la clase
		volver al día siguiente

1. _____

2. _____

3. _____

4. _____

5. _____

6. _____

7. _____

8. _____

[4] COMMON EXPRESSIONS WITH PREPOSITIONS

al aire libre   *outdoors, in the open air*
A los niños les gusta jugar **al aire libre**.   *The children like to play outdoors.*

a menudo   *often*
Veo a mis primos **a menudo**.   *I see my cousins often.*

a pie   *on foot*
Él va a la escuela **a pie**.   *He goes to school on foot.*

a tiempo   *on time*
El tren llega **a tiempo**.   *The train arrives on time.*

a veces   *sometimes*
A veces me gusta dormir la siesta.   *Sometimes I like to take a nap.*

con cuidado   *carefully*
Escribo la tarea **con cuidado**.   *I write the assignment carefully.*

de memoria   *by heart*
Él sabe la dirección **de memoria**.   *He knows the address by heart.*

De nada.   *You're welcome.*
Muchas gracias. **De nada**.   *Thanks a lot. You're welcome.*

de nuevo   *again*
Escribí la oración **de nuevo**.   *I wrote the sentence again.*

de pie   *standing*
Todos están **de pie**.   *Everyone is standing.*

de pronto
de repente   }   *suddenly*

De repente empezó a llover.   *Sudddenly, it started to rain.*

en punto   *sharp*
Es la una **en punto**.   *It's one o'clock sharp.*

en serio   *seriously*
Él toma todo **en serio**.   *He takes everything seriously.*

en venta   *for sale*
El coche de mi tío está **en venta**.   *My uncle's car is for sale.*

en vez de   *instead of*
Ella descansó **en vez de** trabajar.   *She rested instead of working.*

EXERCISE V

Norma is describing a camping trip in her diary. Write the expressions that are needed to complete the entry in her diary.

El club de la escuela va a acampar _____. _____ van a la playa
                                    1. (often)   **2.** (sometimes)

_____ ir a las montañas. No importa, porque a mí me gusta estar
   3. (instead of)

_____. El autobús siempre sale de la escuela _____ : a las siete
   4. (outdoors)   **5.** (on time)

de la mañana _____. En el autobús la consejera del club explicó
                  6. (sharp)

_____ las reglas _____. Ya las sé _____. Ella
   7. (again)   **8.** (carefully)   **9.** (by heart)

toma _____ su responsabilidad. Ella viajó _____
        10. (seriously)   **11.** (standing)

_____ sentarse.
   12. (instead of)

Cuando llegamos a la playa, fuimos al campamento _____ . _____
$\qquad\qquad\qquad\quad$ *13.* (on foot) $\qquad\qquad$ *14.* (suddenly)

comenzó a hacer mucho frío. Gladys me prestó un suéter. Le di las gracias y ella contestó:

—_____ .
$\quad$ *15.* (you're welcome)

M A S T E R Y $\quad$ E X E R C I S E S

EXERCISE W

Read this story. Select the preposition that should be used in each sentence. Note that in some cases a preposition may not be needed.

A una señora le gusta andar _____ pie cuando va _____ mercado todos los días. _____
$\qquad\qquad\qquad\quad$ *1.* (a/de) $\qquad\qquad\quad$ *2.* (al/a la) $\qquad\qquad\qquad\quad$ *3.* (A/De)

menudo lleva _____ su hija _____ ella. Prefiere _____ estar _____ aire libre,
$\qquad\quad$ *4.* (a/) $\qquad\quad$ *5.* (a/con) $\qquad\qquad$ *6.* (a/) $\qquad$ *7.* (en el/al)

especialmente cuando cesa _____ llover. _____ veces pasa por el parque en vez _____
$\qquad\qquad\qquad\quad$ *8.* (a/de) $\qquad\quad$ *9.* (De/A) $\qquad\qquad\qquad\quad$ *10.* (a/de)

tomar una ruta más directa _____ centro. Un día _____ salir de su casa _____
$\qquad\qquad\qquad\quad$ *11.* (al/a la) $\qquad\qquad$ *12.* (al/a) $\qquad\qquad$ *13.* (a los/a las)

ocho y media _____ mañana, ella comenzó _____ andar por el parque. Cerca _____
$\qquad\quad$ *14.* (del/de la) $\qquad\qquad\qquad\quad$ *15.* (a/de) $\qquad\qquad$ *16.* (del/de la)

entrada vio _____ la niña _____ vecino. Corrió _____ ayudarla. Trató _____
$\qquad\quad$ *17.* (a/) $\qquad\quad$ *18.* (del/de la) $\qquad\qquad$ *19.* (a/) $\qquad\qquad$ *20.* (/de)

hablarle _____ niña pero la niña empezó _____ llorar.
$\qquad\quad$ *21.* (al/a la) $\qquad\qquad\qquad\quad$ *22.* (a/de)

_____ fin la niña dijo: —Yo no debo _____ hablarle _____ usted porque no la conozco
23. (Al/A la) $\qquad\qquad\qquad\quad$ *24.* (a/) $\qquad\qquad$ *25.* (/a)

_____ usted—. La señora prometió _____ ayudar _____ niña _____ encontrar la casa
26. (a/) $\qquad\qquad\qquad$ *27.* (a/) $\qquad\qquad$ *28.* (al/a la) $\qquad$ *29.* (a/)

_____ tía. Después _____ andar por unos minutos la señora le preguntó: —¿Qué hora es?—
30. (del/de la) $\quad$ *31.* (de/)

La niña contestó: —Yo no sé _____ decir la hora—. La señora prometió _____ enseñarle
$\qquad\qquad\qquad\quad$ *32.* (/a) $\qquad\qquad\qquad\quad$ *33.* (de/)

_____ decir la hora. _____ repente la niña dejó _____ andar. Vio _____ un perro.
34. (/a) $\qquad\qquad$ *35.* (De/A) $\qquad\qquad$ *36.* (/de) $\qquad\qquad$ *37.* (a/)

EXERCISE X

Simón is a new neighbor who has just moved to your area from Colombia. Answer his questions.

1. ¿Hace calor en los meses del verano?

   _____

2. ¿A qué hora salen los niños a jugar?

   _____

3. ¿De qué color es tu motocicleta?

   _____

4. ¿A qué hora del día tienes la lección de tenis?

   _____

5. ¿Escuchas los discos de tus amigos?

   _____

6. ¿Cuál es el periódico más popular de la ciudad?

   _____

7. ¿Viven tus compañeros de escuela cerca de aquí?

   _____

8. ¿Cuáles son los colores de la escuela?

   _____

9. ¿A qué hora empiezas a trabajar?

   _____

10. ¿Quién es el profesor de historia?

    _____

EXERCISE Y

Carl is helping his sister study for a Spanish test. He asks her how to say a variety of things in Spanish. Express her answers.

EXAMPLE: How would you say that you're learning to speak Spanish?
   Aprendo a hablar español.

1. How would you ask a young lady if she plays tennis?

   _____

2. How would you ask your teacher if she is going to explain the assignment?

   _____

3. How would you say that it is John's sweater?

_____

4. How would you say that they can go to the movies tonight?

_____

5. How would you ask whose bicycle it is?

_____

6. How would you ask if it stopped snowing?

_____

7. How would you say that he intends to go to the pool tomorrow?

_____

8. How would you ask if they prefer to go to the beach or to the mountains?

_____

9. How would you say that the watch is made of gold?

_____

10. How would you say that you have just read a good book?

_____

11. How would you say that you are trying to call Alicia's brother?

_____

12. How would you ask what they do upon getting up?

_____

13. How would you say that you are starting to go to the gym every day?

_____

14. How would you ask if you should pay before or after eating?

_____

15. How would you say that she is coming to see Antonia's friends?

_____

Part three

Adjective/Adverb and Related Structures

Chapter 20
Adjectives

FRANCIA

PORTUGAL ESPAÑA
○ Madrid Barcelona •
ITALIA
Islas Baleares
• Sevilla

[1] AGREEMENT OF ADJECTIVES

Adjectives describe nouns and agree in number (singular or plural) and gender (masculine or feminine) with the nouns they modify.

a. Adjectives ending in *-o* change *-o* to *-a* when describing a feminine singular noun.

Carlos es alto.	*Carlos is tall.*
María es alta.	*María is tall.*

b. Adjectives ending in *-e* remain the same when describing a feminine singular noun.

Él es valiente.	*He's brave.*
Ella es valiente.	*She's brave.*
El muchacho es inteligente.	*The boy is intelligent.*
La muchacha es inteligente.	*The girl is intelligent.*

c. Adjectives of nationality that end in a consonant add an *-a* when describing a feminine singular noun.

Paul es francés.	*Paul is French.*
Claire es francesa.	*Claire is French.*

d. The plural of adjectives, like the plural of nouns, is formed by adding *-s* if the adjective ends in a vowel, or *-es* or *-as* if the adjective ends in a consonant.

SINGULAR	PLURAL
Carlos es alto. María es alta.	Carlos y Pedro son altos. María y Anita son altas.
El muchacho es inteligente. La muchacha es inteligente.	Los muchachos son inteligentes. Las muchachas son inteligentes.
Paul es francés. Claire es francesa.	Paul y Pascal son franceses. Claire y Paulette son francesas.

NOTE:

1. Adjectives ending in *-o* have four forms.

   rico, rica, ricos, ricas

2. Adjectives ending in *-e* (or a consonant) have two forms, one for the singular and one for the plural.

SINGULAR	PLURAL	MEANING
cortés	corteses	*courteous*
débil	débiles	*weak*
fuerte	fuertes	*strong*

3. Adjectives of nationality ending in a consonant have four forms.

    español, española, españoles, españolas

4. Adjectives of nationality with an accent mark on the last syllable drop the accent mark in the feminine singular and in both plural forms.

    alemán, alemana, alemanes, alemanas   *German*

    francés, francesa, franceses, francesas   *French*

    inglés, inglesa, ingleses, inglesas   *English*

5. Adjectives that modify two or more nouns of different gender use the masculine plural.

    Yassir y Alice son altos.   *Yassir and Alice are tall.*

    Yassir y Alice son españoles.   *Yassir and Alice are Spanish.*

EXERCISE A

Gregorio, an exchange student in your school, is describing his new friends to you. Tell what he says about them.

EXAMPLE: Javier / interesante
            Javier **es interesante.**

1. Jeffrey / fuerte

_____

2. Cathy / bonito

_____

3. Gloria y Claudia / colombiano

_____

4. Inés / cortés

_____

5. Marco / simpático

_____

6. Pauline / francés

_____

7. Enrique y Lourdes / alto

_____

8. Omar / responsable

_____

9. Las hermanas Dini / popular

_____

10. Kyoko y Mei Ling / divertido

_____

EXERCISE B

At a regional meeting of new exchange students in your area, you introduce them and tell their nationalities.

EXAMPLE: Fritz / alemán
          Fritz **es alemán.**

1. Salvador / español

_____

2. Gina / italiano

_____

3. Edson y Milton / brasileño

_____

4. Yoko / japonés

_____

5. Claudine y Marie / francés

_____

6. Sara / inglés

_____

7. José y Pilar / puertorriqueño

_____

8. Brigitte y Eva / alemán

_____

EXERCISE C

How would you describe your friends? Using the adjectives below, write six sentences about your friends or classmates.

alto	cortés	guapo	responsable
bajo	diligente	independiente	serio
cómico	divertido	inteligente	simpático

EXAMPLE: Elena y Migdalia son **guapas** y **responsables**.

1. _____

2. _____

3. _____

4. _____

5. _____

6. _____

EXERCISE D

Describe the differences between you and your siblings or best friend. Use the adjectives below.

alegre	diligente	gordo	perezoso
cómico	divertido	independiente	quieto
delgado	generoso	melancólico	serio

EXAMPLE: Yo soy **cómico** y mi hermana es **seria**.

1. _____

2. _____

3. _____

4. _____

5. _____

[2] POSITION OF ADJECTIVES

a. Descriptive adjectives generally follow the noun they describe.

una chica **guapa**	*a pretty girl*
un niño **bueno**	*a good boy*
un señor **mexicano**	*a Mexican man*

b. Adjectives expressing number or quantity generally come before the noun.

algunos chicos	*some boys*
cada año	*each year*
mucho dinero	*much money*
tres muchachas	*three girls*

EXERCISE E

You're talking to a blind date on the telephone. Answer his or her questions.

1. ¿Eres alto(a) o bajo(a)?

_____

2. ¿De qué color tienes los ojos?

_____

3. ¿Y el pelo?

_____

4. ¿Tienes el pelo largo o corto?

_____

5. ¿Eres divertido(a) o serio(a)?

_____

6. ¿Eres paciente?

_____

7. ¿Tienes muchos amigos?

_____

8. ¿Cuántas clases tomas?

_____

9. ¿Son aburridas las clases?

_____

10. ¿Es grande tu familia?

_____

11. ¿Cuántos hermanos y hermanas tienes?

_____

EXERCISE F

Prepare a list of things you need to redecorate your bedroom.

EXAMPLE: una cama / doble
                   una cama **doble**

1. un escritorio / grande

_____

2. una silla / cómodo

_____

3. butaca / rojo, dos

_____

4. una alfombra / negro

_____

5. unas cortinas / bonito

_____

6. lámpara / tres, bueno

_____

7. un estante / fuerte

_____

8. una mesa / pequeño, redondo

_____

9. almohada / duro, tres

_____

10. un televisor / nuevo

_____

EXERCISE G

Make a list of things you see in the beautiful garden outside your window.

EXAMPLE: jardín / uno, bonito
            un jardín **bonito**

1. rosa / tres, rojo

_____

2. geranio / alguno, rosado, rojo

_____

3. planta / mucho, verde

_____

4. árbol / dos, viejo

_____

5. pájaro / uno, alegre

_____

6. clavel / mucho, blanco

_____

7. insecto / mucho, feo

_____

EXERCISE H

While vacationing in Germany, Lisa wrote to her pen pal in Costa Rica. Complete Lisa's letter by choosing the appropriate adjectives from the list of choices for each paragraph. Notice that adjectives in each group are listed alphabetically.

nos. 1–8	*nos. 9–16*	*nos. 17–22*
bello	antiguo	alemán
bonito	cómico	divertido
colombiano	formidable	nuevo
dos	interesante	otro
grande	libre	sincero
idéntico	mucho	tres
moderno	serio	
nuevo	simpático	

Querida Lucía:

Hay _____ alumnos _____ en mi clase de matemáticas. Ellos
        1.   *2.*

tienen quince años y son hermanos, pero no son gemelos _____ . Se llaman Lola y
                                                         3.

Luis. Vienen de Bogotá, Colombia, y son _____ . Ahora viven en un
                                       4.

_____ apartamento _____ y _____ cerca de
      5.   *6.*   *7.*

un jardín _____ .
        8.

Lola es muy _____ , pero Luis es más _____ . Lola dice que los
              9.   *10.*

deportes son _____ , pero Luis prefiere pasar su tiempo _____ en la
              11.   *12.*

biblioteca porque le gustan las novelas _____ . A mí me gusta pasar _____
                               13.   *14.*

horas con ellos porque son muy _____ y _____ .
                           15.   *16.*

Mañana vamos a ver una película _____ . En _____ carta te escribo
                               17.   *18.*

más de mis amigos _____ y de sus _____ perros
                     19.   *20.*

_____ .
      21.

                                              Tu amiga _____ ,
                                                           22.

                                              Luisa

[3] SHORTENING OF ADJECTIVES

a. The following adjectives drop the final *-o* when used before a masculine singular noun:

uno	*one, a, an*	un amigo	*one (a) friend*
bueno	*good*	un buen amigo	*a good friend*
malo	*bad*	un mal año	*a bad year*
primero	*first*	el primer día	*the first day*
tercero	*third*	el tercer piso	*the third floor*
alguno	*some*	algún día	*some day*
ninguno	*no, not any*	ningún dinero	*no money*

NOTE:

1. The complete form of the adjective is used when:

(a) it follows a masculine singular noun.
un muchacho malo   *a bad boy*

(b) it modifies a feminine or plural noun.
una muchacha buena   *a good girl*
algunos libros   *some books*

(c) a preposition comes between the adjective and the noun.
el primero de junio   *June 1*

2. The adjectives *alguno* and *ninguno* require an accent mark when the *-o* is dropped: *algún, ningún.*

b. *Ciento* becomes *cien* before any plural noun and before the numbers *mil* (thousand) and *millón* (million). The short form is not used with multiples of *ciento (doscientos, trescientos, etc.)* or in combination with any other number *(ciento diez)*:

cien libros (muchachas)   *one (a) hundred books (girls)*
cien mil años   *one (a) hundred thousand years*
cien millones de dólares   *one (a) hundred million dollars*

BUT

cuatrocientos alumnos   *four hundred students*
cuatrocientas personas   *four hundred people*
ciento veintiséis dólares   *one (a) hundred twenty-six dollars*

c. *Santo* becomes *San* before the name of a male saint, unless the name begins with *To-* or *Do-*.

San Francisco   *Saint Francis*
San José   *Saint Joseph*

BUT

Santo Tomás   *Saint Thomas*
Santo Domingo   *Saint Dominic*

NOTE: The feminine form of *santo* is *santa*.

Santa María   *Saint Mary*

d. *Grande* becomes *gran* before a singular noun and means "great." When *grande* follows the noun, it means "large" or "big."

un gran hombre   *a great man*

una gran mujer   *a great woman*

BUT

una casa grande   *a large house*

EXERCISE 1

Select the correct form of each adjective in parentheses to complete Adriana's description of her cousin Esteban.

Esteban es mi primo, pero somos _____ amigos también. Él es el

1. (buen / buenos)

_____ hijo de mis tíos Pedro y Beatriz. Yo soy la _____ hija de mis

2. (primer / primero)   *3. (primer / primera)*

padres. Vivimos en el mismo edificio: yo vivo en el _____ piso y mis tíos viven en

4. (primer / primera)

el _____ . _____ amigos creen que Esteban y yo somos hermanos.

5. (tercer / tercero)   *6. (Algún / Algunos)*

Cuando yo tengo _____ _____ día, Esteban es la

7. (un / uno)   *8. (mal / malo)*

_____ persona con quien hablo. Este verano pensamos hacer un viaje juntos a

9. (primer / primera)

_____ Francisco y a _____ Monica. Yo tengo

10. (San / Santo)   *11. (San / Santa)*

_____ dinero ahorrado, pero Esteban no tiene _____ dinero

12. (algún / alguno)   *13. (ningún / ninguno)*

todavía. Necesitamos _____ setenta y cinco dólares. Yo tengo ya

14. (cien / ciento)

_____ dólares en el banco. Mi tía dice que Esteban no puede ahorrar ni

15. (cien / ciento)

_____ centavo. Su cumpleaños es el _____ de julio. Siempre

16. (un / uno)   *17. (primer / primero)*

recibe _____ regalos de dinero. Va a ser _____ verano

18. (algún / algunos)   *19. (un / uno)*

_____ si no hago _____ excursión.

20. (mal / malo)   *21. (ningún / ninguna)*

EXERCISE J

Roberto has just learned that many Spanish speakers are named after a saint. Write the name of the saint after whom Roberto's friends were named.

1. Guillermo

_____

2. Cecilia

_____

3. Fernando

_____

4. Luis

_____

5. Domingo

_____

6. Juan

_____

7. Tomás

_____

8. Teresa

_____

9. María

_____

10. Alfonso

_____

MASTERY EXERCISES

EXERCISE K

Gloria shows you her closet. Describe some of the things you see, using the adjectives below.

cien	largo	pequeño
grande	negro	sucio
japonés	nuevo	viejo

EXAMPLE: nuevo
un sombrero nuevo

1. _____

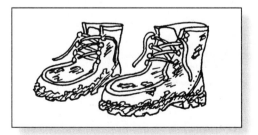

2. _____

3. _____

4. _____

5. _____

6. _____

7. _____

8. _____

EXERCISE L

Express in Spanish what Ricardo says about his summer vacation.

1. Today is the first of August.

   _____

2. The long vacation now seems very short.

   _____

3. During the third week, my family and I took a short trip.

   _____

4. We visited the beautiful mountains in the north.

   _____

5. We spent many happy hours walking in the big woods.

   _____

6. I liked to look at the great blue sky through the tall green trees.

   _____

7. At night there were many bright stars in the dark sky.

   _____

8. One night there were more than one hundred thousand stars.

   _____

9. There is no more time to take another trip.

   _____

10. We met many interesting and nice people.

    _____

11. My parents like to go to different places each year.

    _____

12. Some day I hope to visit a tropical island with white sand and blue sea.

    _____

Chapter 21
Adverbs and Adverbial Phrases

Adverbs describe the action expressed by a verb. They explain how, in what way, when, where, or why the action takes place. Adverbs also modify adjectives and other adverbs. They don't change form according to gender and number. Adverbial phrases are groups of words that together function as an adverb.

[1] ADVERBS AND ADVERBIAL PHRASES OF MODE

a. Adverbs of mode (those answering the question *how?* or *in what way?*) are generally formed by adding *-mente* to the feminine singular form of an adjective.

ADJECTIVE	ADVERB
correcta *correct* **fácil** *easy*	**correctamente** *correctly* **fácilmente** *easily*

NOTE:

1. Adjectives that have an accent mark keep the accent mark when they are changed to adverbs.

   rápida   rápidamente

2. The adjectives *bueno* and *malo* form adverbs irregularly.

   bueno *good*   bien *well*
   mal *bad*   mal *badly*

   Es un carro **bueno**,   *It's a good car,*
   pero Pedro conduce **mal**.   *but Pedro drives badly.*

b. Adverbial phrases of mode are usually formed as follows:

   de manera + *adjective*
   Él habla **de manera extraña**.   *He talks in a strange way.*

   de modo + *adjective*
   Él habla **de modo extraño**.   *He talks in a strange way.*

EXERCISE A

After Migdalia's first singing recital, people commented on her talent. Complete each comment by writing the appropriate form of the adverb.

EXAMPLE: su profesor de música: correcto
            Ella canta **correctamente**.

1. sus padres: divino

   Ella canta _____  divinamente _____ .

2. su hermano: malo

Ella canta ___malomente___.

3. sus abuelos: alegre

Ella canta ___alegremente___.

4. su novio: dulce

Ella canta ___dulcemente___.

5. una amiga: suave

Ella canta ___suavemente___.

6. otro cantante: bueno

Ella canta ___buenomente___.

EXERCISE B

A classmate asks how you do different things. Answer his or her questions using the cue given in parentheses.

EXAMPLE: ¿Cómo completas tus tareas? *(diligente)*
   Yo completo mis tareas **diligentemente.**

1. ¿Cómo almuerzas? *(rápido)*

___Yo almuerzo rápidamente.___

2. ¿Cómo hablas a tu novio(a)? *(dulce)*

___Yo hablo a tu novia dulce.___

3. ¿Cómo patinas? *(malo)*

___Yo patino malómente___

4. ¿Cómo caminas a las clases? *(lento)*

___Yo camino a las clases lentomente___

5. ¿Cómo saludas a tus amigos? *(cordial)*

___Yo saludo a tus amigos cordialmente___

6. ¿Cómo comprendes a la maestra de español? *(fácil)*

___Yo comprondo a la maestra de español fácilemente___

[2] ADVERBS AND ADVERBIAL PHRASES OF TIME OR FREQUENCY

a. Adverbs of time or frequency

ahora   *now*

anoche   *last night*

ayer   *yesterday*

¿cuándo?   *when?*

entonces	*then*	pronto	*soon*
hoy	*today*	siempre	*always*
luego	*then, next*	tarde	*late*
mañana	*tomorrow*	temprano	*early*
nunca	*never*	todavía	*still, yet*

b. Adverbial phrases of time or frequency

algún día	*some day*	muchas veces	*often*
a veces	*sometimes*	pocas veces	*seldom*
esta noche	*tonight*	primero	*first*
este fin de semana	*this weekend*	todos los días	*every day*
más tarde	*later*		

EXERCISE C

Tell when, or how frequently, you do or are going to do the following things. For each statement, use the suggested adverb or adverbial phrase.

EXAMPLES: bañarse / todos los días.
Yo me baño todos los días.

descansar / mañana
Yo voy a descansar mañana.

1. ir de compras / este fin de semana
Yo voy de compras este fin de semana

2. estudiar para un examen / esta noche
Yo estudio para un examen esta noche.

3. llegar a tiempo a la escuela / siempre
Yo llego a tiempo a la escuela siempre.

4. ser rico / algún día
Yo soy rico algún día

5. escribir el ejercicio / ahora
Yo escribo el ejercicio ahora.

6. visitar a los abuelos / pronto
Yo visito a los abuelos pronto.

7. recibir malas notas / pocas veces
Yo recibo malas notas pocas veces

8. pelear con los padres / nunca
Yo peleo con los padres nunca.

EXERCISE D

Using the expressions given, tell how frequently you do these things.

sometimes

a veces	nunca	siempre
muchas veces	pocas veces	todas los días

EXAMPLE: lavar los platos
Nunca lavo los platos.

1. preparar la tarea

Yo preparo la tarea a veces.

2. ir al supermercado

Yo voy al supermercado muchas veces

3. cocinar

Yo cocino nunca.

4. arreglar su cuarto

Yo arreglo su cuarto Siempre.

5. pasar la aspiradora

Yo paso la aspiradora pocas veces.

6. lavar el carro

Yo lavo el carro a veces

7. trabajar en el jardín

Yo trabajo en el jardín todas los días

[3] ADVERBS AND ADVERBIAL PHRASES OF PLACE

a. Common adverbs of place (answering the question *where?*)

abajo *below, downstairs*	derecho *straight ahead*
¿adónde? *(to) where?*	detrás *behind*
allí *there*	¿dónde? *where?*
aquí *here*	enfrente *in front of, opposite*
arriba *above, upstairs*	

b. Common adverbial phrases of place

a la derecha *to the right*	delante de *in front of, ahead of*
a la izquierda *to the left*	detrás de *behind*
debajo de *beneath*	frente a *facing, in front of*

EXERCISE E

You are helping a new friend become familiar with the downtown area of your city. Use the map below to tell him the location of the buildings listed. Express the location using an adverbial phrase.

EXAMPLE: el banco
El banco **está detrás del cine**.

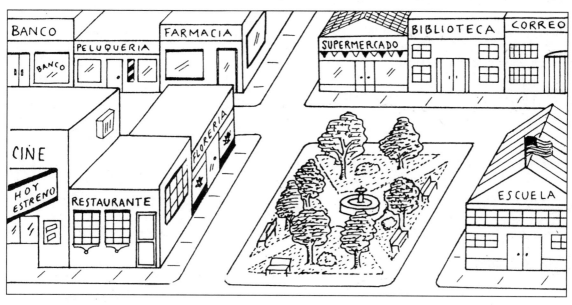

1. la florería

La florería esta cerca restaurante

2. la biblioteca

La biblioteca está cerca el correo,

3. el restaurante

El restaurante esta cerca d'cine

4. el correo

El correo esta cerca de la biblioteca

5. el parque

El parque está en la center de (town)

6. la escuela

La escuela está cerca de el parque,

7. el cine

El cine está cerca de restaurante

MASTERY EXERCISES

EXERCISE F

In each group, select the adverb that is in a different category (mode, time, or place) from the other three and write it in the space provided.

EXAMPLE: alegremente, libremente, **temprano**, lentamente

1. ayer, siempre, correctamente, entonces   _____

2. débilmente, ahora, luego, nunca   _____

3. ¿adónde?, dulcemente, bien, rápidamente   _____

4. ¿cuándo?, hoy, nunca, tristemente   _____

5. diligentemente, tarde, sinceramente, perezosamente   _____

6. pronto, aquí, abajo, ¿dónde?   _____

7. allí, arriba, ¿dónde?, fácilmente   _____

8. ¿por qué?, anoche, todavía, mañana   _____

9. felizmente, mal, rápidamente, ¿cuándo?   _____

10. difícilmente, a la derecha, allí, derecho   _____

EXERCISE G

You're talking about your language class. Complete each sentence with the appropriate adverb.

EXAMPLE: No comprendemos a Jorge cuando habla.
           Él habla **rápidamente**.

1. Yo hago la tarea sin errores.
   Yo hago la tarea _perfectamente_.

2. Yo estudio siete días a la semana.
   Yo estudio _mucho_.

3. La maestra dice «por favor» y «gracias» a los alumnos.
   Ella habla _en español, bien_.

4. Nosotros comprendemos todo lo que dice la profesora.
   Nosotros comprendemos _mucho_.

5. La maestra tiene una voz bonita.

Ella canta ___bonitamente___.

6. A Roberto le gusta hablar.

Él habla ___mucho___ en la clase.

7. Mi amigo no recibe buenas notas.

Él sale ___mal___ en todos los exámenes.

EXERCISE H

Tell where the objects in the picture below are located. Use adverbial phrases of place in your sentences.

EXAMPLE: **El vaso está al lado de la leche.**

1. El guante de béisbol ___está debajo de la mesa___.

2. Los gatos ___está izquierdo de el perro___.

3. La niña _está detras de el árbol._

4. Las papitas _está la derecha de hamburguesa._

5. El automóvil _está delante de la bicicleta._

EXERCISE I

Express the following in Spanish.

1. The team is going to arrive soon.

   El equipo ~~esta~~ va a llegar pronto.

2. Ricardo invites his friends often.

   Ricardo invita ~~su~~ a sus amigos ~~a~~ ~~es~~ muchas veces

3. They always come to his house happily.

   Ellos siempre venido a su casa contentamente.

4. Now Ricardo has to work rapidly.

   ~~Ahora~~ Ahora Ricardo ~~tiene~~ tiene a trabajo rapidamente.

5. He cooks well, but he rarely eats the food.

El cocino bien, pero su raramente comer el alimento.

6. He greets his friends cordially at the door.

El saluda su amigos cordialmente en la puerta.

7. First he opens the soda; then he carefully puts the food on the table.

Prima el se abre el refresco; entonces pone cuidadosamente el alimento en la mesa.

8. The party turned out *(salir)* perfectly.

La fiesta resultado saliramente.

Chapter 22
Numbers

[1] CARDINAL NUMBERS

a. 0 to 99

0	cero	13	trece	26	veintiséis (veinte y seis)
1	uno	14	catorce	27	veintisiete (veinte y siete)
2	dos	15	quince	28	veintiocho (veinte y ocho)
3	tres	16	dieciséis (diez y seis)	29	veintinueve (veinte y nueve)
4	cuatro	17	diecisiete (diez y siete)	30	treinta
5	cinco	18	dieciocho (diez y ocho)	31	treinta y uno (and so on)
6	seis	19	diecinueve (diez y nueve)	40	cuarenta
7	siete	20	veinte	50	cincuenta
8	ocho	21	veintiuno (veinte y uno)	60	sesenta
9	nueve	22	veintidós (veinte y dos)	70	setenta
10	diez	23	veintitrés (veinte y tres)	80	ochenta
11	once	24	veinticuatro (veinte y cuatro)	90	noventa
12	doce	25	veinticinco (veinte y cinco)	99	noventa y nueve

NOTE:

1. Compound numbers 16 to 99 are connected by *y*.

2. Although numbers 16 to 19 and 21 to 29 may be connected by *y*, they are usually written as one word. Note the spelling changes that occur when these numbers are written as one word.

   diez   dieciséis
   veinte   veintiuno

3. *Uno* and combinations of *uno* (like *veintiuno* and *treinta y uno*) become *un* before masculine nouns and *una* before feminine nouns.

un libro	*one (a) book*
veint**iún** asientos	*twenty-one seats*
treinta y **un** profesores	*thirty-one teachers*
una mesa	*one (a) table*
veint**iuna** camisas	*twenty-one shirts*
treinta y **una** sillas	*thirty-one chairs*
veint**iún** asientos	*twenty-one seats*

EXERCISE A

As you leave a summer camp in Mexico, your new friends give you their telephone numbers. Rewrite them using Spanish words.

EXAMPLE: Silvia 5-47-08-23
cinco - cuarenta y siete - cero ocho - veintitrés

1. Arturo 6-31-74-92
seis - treinta y uno - setenta y cuatro - noventa y dos

2. Raquel 3-65-22-81
tres - sesenta y cinco - veintidós - ochenta y uno

3. Emilio 7-27-00-48
siete - veintisiete - cero cero - cuarenta y ocho

4. Graciela 2-59-11-17
dos - cincuenta y nueve - once - diecisiete

5. Humberto 9-13-36-14
nueve - trese - trenta y seis - catorce

6. Raúl 8-72-12-41
ocho - setenta y dos - doce - cuarenta y uno

7. Linda 9-97-16-67
nueve - noventa y siete - dieciséis - sesenta y sieta

8. Pedro 5-33-21-86 ·
cinco - trenta y tres - vientiuno - ochenta y seis

EXERCISE B

While touring Spain, you help the tour guide give out the room assignments at the hotel.

EXAMPLE: Enrique y José, 57
Para Enrique y José, el **cincuenta y siete**.

1. Louise y Estela, 38
Para Louise y Estela, el treinta y ocho

2. Elisa y Jane, 71
Para Elisa y Jane, el setenta y uno

3. Billy y Tomás, 43
Para Billy y Tomás, el cuarenta y tres

4. Javier y Antonio, 15

Para Javier y Antonio, quince

5. Rita y María, 64

Para Rita y María, sesenta y cuatro

6. Clara y Marcela, 86

Para Clara y Marcela, ochenta y seis

7. Felipe y Hugo, 29

Para Felipe y Hugo, veinte y nueve

EXERCISE C

Use the following map to tell your Spanish-speaking friend the expected high and low temperatures in some major cities of the United States. All temperatures are in degrees Fahrenheit.

EXAMPLE: Los Angeles
     La temperatura alta será setenta y seis grados y la baja sesenta y dos grados.

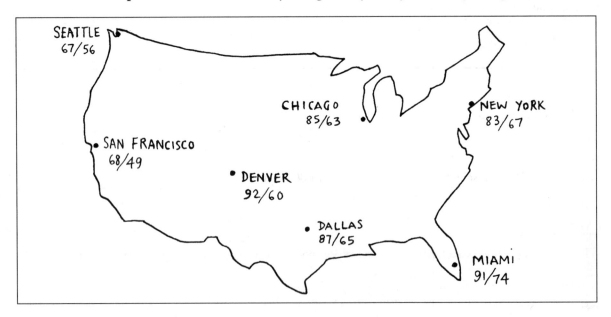

1. Miami

_____

_____

2. Chicago

_____

_____

3. Seattle

_____

_____

4. Denver

_____

_____

5. New York

_____

_____

6. Dallas

_____

_____

7. San Francisco

_____

_____

b. **100 to 1,000,000**

100	cien	800	ochocientos (–as)
101	ciento uno (–a)	900	novecientos (–as)
200	doscientos (–as)	1,000	mil
300	trescientos (–as)	2,000	dos mil
400	cuatrocientos (–as)	2,500	dos mil quinientos
500	quinientos (–as)	100,000	cien mil
600	seiscientos (–as)	1,000,000	un millón (de)
700	setecientos (–as)		

NOTE:

1. *Cien* becomes *ciento* when it's followed by another number from one to ninety-nine.

cien libros	*one hundred books*
cien casas	*one hundred houses*
cien mil habitantes	*one hundred thousand inhabitants*
cien millones	*one hundred million*

BUT

cien**to** veinte libros	*one hundred twenty books*

2. Numbers that express hundreds, like *doscientos* and *trescientos,* become *doscientas* and *trescientas* before a feminine noun.

    doscientas páginas   *two hundred pages*
    trescientas plumas   *three hundred pens*

3. In Spanish, compound numbers higher than a thousand (such as 1,110) are expressed with *mil.* Words like *twelve hundred* have no equivalent in Spanish.

    mil doscientos   *twelve hundred (one thousand two hundred)*
    mil novecientos noventa   *nineteen hundred ninety (one thousand nine hundred ninety)*
    dos mil quinientos   *twenty-five hundred (two thousand five hundred)*

4. No equivalent to the English word *a* or *one* is expressed before *ciento* or *mil,* but the equivalent *un* must be used before *millón. Millón* (pl. *millones*) also requires *de* when a noun follows.

    ciento diez alumnos   *a (one) hundred ten students*
    mil dólares   *a (one) thousand dollars*

    BUT

    un millón de dólares   *a (one) million dollars*
    dos millones de habitantes   *two million inhabitants*

5. In many Spanish-speaking countries, the commas in large numbers change to periods: 1,000 becomes 1.000 and 1,000,000 becomes 1.000.000. The periods in decimal numbers change to commas: 1.10 becomes 1,10.

EXERCISE D

You and a friend are comparing the population of cities around the world. Express the approximate populations of these cities, using Spanish words.

EXAMPLE: Madrid / 3,120,000
            tres millones ciento veinte mil habitantes

1. México, D. F. / 8,236,960

ocho millones, docientos treinta y seis, ~~mil~~ novecientos sesenta

2. París / 2,152,423

dos millones, ciento cincuenta y dos, ~~mil~~ cuatrocientos veinte y tres.

3. Tokio / 11,000,000

once millones

4. Chicago / 2,783,726

dos millones, setecientos ochenta y tres, ~~mil~~ setecientos veinte y seis.

5. San Francisco / 723,959

setecientos veinte y tres mil, novecientos cincuenta y nueve.

6. Barcelona / 1,623,542

un millones, sescientas veinte y tres mil, quinientos cuarenta y dos

7. Buenos Aires / 2,780,092

dos millones, setecientos ocheta y cero mil, noventa y dos

8. New Orleans / 496,938

cuatrocientos noventa y seis mil, novecientos treinta y ocho

9. Atlanta / 393,929

trescientos noventa y tres mil, novecientos viente y nueve.

10. Seattle / 516,259

quinientos diez y seis mil, doscientos cincuenta y nueve.

EXERCISE E

You're using Mexico City as your base for several side trips to other cities. Express in Spanish the approximate distance by car between Mexico City and each of the other cities you plan to visit.

EXAMPLE: Cuernavaca / 82 kilómetros
Cuernavaca está a **ochenta y dos** kilómetros.

1. Acapulco / 305 kilómetros

_____

2. Puebla / 120 kilómetros

_____

3. Veracruz / 424 kilómetros

_____

4. Oaxaca / 516 kilómetros

_____

5. Toluca / 56 kilómetros

_____

6. Guadalajara / 450 kilómetros

_____

7. Querétaro / 257 kilómetros

_____

EXERCISE F

Tell the year in which these family members were born.

EXAMPLE: tu prima favorita
Mi prima favorita **nació en mil novecientos setenta y ocho**.

1. tu padre

_____

2. tu madre

_____

3. tu hermano(a)

_____

4. tu abuelo

_____

5. tu abuela

_____

6. tu tío favorito

_____

7. tú

_____

EXERCISE G

The airlines have just lowered their fares. Tell how much each of these flights will cost one-way (*ida*) and round-trip (*ida y vuelta*).

AEROLINEAS INTERNACIONALES
BOLETOS DE IDA

SAN JUAN	$139	COSTA RICA	$209
CANCÚN	$159	BARCELONA	$299
BUENOS AIRES	$499	CARACAS	$299

EXAMPLE: Caracas
           ida **doscientos noventa y nueve dólares**
           ida y vuelta **quinientos noventa y ocho dólares**

1. Barcelona

   ida _____

   ida y vuelta _____

2. Costa Rica

   ida _____

   ida y vuelta _____

3. San Juan

   ida _____

   ida y vuelta _____

4. Cancún

   ida _____

   ida y vuelta _____

5. Buenos Aires

   ida _____

   ida y vuelta _____

EXERCISE H

Mr. Jiménez is planning his summer vacation and wants to find out the foreign currency exchange rate for various countries. Write down what he finds out in the newspaper.

EXAMPLE: Francia / 5 francos
           Un dólar es igual a cinco francos.

1. Argentina / 1 peso

   _____

2. Chile / 430 pesos

   _____

3. Colombia / 929 pesos

   _____

4. Costa Rica / 152 colones

   _____

5. España / 132 pesetas

   _____

6. México / 3,115 nuevos pesos

_____

7. Nicaragua / 5 córdobas

_____

8. Paraguay / 1,887 guaraníes

_____

9. República Dominicana / 13 pesos

_____

10. Venezuela / 112 bolívares

_____

EXERCISE I

You're preparing a surprise party for a friend and you're writing the details in Spanish in your diary. Complete the sentences using the correct form of _uno_.

1. Mañana Federico cumple treinta y _____ años.

2. Invitamos a cincuenta y _____ personas.

3. Hay cuarenta y _____ globos.

4. Necesitamos treinta y _____ velas para el pastel.

5. Vamos a necesitar _____ silla más.

6. Podemos comer el pastel con _____ cuchara.

EXERCISE J

You're working at a hotel that is going to be refurbished. Complete the following sentences with _cien_ or _ciento_.

1. Hay _____ cuartos en el hotel.

2. _____ cincuenta y cinco personas van a pasar la noche en el hotel.

3. Unos cuartos cuestan _____ dólares la noche.

4. Otros cuartos cuestan _____ veinte y cinco dólares.

5. La reparación va a durar _____ días.

[2] ARITHMETIC EXPRESSIONS

The following expressions are used in arithmetic problems in Spanish:

y, más   *plus* (+)

menos   *minus* (−)

por   *(multiplied) by, "times"* (×)

dividido por   *divided by* (÷)

son, es igual a   *equals* (=)

EXERCISE K

Express the following in Spanish.

1. 35 + 70 = 105

treinta y cinco y setenta son ciento cinco

2. 187 + 542 = 729

cientos ochenta y siete y quinientos cuarenta y dos son setecientos veinte y nueve

3. 691 − 255 = 436

seiscientos noventa y uno menos doscientos cincuenta y cinco son cuatrocientos treinta y seis

4. 1,323 − 1,022 = 301

mil trescientos veinte y tres menos mil veinte y dos son tresciento uno.no

5. 1,968 + 2,741 = 4,709

mil novecientos sesenta y ocho y dos mil setecientos nueve

6. 636 × 25 = 15,900

seiscientos treinta y seis por veinte y cinco son quince mil novecientos.

7. 338 ÷ 26 = 13

trescientos treinta y ocho dividido por veinte y seis son trece

8. 700 + 300 = 1,000

setecientos y trescientos son mil.

9. 500 + 400 = 900

quiniento y cuatrociento so novecieuto

10. 900 − 350 = 550

novecieuto menos trescientos cuarenta son
quinientos cuarenta

11. 900 + 800 = 1,700

novecieuto y ochocieuto son mil setecieuto

12. 110 + 115 = 225

ciento diez y ciento cuince son doscientos
veinte y cinco

13. 743 − 243 = 500

setecientos cuarenta y tres menos doscientos
cuarenta y tres son quiniento,

14. 20,000 ÷ 100 = 200

veinte mil dividido por cien son doscienta

15. 800,000 + 200,000 = 1,000,000

ochocieuto mil y doscieuto mil son un millón

16. 1,400,000 + 600,000 = 2,000,000

un millones cuatrociento mil y seiscieuto mil son
dos millón

17. 2,400 ÷ 12 = 200

dos mil cuatrocieuto dividido por doce son
doscieuto

18. 5,000 ÷ 500 = 10

cinco mil dividido por quiniento son diez

19. 930 × 17 = 15,810

novecientos treinta por diecisiete son quince mil
ochocieuto diez

20. 359 × 26 = 9,334

> trescientos cincuenta y nueve por veinte y seis son
> nueve mil trescientos treinta y cuatro.

[3] ORDINAL NUMBERS

1°	primero (-a), primer	1st	*first*
2°	segundo (-a)	2nd	*second*
3°	tercero (-a), tercer	3rd	*third*
4°	cuarto (-a)	4th	*fourth*
5°	quinto (-a)	5th	*fifth*
6°	sexto (-a)	6th	*sixth*
7°	séptimo (-a)	7th	*seventh*
8°	octavo (-a)	8th	*eighth*
9°	noveno (-a)	9th	*ninth*
10°	décimo (-a)	10th	*tenth*

NOTE:

1. All ordinal numbers agree in gender (*m./f.*) and number (*sing./pl.*) with the nouns to which they refer.

el séptimo mes	*the seventh month*
la séptima semana	*the seventh week*

2. The numbers *primero* and *tercero* drop the final *-o* when they come before a masculine singular noun.

el primer hombre	*the first man*
el tercer mes	*the third month*

   BUT

la primera semana	*the first week*
la tercera vez	*the third time*

3. If a preposition comes between *primero* or *tercero* and the noun, the full form is used.

el primero de mayo	*May 1*

4. Ordinal numbers are generally used to express rank order only from the first to the tenth in a series. Numbers above ten have ordinal forms, too, but they are seldom used. Instead, a cardinal number is placed after the noun, and the word *número* is understood.

la sexta lección	*the sixth lesson*
Felipe Segundo	*Felipe II (Felipe the Second)*

   BUT

la lección catorce	*the fourteenth lesson* or *lesson (number) fourteen*
Alfonso Doce	*Alfonso XII (Alfonso the Twelfth)*

EXERCISE L

You step into a hotel elevator. Tell on which floor each of the following places is located. Use the word *piso* in your response.*

```
  (PB) | PERIÓDICOS          (10) | _____
  (1)  | PELUQUERÍA          (11) | _____
  (2)  | PISCINA             (12) | _____
  (3)  | BAR/DISCOTECA       (13) | OFICINAS
  (4)  | TIENDAS             (14) | _____
  (5)  | SALÓN MARTEL        (15) | _____
  (6)  | _____    (16) | _____
  (7)  | TEATRO EL LAGO      (17) | _____
  (8)  | SALÓN DE BANQUETES  (18) | _____
  (9)  | _____    (19) | RESTAURANTE EL LAGO
```

EXAMPLE: El bar **está en el tercer piso**.

1. La piscina _____ .

2. Las tiendas _____ .

3. Las oficinas _____ .

4. La peluquería _____ .

5. El restaurante _____ .

6. El Salón de Banquetes _____ .

7. El Salón Martel _____ .

8. El teatro _____ .

9. La discoteca _____ .

10. Los periódicos _____ .

---

* In most Spanish-speaking countries, the first floor (or ground floor) is called *planta baja (PB);* the second floor, *primer piso;* and so forth.

EXERCISE M

You're helping a younger brother learn the order of the months. Tell what position each month occupies in the calendar year.

EXAMPLE: abril
el cuarto mes

1. junio

   el sexto mes

2. septiembre

   el noveno mes

3. enero

   el primero mes

4. diciembre

   el mes doce

5. febrero

   el mes segundo

6. octubre

   el mes déeimo

7. julio

   el mes séptimo

8. marzo

   el mes tercero

9. agosto

   el mes octavo

10. mayo

    el mes quinto

11. noviembre

    el mes once

EXERCISE N

Write the sentences, changing the number in parentheses into a Spanish word.

1. Siéntate en el *(3°)* asiento.

_____

2. Saliste mal en la *(5°)* prueba.

_____

3. Naciste en junio, el *(6°)* mes del año.

_____

4. Acabas de celebrar tu cumpleaños *(15°)*.

_____

5. Vives es un apartamento en el *(1°)* piso.

_____

6. Caminas a la escuela por la Calle *(8°)*.

_____

7. El español es tu *(3°)* clase del día.

_____

8. Estudias el *(2°)* semestre de español.

_____

9. Estamos en la *(10°)* lección.

_____

10. Debes hacer el *(4°)* ejercicio.

_____

[4] FRACTIONS

$\frac{1}{2}$ un medio, medio (-a), una mitad de	*(a/one) half, half of*
$\frac{1}{3}$ un tercio, una tercera parte de	*(a/one) third, the third part of*
$\frac{1}{4}$ un cuarto, una cuarta parte de	*(a/one) fourth, a quarter of*
$\frac{2}{3}$ dos tercios, las dos terceras partes de	*two-thirds, two-thirds of*
$\frac{3}{4}$ tres cuartos, las tres cuartas partes de	*three-fourths, three quarters of*
$\frac{4}{5}$ cuatro quintos, las cuatro quintas partes de	*four-fifths of*
$\frac{1}{10}$ un décimo, la décima parte de	*(a/one) tenth, a tenth of*

NOTE:

1. Except for *medio* and *tercio*, noun fractions are formed with ordinal numbers up through *décimo* (tenth). Thereafter, the ending *-avo* is usually added to the cardinal number to express fractions smaller than a tenth.

   $\frac{1}{12}$ un doceavo, una doceava parte de   *(a/one) twelfth of*

2. Fractions are masculine nouns.

   3 $\frac{1}{3}$ tres y un tercio   *three and one-third*

   When the fraction precedes the thing divided, it may be used with the feminine noun *parte*, unless a unit of measure is expressed:

   una tercera **parte** (un tercio) del libro   *a third of the book*

   BUT

   un tercio de libra   *a third of a pound*

3. The adjective *medio* (*-a*) means "half," while the noun *la mitad* (*de*) means "half (of)."

   media docena de huevos   *half a dozen eggs*
   la mitad de la clase   *half of the class*

EXERCISE O

Copy the following shopping list, writing out fractions in full.

Lista de compras
½ docena de huevos
½ galón de leche
¼ libra de jamón
3/4 libra de queso
½ pan
1½ libra de galletas
½ melón
½ sandía

1. _____

2. _____

3. _____

4. _____

5. _____

6. _____

7. _____

[5] MULTIPLES

Terms that indicate that one quantity is a multiple of another are used in the same manner as their English equivalents.

una vez _once_	simple _single, simple_
dos veces _twice_	doble _double_
tres veces _three times_	triple _triple_

Me visitó una vez.	_She visited me once._
Lo leí dos veces.	_I read it twice._
Escribí el doble de lo que escribiste tú.	_I wrote twice as much as you._

NOTE:

1. Adverbial phrases expressing the number of times that an event occurs are formed by a cardinal number and the feminine noun _vez_ (a time).

Leí el libro tres veces.	_I read the book three times._

2. Multiples like _doble, triple_ may be either adjectives or nouns.

Es una máquina de **doble** motor.	_It's a double-motor machine._
Este carro cuesta hoy el **doble**.	_This car costs twice as much today._

EXERCISE P

You overhear your younger sister tell a friend how many times she has done some activities. Tell what she says using the cues in parentheses.

EXAMPLE: ir al parque zoológico _(10)_
            Fui al parque zoológico **diez veces**.

1. volar en avión _(5)_

_____

2. esquiar _(20)_

_____

3. ver la película «Fantasma» _(2)_

_____

4. jugar al fútbol _(50)_

_____

5. comer al aire libre _(8)_

_____

6. ir a la playa *(100)*

_____

7. preparar la cena *(1)*

_____

M A S T E R Y   E X E R C I S E S

EXERCISE Q

Your parents have remodeled the house to give you a larger room. Write sentences telling how much different things cost.

1. pintura $790

_____

2. ventanas $1,200

_____

3. muebles $920

_____

4. alfombra $444

_____

5. televisor $389

_____

6. cortinas $56

_____

7. total $3,799

_____

EXERCISE R

You are visiting a cousin in Spain. She mentions several tourist attractions and indicates how many times she has visited each one of them. Use the cues in parentheses to express what she says.

EXAMPLE: el Escorial (3)
                  Visité al Escorial tres veces.

1. el Valle de los Caídos *(5)*

_____

2. el Museo del Prado *(12)*

_____

3. la Plaza Mayor *(20)*

_____

4. el Palacio Real *(1)*

_____

5. la cuidad de Toledo *(7)*

_____

6. el Parque del Buen Retiro *(25)*

_____

EXERCISE S

You're writing to a friend about your summer job. Express the following in Spanish.

1. This summer I'm working for the first time.

_____

2. I work 37½ hours a week.

_____

3. My salary is two hundred and eighty-eight dollars.

_____

4. I have a half-hour for lunch.

_____

5. I work in a large store on Fifth Avenue.

_____

6. There are more than seventy-five employees.

_____

7. One-half of the employees are students.

_____

8. Five hundred people enter the store each day.

_____

9. My first day there I sold fifteen thousand dollars in merchandise.

_____

10. The company earns more than three million dollars a year.

_____

11. Two-thirds of the people use credit cards.

_____

12. The telephone number of the store is 555-9321.

_____

13. The store opened in 1976 on Forty-eighth Street.

_____

14. One-quarter of their business is by telephone.

_____

15. I will work for eleven weeks.

_____

16. I will work 412¹/₂ hours this summer.

_____

Chapter 23
Times and Dates

[1] TIME EXPRESSIONS

a. *¿Qué hora es?* is equivalent to "What time is it?"

b. In expressing time, "It is" is expressed by *Es la* (for one o'clock), and *Son las* for other hours (two o'clock, three o'clock, and so on).

Es la una.	*It's one o'clock.*
Son las dos (tres).	*It's two (three) o'clock.*

c. Time after or past the hour (up to half past) is expressed by the hour + *y*, followed by the number of minutes. "Half past" is expressed by *y media;* "a quarter past" is expressed by *y cuarto.*

Es la una **y** diez.	*It's ten (minutes) after one. It's 1:10.*
Son las seis **y media.**	*It's half past six. It's 6:30.*
Son las diez **y cuarto.**	*It's a quarter after ten. It's 10:15.*

d. After half past, the time is expressed in terms of the following hour *menos* (minus) the minutes.

Son las dos **menos** veinte.	*It's twenty minutes to two. It's 1:40.*
Son las nueve **menos** cuarto.	*It's a quarter to nine. It's 8:45.*

e. The expression *de la mañana* corresponds to English A.M. (in the morning). *De la tarde* (in the afternoon) and *de la noche* (in the evening) correspond to English P.M. *En punto* means "sharp" or "on the dot."

Son las ocho **de la mañana.**	*It's 8:00 A.M.*
Es la una **de la tarde.**	*It's 1:00 P.M.*
Son las ocho **de la noche en punto.**	*It's 8:00 P.M. sharp.*

NOTE:

1. Instead of *media* and *cuarto*, the number of minutes may be used *(treinta, quince).*

Son las cinco y *treinta.*	*It's five-thirty. It's half past five.*
Es la una y **quince.**	*It's one-fifteen. It's a quarter past one.*

2. It's not uncommon to hear times like 12:45 and 12:50 expressed with *y.*

Son las doce y **cuarenta y cinco.**	*It's twelve-forty-five.*
Son las doce y **cincuenta.**	*It's twelve-fifty.*

f. Common time expressions

¿Qué hora es?	*What time is it?*
¿A qué hora?	*At what time?*
a las dos (tres)	*at two (three) o'clock*

de la mañana	*in the morning, A.M.*		a medianoche	*at midnight*
de la tarde	*in the afternoon, P.M.*		Es tarde.	*It's late.*
de la noche	*at night, P.M.*		Es temprano.	*It's early.*
Es mediodía.	*It's noon.*		a tiempo	*on time*
a mediodía	*at noon*		en punto	*exactly, sharp*
Es medianoche.	*It's midnight.*			

EXERCISE A

You're teaching your younger sister to tell time in Spanish. Express the hours indicated on the clocks.

EXAMPLE: Son las **diez menos cuarto.**

1. _____

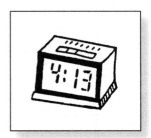

3. _____

2. _____

4. _____

5. _____

_____

6. _____

_____

7. _____

_____

8. _____

_____

9. _____

_____

10. _____

_____

11. _____

_____

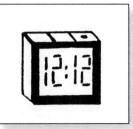

12. _____

_____

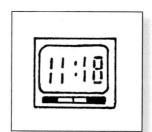

13. _____

_____

14. _____

_____

15. _____

_____

16. _____

_____

17. _____

_____

18. _____

_____

19. _____

_____

20. _____

_____

EXERCISE B

Tell at what time in the morning, afternoon, or evening you usually do the following activities.

EXAMPLE: desayunarse
Me desayuno a las seis y media **de la mañana**.

1. ir a la escuela

   _____

2. almorzar

   _____

3. preparar la tarea

   _____

4. jugar con los amigos

   _____

5. salir de la escuela

   _____

6. cenar

   _____

7. ver su programa favorito de televisión

   _____

8. acostarse

   _____

9. practicar un deporte

   _____

10. bañarse

   _____

EXERCISE C

You don't know where the day has gone. Using the notes below, tell at what time you completed each activity.

EXAMPLE: Tú ayudas a tu papá a lavar el carro. Son las ocho y media cuando empiezan. Tardan una hora y media en lavar el carro. ¿Qué hora es?
Son las diez.

1. Tú acompañas a tu mamá al supermercado. Salen de la casa a las diez y cuarto. Regresan a casa ochenta minutos después. ¿Qué hora es?

   _____

2. Tu amiga te llama por teléfono a las doce menos cinco. Hablan por quince minutos. ¿A qué hora terminan de hablar?

_____

3. A la una tú arreglas tu cuarto. Necesitas setenta y cinco minutos. ¿Qué hora es?

_____

4. Tienes que sacar un libro de la biblioteca. Sales de tu casa a las tres menos cuarto y vuelves a la casa en dos horas y media. ¿A qué hora vuelves a casa?

_____

5. Después de cenar, estudias para un examen por tres horas y quince minutos. Empiezas a estudiar a las siete y diez. ¿Qué hora es cuando terminas de estudiar?

_____

[2] DATES

a. Days of the week (*Los días de la semana*)

lunes *Monday*	viernes *Friday*
martes *Tuesday*	sábado *Saturday*
miércoles *Wednesday*	domingo *Sunday*
jueves *Thursday*	

NOTE:

1. **"On" before a day of the week is expressed by *el* for the singular and *los* for the plural.**

el lunes *on Monday*	los lunes *on Mondays*
el viernes *on Friday*	los viernes *on Fridays*
el sábado *on Saturday*	los sábados *on Saturdays*
el domingo *on Sunday*	los domingos *on Sundays*

2. **Days of the week whose names end in *-s* do not change their form in the plural.**

3. **The days of the week are not capitalized in Spanish.**

b. Months (*Los meses*)

enero *January*	julio *July*
febrero *February*	agosto *August*
marzo *March*	septiembre *September*
abril *April*	octubre *October*
mayo *May*	noviembre *November*
junio *June*	diciembre *December*

NOTE: **Like the days of the week, the months are written with lowercase (small) letters in Spanish.**

c. Dates

¿Cuál es la fecha de hoy?   }   *What is today's date?*
¿A cuántos estamos hoy?

Es el primero de enero.   }   *It's January 1.*
Estamos a primero de enero.

Es el dos de febrero   *It's February 2.*
Es el tres (cuatro) de mayo.   *It's May 3 (4)*
mil ochocientos doce   *1812*
el quince de abril de   *April 15, 1996*
mil novecientos noventa y seis

NOTE:

1. Cardinal numbers are used for all dates except *primero* (first).

    el **primero** de abril   *April 1*
    el tres (cuatro, cinco) de abril   *April 3 (4,5)*

2. The year is expressed in Spanish by thousands and hundreds, not by hundreds alone as in English.

3. The date and month are connected by the preposition *de.* The month and the year are also connected by *de.*

    el diez **de** junio **de**   *(on) June 10, 1840*
    mil ochocientos cuarenta

    With dates, *el* corresponds to "on."

EXERCISE D

You're telling an exchange student at your school about important dates in the United States. Give the Spanish equivalent for the dates indicated.

1. February 22

_____

2. December 25

_____

3. February 14

_____

4. January 1

_____

5. October 12

_____

6. July 4

_____

7. November 11

_____

8. April 1

_____

9. October 31

_____

10. February 12

_____

EXERCISE E

You're reading a list of Mexican national holidays. Express these dates in Spanish.

1. May 5

_____

2. September 16

_____

3. November 20

_____

4. May 1

_____

5. February 5

_____

6. March 21

_____

7. January 1

_____

8. December 25

_____

EXERCISE F

Tell the date of birth (including the year) of the following members of your family.

EXAMPLE: tu tía favorita
            Mi tía favorita **nació** el **dos de agosto** de **mil novecientos sesenta y uno**.

1. tu madre

Mi madre _____ .

2. tu padre

Mi padre _____ .

3. tu abuelo materno

Mi abuelo materno _____ .

4. tu abuela paterna

Mi abuela paterna _____ .

5. tu hermano(-a)

Mi hermano(-a) _____ .

6. tu primo(-a) favorito(-a)

Mi primo(-a) favorito(-a) _____ .

7. tú

Yo _____ .

EXERCISE G

Express the following dates in Spanish.

1. March 15, 1271

_____

2. February 2, 1588

_____

3. April 17, 1942

_____

4. May 23, 1848

_____

5. July 4, 1776

_____

6. January 30, 1660

_____

7. July 18, 1395

_____

8. December 13, 1969

_____

9. June 22, 1453

_____

10. March 25, 1124

_____

MASTERY EXERCISES

EXERCISE H

A friend is helping you study for a Spanish test. Answer the questions your friend asks.

1. Si hoy es lunes, ¿qué día es mañana?

_____

2. ¿Cuál es el segundo mes del año?

_____

3. ¿En qué mes celebramos la Navidad?

_____

4. ¿Cuál es el noveno mes del año?

_____

5. Si hoy es jueves, ¿qué día fue ayer?

_____

6. ¿Cuáles son los meses que tienen treinta días?

_____

7. ¿Qué mes tiene veintiocho o veintinueve días?

_____

8. ¿Qué meses tienen treinta y un días?

_____

9. ¿En qué días no hay clases?

_____

10. ¿En qué días vas a la escuela?

_____

11. ¿Cuál es la fecha de hoy?

_____

12. ¿En qué mes celebramos la fiesta nacional de los Estados Unidos?

_____

13. ¿Cuál es el séptimo mes del año?

_____

14. ¿En qué mes celebramos el Año Nuevo?

_____

15. ¿En qué fecha celebras tu cumpleaños?

_____

EXERCISE I

You're telling a friend about your summer plans. Express the following in Spanish.

1. On July 1, my family and I are going to travel by train.

_____

2. The train leaves at 10:30 A.M. sharp.

_____

3. The train always leaves on time.

_____

4. They serve dinner on the train at 6:00 P.M.

_____

5. At 8:00 there is a movie.

_____

6. We leave on Thursday and arrive in Chicago early on Saturday.

_____

7. The party is on Sunday at one o'clock in the afternoon.

_____

8. The party will end at five o'clock in the afternoon.

_____

9. The party is for my grandfather. He was born on July 4, 1924.

_____

_____

10. On Sunday nights my family goes to bed early.

_____

11. We have to wake up at 5:45 A.M. on Monday.

_____

12. We have to be in the train station at 7:00 A.M. because the train leaves at 7:20.

_____

_____

13. We leave on Monday and arrive home on Wednesday.

_____

14. My father has to go to work at midnight on Wednesday.

_____

15. Our trip ends on July 7.

_____

Chapter 24
Interrogatives

[1] INTERROGATIVES

a. Common interrogative expressions

¿qué? *what?*

¿quién (-es)? *who?*

¿a quién (-es)? *whom? to whom?*

¿de quién (-es)? *whose? of whom?*

¿con quién (-es)? *with whom?*

¿cuál (-es)? *which? which one(s)?*

¿cuándo? *when?*

¿cuánto (-a)? *how much?*

¿cuántos (-as)? *how many?*

¿cómo? *how?*

¿por qué? *why?*

¿dónde? *where?*

¿de dónde? *(from) where?*

¿adónde? *(to) where?*

NOTE:

1. All interrogative words have a written accent.

2. In Spanish, questions have an inverted question mark (¿) at the beginning and a standard one (?) at the end.

3. When interrogatives (words such as *¿qué?, ¿cuándo?, ¿dónde?*) are used in a question, the subject-verb order is reversed from the order in statements.

¿Qué hacen ellos?	*What are they doing?*
Ellos bailan.	*They are dancing.*
¿Dónde está María?	*Where is Mary?*
Ella está aquí.	*She is here.*

EXERCISE A

You're talking to a new student in your class for the first time. Write the questions that he has answered.

1. Me llamo Enrique Casas.

_____

2. Yo soy de Colombia.

_____

3. Vivo en la calle Oak.

_____

4. Vivo con mis padres y mis dos hermanos.

_____

5. Llegué a los Estados Unidos el mes pasado.

_____

6. Tengo quince años.

_____

7. Me gustan el tenis y el fútbol.

_____

8. Tengo seis clases.

_____

9. Son el inglés, la historia, la biología, las matemáticas, el español y la educación física.

_____

10. El señor Época es mi profesor de historia.

_____

11. Me gusta más la clase de inglés.

_____

12. Después de las clases voy al parque.

_____

13. Voy al parque porque me gusta remar en el lago.

_____

b. Both _¿qué?_ and _¿cuál?_ are equivalent to English "what?" and "which?," but the two words are not usually interchangeable in Spanish.

(1) _¿Qué?_ seeks a description, definition, or explanation.

¿**Qué** es eso?   _What is that?_

(2) _¿Cuál?_ implies a choice or selection.

¿**Cuál** perfume prefiere Ud.?   _Which perfume do you prefer?_

NOTE: **It's common practice in modern Spanish to substitute** _¿qué?_ **for** _¿cuál?_.

¿**Qué** camisa prefiere José? ⎫
¿**Cuál** camisa prefiere José? ⎭   _Which shirt does José prefer?_

EXERCISE B

Underline the interrogative word that is needed in each question.

1. ¿(Cuál / Qué) es esto?

2. ¿(Cuál / Qué) comes por la mañana?

3. ¿(Cuál / Qué) día es hoy?

4. ¿(Cuál / Cuáles) son los meses del año?

5. ¿(Cuál / Qué) es tu número de teléfono?

6. ¿(Cuál / Cuáles) postres te gustan más?

7. ¿(Cuál / Qué) vas a hacer con el dinero?

8. ¿(Cuál / Qué) haces cuando llueve?

9. ¿(Cuál / Qué) comes en un restaurante mexicano?

10. ¿(Cuál / Qué) libros leíste el año pasado?

EXERCISE C

While Linda is trying to study, her little sister is looking through a book that has many words she doesn't understand. According to the answers given, write the questions Linda's sister asks.

EXAMPLE: Un clavel es una flor.
　　　　　　 ¿Qué es un clavel?

1. Un pasaporte es un documento.

_____

2. Una vaca es un animal.

_____

3. Una manzana es una fruta.

_____

4. El oro es un metal.

_____

5. Un diccionario es un libro.

_____

c. *¿Quién (-es)?, ¿a quién (-es)?,* and *¿de quién (-es)?*

(1) *¿Quién (-es)?* (who?) is used as the subject of the sentence.

¿**Quién** es este alumno?	*Who is this student?*
¿**Quiénes** son estos alumnos?	*Who are these students?*

(2) *¿A quién (-es)?* (whom?, to whom?) is used as the object of the verb (either direct or indirect object).

¿**A quién** ve Ud.?	*Whom do you see?*
¿**A quiénes** habla Ud.?	*To whom are you speaking?*

(3) ¿**De quién** (-es) (whose?) is used to express possession.

¿**De quién** es el libro?	*Whose book is it? (Of whom is the book?)*
¿**De quién** (-es) son los libros?	*Whose books are they? (Of whom are the books?)*

EXERCISE D

Pablo never listens carefully when his friends are talking and always has to ask whom they're speaking about. Write the questions Pablo asks to find out who does the following.

EXAMPLE: Daniel juega al fútbol.
             ¿**Quién** juega al fútbol?

1. Mis hermanas van a una fiesta.

_____

2. Carlos trabaja en el cine.

_____

3. Nosotros vamos al cine esta noche.

_____

4. Rosa no habla con su hermano.

_____

5. Alberto quiere vender su bicicleta.

_____

6. Yo tengo que estudiar para un examen.

_____

7. Mis tíos llegan mañana.

_____

EXERCISE E

You're with a friend at a party, but you don't know many of the people there. Write what you ask your friend about the other people at the party. They're indicated in parentheses.

EXAMPLE: Marta / hablar *(Gerardo y Hugo)*
            ¿A quiénes habla Marta?

1. Gloria / mirar *(su novio)*

_____

2. Vincent y Sara / ver *(los señores Junco)*

_____

3. Carmen / hablar *(Jorge y Fergus)*

_____

4. tú / saludar *(Pilar)*

_____

5. la señora Junco / servir café *(Jamal y Tony)*

_____

6. Esteban / llamar *(sus padres)*

_____

EXERCISE F

After the party, Mrs. Junco finds that several guests left things at the house. Write what Mrs. Junco asks her daughter, Raquel.

EXAMPLE: **¿De quién** es la bolsa?

1. _____

2. _____

3. _____

4. _____

5. _____

d. *¿Dónde?, ¿adónde?,* and *¿de dónde?*

    (1) *¿Dónde?* (where?) **expresses location.**

        ¿Dónde está Ana?   *Where's Ana?*

    (2) *¿Adónde?* (to where?) **expresses motion to a place.**

        ¿Adónde va Ud.?   *Where are you going?*

    (3) *¿De dónde?* (from where?) **expresses origin.**

        ¿De dónde es Ud.?   *Where are you from?*

EXERCISE G

When Julio's grandmother comes to visit, she wants to know where everyone is. Based on Julio's answers, tell what she asks him.

EXAMPLE: Mi papá está en el jardín.
            ¿**Dónde está** tu papá?

1. Mi mamá está en la cocina.

   _____

2. Mis hermanas están en el centro.

   _____

3. Mis amigos están en el parque.

   _____

4. Alfredo está en su dormitorio.

   _____

5. El perro está en el sótano.

   _____

EXERCISE H

As you go home on the last day of school, a friend asks you about other people's summer plans. Write down his questions.

EXAMPLE: Ricardo
            ¿**Adónde va** Ricardo durante las vacaciones?

1. Sue y Helen

   _____

2. tú

   _____

3. la señora Núñez

   _____

4. los hermanos Pirelli

   _____

5. Álvaro y su familia

   _____

EXERCISE I

You invite your cousin to an international fair at your school, where dishes from different countries are being served. Tell what she asks you about each dish.

EXAMPLE: los tacos
           ¿De dónde son los tacos?

1. la paella

_____

2. el asopao

_____

3. los frijoles negros

_____

4. el arroz con pollo

_____

5. la pizza

_____

6. las empanadas

_____

MASTERY EXERCISES

EXERCISE J

A friend is helping you study for a Spanish test. She gives you cards that contain statements. You
are to form questions using an interrogative expression in place of the word(s) in boldface.

EXAMPLE: José vive **en Colorado.**
           ¿Dónde vive José?

1. **Pedro** es muy aplicado.

   ¿_____ es muy aplicado?

2. El cuaderno es **de Ana.**

   ¿_____ es el cuaderno?

3. Mis bebidas favoritas son **los jugos y las gaseosas.**

   ¿_____ son tus bebidas favoritas?

4. Guatemala está **en la América Central**.

¿_____ está Guatemala?

5. Hoy es **el catorce de noviembre**.

¿_____ es la fecha de hoy?

6. El director va **a Italia**.

¿_____ va el director?

7. Un resfriado es **una enfermedad**.

¿_____ es un resfriado?

8. Pienso visitar **a Inglaterra**.

¿_____ país piensas visitar?

9. La señora admira **el vestido de seda**.

¿_____ vestido admira la señora?

10. Hay **cincuenta y dos** semanas en un año.

¿_____ semanas hay en un año?

11. Juana tiene **dos** pares de zapatos.

¿_____ pares de zapatos tiene Juana?

12. Da un paseo **con su hija**.

¿_____ da un paseo?

13. **La bicicleta** vale doscientos dólares.

¿_____ vale doscientos dólares?

14. **Los alumnos** traducen mal.

¿_____ traducen mal?

15. Javier besó **a su abuela**.

¿_____ besó Javier?

16. Almuerzan **porque tienen hambre**.

¿_____ almuerzan?

17. Pablo invitó **a Luisa y Alfredo**.

¿_____ invitó Pablo?

18. Francisco tiene **dolor de muelas**.

¿_____ tiene Francisco?

19. Mi abuelo cenó **a las seis y cuarto**.

¿_____ cenó tu abuelo?

20. Los alumnos abrieron **las ventanas**.

¿_____ abrieron las ventanas?

EXERCISE K

An exchange student from Argentina will be staying with your family. Write the questions that you'll ask her when you meet for the first time. From the list below, be sure to use a different interrogative expression in each question.

¿adónde?	¿cuál(es)?	¿cuánto?	¿dónde?	¿qué?
¿cómo?	¿cuándo?	¿de dónde?	¿por qué?	¿quién(es)?

1. _____

2. _____

3. _____

4. _____

5. _____

6. _____

7. _____

8. _____

9. _____

10. _____

EXERCISE L

You find a message on your answering machine but you cannot understand certain words in the message. Write the questions that you want to ask as you hear the following message.

1. Habla ******.

_____

2. Son las ****** de la tarde.

_____

3. Estoy en el Hotel ******.

_____

4. Viajo con dos ******.

_____

5. Son muy ******.

_____

6. Ellas se llaman ****** y ******.

_____

7. Vamos a pasar ****** días en esta ciudad.

_____

8. Espero ******.

_____

9. Llámame al número ******.

_____

10. Esta noche vamos al ******.

_____

11. Mis ****** mandan muchos saludos.

_____

EXERCISE M

You and several friends are going to interview a group of Spanish-speaking students who are visiting your school for a month. You will then publish their answers in the school newspaper. Express the following questions in Spanish.

1. What's your name?

_____

2. Where are you from?

_____

3. How old are you?

_____

4. How do you spend your free time?

_____

5. What subjects are you studying in school?

_____

6. Where do you live?

_____

7. How many weeks will you spend at our school?

_____

8. Where are you going next month?

_____

9. What's your favorite sport?

_____

10. Why did you come to the United States?

_____

11. What do you hope to learn here?

_____

12. When will the group return home?

_____

13. Whom do you want to meet?

_____

14. Where does the group want to go?

_____

15. Whose idea was it to come to the United States?

_____

16. What do you like most about the trip?

_____

Chapter 25
Exclamations

Exclamatory words, like interrogative words, have written accents. The most common exclamatory words are:

¡Qué...!   *What . . . ! What a . . . ! How . . . !*

¡Cuánto (-a)...!   *How much . . . !*

¡Cuántos (-as)...!   *How many . . . !*

¡**Qué** libro!	*What a book!*
¡**Qué** grande es!	*How large it is!*
¡**Cuántos** perros tienen!	*How many dogs they have!*
¡**Qué rápido** corre el coche!	*How fast the car runs!*

NOTE:

1. Exclamatory sentences have an inverted exclamation mark (¡) at the beginning and a standard one (!) at the end.

2. If there is an adjective next to a noun, the exclamation is made more intense by placing *tan* or *más* before the adjective.

   ¡Qué niño *tan (más)* inteligente!   *What an intelligent child!*

EXERCISE A

Two friends are raving about their vacation in Puerto Rico. Write what they say.

EXAMPLE: isla / bonita
            ¡**Qué** isla **tan (más)** bonita!

1. vacaciones / fabulosas

_____

2. sol / fuerte

_____

3. piscina / grande

_____

4. clima / agradable

_____

5. deliciosa / ser / la comida

_____

6. playas / hay

_____

7. simpáticos / ser / los puertorriqueños

_____

8. bien / pasar / nosotros / las vacaciones

_____

EXERCISE B

You take your younger brother to the zoo. Write what he exclaims upon seeing the following.

EXAMPLE: tren / moderno
                 ¡Qué tren **más** moderno!

1. cola / larga

2. tigre / feroz

_____   _____

3. globos / bonitos

4. pájaros / tranquilos

_____   _____

5. oso / grande

6. monos / cómicos

7. pavo real / elegante

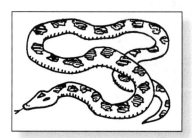

8. serpiente / larga

9. patos / graciosos

10. zoológico / interesante

EXERCISE C

You and some friends are returning home from a gathering where you heard about the trip another friend made last summer. Select the correct exclamatory word.

1. ¡(Qué / Cuánto) aburrido! Pasó el verano con su familia.

2. ¡(Qué / Cuánto) viaje más emocionante!

3. ¡(Cuántos / Cuántas) fotos sacó!

4. ¡(Qué / Cuánto) lugares más interesantes visitó!

5. ¡(Cuántos / Cuántas) cosas bonitas compró!

6. ¡(Qué / Cuánto) dinero costó!

7. ¡(Qué / Cuánto) cuentos más divertidos tiene del viaje!

8. ¡(Qué / Cuánto) simpática es su familia!

MASTERY EXERCISES

EXERCISE D

You've just returned from a soccer game. Your friend watched it on television and agrees with your comments. Tell what your friend exclaims when he hears your comments.

EXAMPLE:　Era un partido aburrido.
　　　　　¡**Qué** partido **más (tan)** aburrido!

1. Los futbolistas jugaron mal.

_____

2. Necesitan más práctica.

_____

3. El estadio es muy moderno.

_____

4. Mucha gente salió temprano.

_____

5. Perdieron muchos fanáticos.

_____

6. Parecía un partido aficionado.

_____

EXERCISE E

Your friend is going to a Spanish-speaking country and wants to learn some expressions she can use during her trip. Express the following in Spanish.

1. What a beautiful day!

_____

2. What a delicious meal!

_____

 3. What a beautiful photo!

_____

 4. How great!

_____

 5. What a party!

_____

 6. What a beautiful house you have!

_____

 7. How quickly the days pass!

_____

 8. It's so hot!

_____

 9. What good friends I have!

_____

10. What a good restaurant!

_____

Chapter 26
Possession

[1] EXPRESSING POSSESSION

a. Possession is normally expressed in Spanish by *de* + the possessor.

el libro **de Juan**	*John's book*
la casa **de los señores Camacho**	*the Camachos' house*
los regalos **de los niños**	*the children's gifts*
el suéter **de mi hermana**	*my sister's sweater*

b. When the preposition *de* is followed by the definite article *el,* the contraction *del* is formed.

el juguete **del** niño	*the boy's toy*

c. When followed by a form of *ser,* ¿*De quién (-es)...?* is equivalent to the English interrogative "Whose?".

¿**De quién es** la pelota?	*Whose ball is it?*
¿**De quién son** los guantes?	*Whose gloves are they?*
¿**De quiénes es** el coche nuevo?	*Whose new car is it?*
¿**De quiénes son** las revistas?	*Whose magazines are they?*

EXERCISE A

While visiting your house, Antonio wants to know whom the various things he sees there belong to. Using the cues provided, write Antonio's questions.

EXAMPLE: el televisor
¿**De quién es** el televisor?

1. los libros

_____

2. la muñeca

_____

3. los patines

_____

4. los relojes

_____

5. las llaves

_____

6. las camisetas

_____

7. las revistas

_____

8. la calculadora

_____

9. los anteojos

_____

10. el estéreo

_____

EXERCISE B

Using the cues provided, answer the questions Antonio asked you in Exercise A.

EXAMPLE   el televisor / mi papá
           El televisor **es de** mi papá.

1. los libros / María

_____

2. la muñeca / mi hermana

_____

3. los patines / mi primo

_____

4. los relojes / mis padres

_____

5. las llaves / mi abuela

_____

6. las camisetas / mis hermanos

_____

7. las revistas / el vecino

_____

8. la calculadora / mi madre

_____

9. los anteojos / mi abuelo

_____

10. el estéreo / mi mamá

_____

EXERCISE C

While sitting in the dentist's waiting room, Gloria comments on the people she sees there. Tell what she says.

EXAMPLE: las uñas / la señora / largo
Las uñas **de** la señora **son largas**.

1. el sombrero / el niño / grande

_____

2. los zapatos / la chica / feo

_____

3. la pulsera / la enfermera / bonito

_____

4. la máscara / el dentista / cómico

_____

5. el suéter / el señor / ridículo

_____

[2] POSSESSIVE ADJECTIVES

SINGULAR	PLURAL	MEANING
mi amigo (-a)	**mis amigos (-as)**	*my*
tu amigo (-a)	**tus amigos (-as)**	*your* (fam. sing.)
su amigo (-a)	**sus amigos (-as)**	*his, her, its, their; your* (formal)
nuestro amigo	**nuestros amigos**	*our*
nuestra amiga	**nuestras amigas**	
vuestro amigo	**vuestros amigos**	*your* (fam. pl.)
vuestra amiga	**vuestras amigas**	

NOTE:

1. Possessive adjectives agree in gender (masculine or feminine) and number (singular or plural) with the person or thing possessed, not with the possessor.

nuestra madre	*our mother*
nuestras madres	*our mothers*
su libro	*his, her, its, their, your (formal), your (pl.) book*
sus libros	*his, her, its, their, your (formal), your (pl.) books*

2. *Nuestro* and *vuestro* have four forms. The other possessive adjectives have two forms.

EXERCISE D

Complete the description that Pedro wrote about a member of his family by inserting the appropriate possessive adjective in the spaces.

_____ familia y yo vivimos en la ciudad. _____ casa no es muy
     1.   *2.*

grande. Yo comparto _____ dormitorio con uno de _____
                      3.   *4.*

hermanos. _____ nombre es Enrique. _____ dormitorio es
           5.   *6.*

amplio pero tengo que guardar todas _____ cosas en otro cuarto. Enrique tiene
                                                  7.

muchos juguetes pero él tiene la costumbre de dejar _____ cosas en los otros cuartos
                                                            8.

de la casa. Enrique nunca usa _____ propia ropa. Le gusta usar _____
                              9.   *10.*

ropa. Usa _____ camisas y _____ suéteres. Aunque Enrique es
               11.   *12.*

_____ hermano menor, _____ talla es la misma. También le
        13.   *14.*

gusta molestar a _____ hermanas. Siempre usa _____ cámara para
                     15.   *16.*

sacar fotos. Entonces ellas esconden _____ fotos. _____ papás van a
                                17.   *18.*

darle a Enrique _____ propia cámara para _____ cumpleaños.
                  19.   *20.*

EXERCISE E

Roberta and some friends are returning from a camping trip. As they unpack the car, Roberta indicates whom the different things belong to. Use the appropriate possessive adjective to tell what she says.

EXAMPLE: una linterna / de Roberta
                Es mi linterna.

1. una cámara / de Alfredo

_____

2. una grabadora / de nosotros

_____

3. unas revistas / de Gregorio

_____

4. una mochila / de Alfredo y Javier

_____

5. los anteojos / de Roberto

_____

6. unas monedas / de Pepe

_____

EXERCISE F

Teresa is guessing who's who in the Jiménez family, but she doesn't know how to read a family tree. Help Teresa figure out the correct family relationships among the following people.

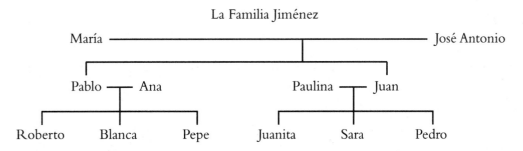

La Familia Jiménez

EXAMPLES: María es la madre de Pepe.
No, María no es la madre de Pepe. **Ella es su abuela.**
OR: **No, María no es** la madre de Pepe. **Ella es la madre de Juan y de Pablo.**

1. Pablo es el padre de María.

_____

2. Blanca es la hermana de Ana.

_____

3. Juan y Paulina son los padres de María y José Antonio.

_____

4. María y José Antonio son los primos de Juanita, Sara y Pedro.

_____

5. Pedro es el hermano de Roberto, Blanca y Pepe.

_____

6. Juanita y Sara son las primas de Pedro.

_____

M A S T E R Y   E X E R C I S E S

EXERCISE G

Answer these questions that your parent asks you about some new friends of yours. Use the appropriate possessive adjective in your responses.

1. ¿Cómo se llaman tus amigos nuevos? *(Jorge y Paco)*

   _____

2. ¿Cuáles son sus apellidos? *(Nogales, Fuentes)*

   _____

3. ¿Dónde está su casa? *(la calle Olmo)*

   _____

4. ¿Qué es su padre? *(ingeniero)*

   _____

5. ¿Viven cerca de tu tío Daniel? *(sí)*

   _____

6. ¿Cuántas personas hay en su familia? *(5)*

   _____

7. ¿Son miembros de tu equipo de baloncesto? *(sí)*

   _____

8. ¿Salen bien en sus exámenes? *(sí)*

   _____

9. ¿Conocen a tus otros amigos? *(sí)*

   _____

10. ¿Cuándo vas a su casa? *(mañana)*

    _____

EXERCISE H

Anita is talking to a student from Argentina. Express what she says in Spanish.

1. There are many students in our school.

   _____

2. My classes are small; your classes are large.

_____

3. Ricardo's teachers arrive on time.

_____

4. He leaves his bicycle in the schoolyard.

_____

5. My friends and I walk to school.

_____

6. Our houses are near the school.

_____

7. Whose photo is that?

_____

8. Is your sister's boyfriend tall?

_____

9. Nilda's brothers are very tall.

_____

10. Can you come to my house after school?

_____

11. You have to meet my parents.

_____

12. When do you celebrate your birthday?

_____

13. Ricardo's birthday is tomorrow.

_____

14. I bought his gift last night.

_____

15. His friends are very nice.

_____

16. Our classes are very interesting today.

_____

17. Patricia's teacher is strict.

_____

18. I like your watch.

_____

19. Do you like my new shoes?

_____

20. I want to be your friend.

_____

Chapter 27
Demonstrative Adjectives

Demonstrative adjectives, like other adjectives, agree with their nouns in gender (masculine or feminine) and number (singular or plural).

	MASCULINE	FEMININE	MEANING
SINGULAR	este libro	esta casa	*this*
PLURAL	estos libros	estas casas	*these*

	MASCULINE	FEMININE	MEANING
SINGULAR	ese libro	esa casa	*that (near you)*
PLURAL	esos libros	esas casas	*those (near you)*

	MASCULINE	FEMININE	MEANING
SINGULAR	aquel libro	aquella casa	*that (at a distance)*
PLURAL	aquellos libros	aquellas casas	*those (at a distance)*

NOTE:

1. *Este (esta, estos, estas)* refers to what is near. *Ese (esa, esos, esas)* refers to what isn't so near. *Aquel (aquella, aquellos, aquellas)*, "that" (those), refers to what is remote from both the speaker and the person addressed.

Esta blusa es negra.	*This blouse is black.*
Mary, dame **esa** blusa que tienes en la mano.	*Mary, give me that blouse that you have in your hand.*
Mary, dame **aquella** blusa.	*Mary, give me that blouse over there.*

2. The adverbs *aquí* (here), *ahí* (there), and *allí* ([over] there) correspond to the demonstrative adjectives *este, ese,* and *aquel.*

Pon	este libro **aquí**.	Put	*this book here.*
	ese cuaderno **ahí**.		*that notebook there.*
	aquel lápiz **allí**.		*that pencil over there.*

EXERCISE A

A week before Mother's Day, Federico accompanies his mother to a department store. He tries to find out what she likes. Tell what he asks her.

EXAMPLE: prendedor
¿Te gusta **este** prendedor?

1. aretes

_____

2. pulsera

_____

3. anillos

_____

4. billetera

_____

5. cadenas

_____

6. perfume

_____

7. reloj

_____

8. bolsa

_____

EXERCISE B

Pilar and a friend are visiting a botanical garden. Tell what they say about the plants and flowers they see.

EXAMPLE: árboles / altos
           Esos árboles **son** altos.

1. rosas / delicadas

_____

2. planta / pequeña

_____

3. gladiolas / bonitas

_____

4. orquídeas / exóticas

_____

5. tulipanes / rojos

_____

6. cacto / feo

_____

7. pino / viejo

_____

8. dalia / elegante

_____

EXERCISE C

You and a friend are visiting the observation deck at the tallest building in the city. As you look through the telescope, describe what you see.

EXAMPLE: iglesia / antigua
             Aquella iglesia es antigua.

1. puente / largo

_____

2. barcos / caros

_____

3. estadio / grande

_____

4. calle / corta

_____

5. barrio / interesante

_____

6. estatua / famosa

_____

7. parques / bonitos

_____

8. casas / pequeñas

_____

9. universidad / privada

_____

EXERCISE D

Alice is in a toy store looking for a gift for her brother and sister. She wants to know the price of the things she sees. Tell what she asks.

EXAMPLES: guante de béisbol / aquí
¿**Cuánto cuesta este** guante de béisbol?

juego electrónico / ahí
¿**Cuánto cuesta ese** juego electrónico?

muñecas / allí
¿**Cuánto cuestan aquellas** muñecas?

1. bicicletas / allí

_____

2. calculadoras / ahí

_____

3. osito de peluche / aquí

_____

4. pelota / allí

_____

5. discos / ahí

_____

6. grabadora / aquí

_____

7. raqueta de tenis / ahí

_____

8. radio portátil / ahí

_____

9. casa de muñecas / aquí

_____

10. juego de damas / allí

_____

EXERCISE E

Pepe is helping his mother do the shopping. Answer the questions he asks his mother, using the appropriate demonstrative adjective.

EXAMPLE: ¿Prefieres la sandía de ahí?
Prefiero esa sandía.

1. ¿Te gustan los plátanos de allí?

_____

2. ¿Prefieres los tomates de aquí?

_____

3. ¿Prefieres el melón de allí?

_____

4. ¿Te gustan las manzanas de ahí?

_____

5. ¿Te gusta la piña de aquí?

_____

6. ¿Prefieres las peras de ahí?

_____

7. ¿Quieres las uvas de aquí?

_____

8. ¿Te gusta la fruta de allí?

_____

EXERCISE F

Mr. Molina takes his family on a tour of the city where he went to college. Complete his statements with the appropriate demonstrative adjective.

Yo vivía aquí, en _____ pensión aquí. De _____ ventana en el
                        1.   *2.*

tercer piso veía _____ monumentos que visitamos ayer. En _____
                        3.   *4.*

calle ahí había muchos restaurantes buenos y baratos. Tomaba el desayuno en _____
                                                                                      5.

café; almorzaba en _____ restaurante de aquí y cenaba en _____
                          6.   *7.*

restaurante que está en la esquina. Compraba el periódico en _____ tienda que está al
                                                                      8.

lado de la pensión. Allí había un cine, no existía _____ biblioteca.
                                                            9.

_____ señor que anda ahí vendía los boletos. Vi muchas películas buenas en
        10.

_____ cine. Jugaba fútbol en _____ parque de allí. En el verano iba
                    11.   12.

a nadar en _____ piscina que está dentro del parque. Ahí conocí a
                         13.

_____ señores que Uds. conocieron ayer. ¡Cómo me divertí en
                14.

_____ ciudad!
                15.

MASTERY EXERCISES

EXERCISE G

You're in the cafeteria with a friend who's visiting your school. As you point to the different kinds of food, you comment on them. Use a demonstrative adjective to describe five of the items you see.

carne	galletas	papas fritas	postres
ensaladas	helado	pastel	sopa

EXAMPLE: **Este plátano** es delicioso.
                  Esas hamburguesas tienen queso.
                  Aquel pan es dulce.

1. _____

2. _____

3. _____

4. _____

5. _____

EXERCISE H

You and a Spanish-speaking friend are visiting your sister at her college dormitory. You comment on what you see in her room. Express the following in Spanish.

1. This room isn't very large.

_____

2. That poster (near) is interesting.

_____

3. These books are from the library.

_____

4. She uses that bicycle (near) for exercise.

_____

5. Those stories (distant) are amusing.

_____

6. This computer is new.

_____

7. These tourists are lucky.

_____

8. I gave her those flowers (near).

_____

9. She no longer uses this dictionary.

_____

10. Those photos (distant) are of her friends.

_____

11. These magazines are old.

_____

12. This doll is her favorite.

_____

13. Those records (distant) aren't very good.

_____

14. I don't believe this news.

_____

15. That girl (near) is her best friend.

_____

Part four
Word Study

ESPAÑA

Islas Baleares

Islas Canarias

MÉXICO

REPÚBLICA
DOMINICANA

PUERTO RICO

CUBA

HONDURAS

NICARAGUA

GUATEMALA

EL SALVADOR

COSTA RICA

VENEZUELA

PANAMÁ

COLOMBIA

ECUADOR

PERÚ

BOLIVIA

PARAGUAY

CHILE

URUGUAY

ARGENTINA

EXERCISE B

Match the words in column A with their synonyms in column B. Write the letters in the space provided.

A

_____ *1.* andar

_____ *2.* empezar

_____ *3.* salir

_____ *4.* encontrar

_____ *5.* diligente

_____ *6.* profesor

_____ *7.* error

_____ *8.* completar

_____ *9.* coche

_____ *10.* dormitorio

B

a. terminar

b. maestro

c. aplicado

d. ir a pie

e. falta

f. alcoba

g. automóvil

h. comenzar

i. partir

j. hallar

EXERCISE C

Retell Hector's story by replacing the words in parentheses with their synonyms.

No voy al doctor *(a menudo)* _____ . Nunca *(quiero)* _____ ir al
               1.   **2.**

doctor. Pero la semana pasada tenía *(un catarro)* _____ muy fuerte. Llamé al doctor
                                         3.

para hacer una cita. Mi mamá tenía *(el automóvil)* _____ y tuve que *(caminar)*
                                             4.

_____ a su oficina. Había *(varias)* _____ personas en su
        5.   **6.**

consultorio. El doctor *(empezó)* _____ a examinarme la boca. Me dio una receta.
                               7.

Le di las gracias y él respondió: *(No hay de qué)* _____ .
                                              8.

(Volví) _____ a casa a las cinco. Ahora estoy *(contento)* _____
        9.   **10.**

porque no tengo catarro.

EXERCISE D

Complete the crossword puzzle with the synonym of the words given.

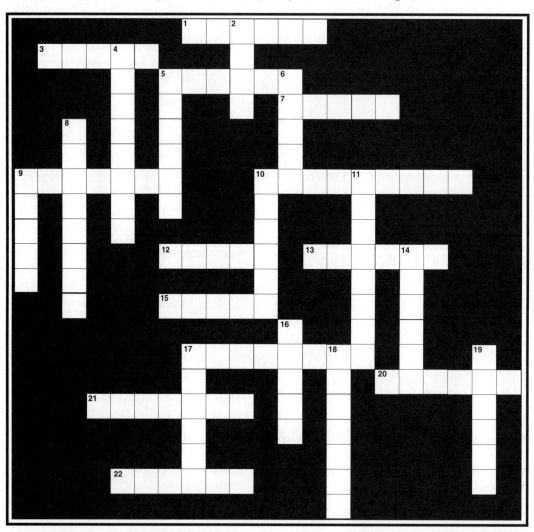

ACROSS	
1. estudiante	**13.** desear
3. error	**15.** niño
5. dormitorio	**17.** maestro
7. montaña	**20.** país
9. andar	**21.** frecuentemente
10. responder	**22.** no hay de qué
12. finalmente	

DOWN	
2. algunos	**11.** comprender
4. completar	**14.** mujer
5. contento	**16.** poseer
6. compañero	**17.** examen
8. mozo	**18.** de nuevo
9. automóvil	**19.** regresar
10. historia	

[2] ANTONYMS (PART I)

An antonym is a word or expression opposite in meaning to another word.

WORD / EXPRESSION	ANTONYM
a menudo, frecuentemente *frequently*	pocas veces *rarely*
abajo *down, downstairs*	arriba *up, upstairs*
abrir *to open*	cerrar *to close*
abuelo *grandfather*	nieto *grandson*
ahora *now*	después *later*
alegre, feliz *happy*	triste *sad*
algo *something*	nada *nothing*
alguien *someone*	nadie *no one*
alguno *some*	ninguno *none*
allí *there*	aquí *here*
alto *high*	bajo *low*
amigo *friend*	enemigo *enemy*
ancho *wide*	estrecho *narrow*
antes de *before*	después de *after*
aplicado, diligente *diligent*	perezoso *lazy*
ayer *yesterday*	mañana *tomorrow*
barato *cheap*	caro *expensive, dear*
bien *well*	mal *badly*
blanco *white*	negro *black*
bueno *good*	malo *bad*
caliente *hot, warm*	frío *cold*
cerca de *near*	lejos de *far from*
comprar *to buy*	vender *to sell*
con *with*	sin *without*
corto *short*	largo *long*
dar *to give*	tomar *to take*
debajo de *under, beneath*	sobre *upon, over*
delante de *in front of*	detrás de *in back of*
derecho *right*	izquierdo *left*
despacio *slowly*	rápidamente *quickly*
día *day*	noche *night*

EXERCISE E

Select the antonym of the word or expression given. Write the words in the space provided.

1. ancho   derecho, bastante, estrecho   _____

2. enemigo   amigo, primo, dueño   _____

3. arriba   hacia, abajo, detrás de   _____

4. mal   demasiado, mucho, bien   _____

5. blanco   plata, negro, alto   _____

6. vender   comprar, valer, prestar   _____

7. despacio   poco a poco, espacio, rápidamente _____

8. nada   alguno, algo, corto   _____

9. bajo   alto, vacío, grande   _____

10. abrir   cenar, celebrar, cerrar   _____

11. frío   nieve, caliente, sur   _____

12. caro   rico, barato, mucho   _____

13. alguien   unos, muchos, nadie   _____

14. más tarde ahora, pocas veces, al fin   _____

15. feliz   contento, gordo, triste   _____

EXERCISE F

Match the word in column A with its antonym in column B. Write the letters in the space provided.

A

_____ 1. frecuentemente

_____ 2. diligente

_____ 3. tomar

_____ 4. derecho

_____ 5. alguno

_____ 6. largo

B

a. nieto

b. dar

c. corto

d. perezoso

e. mañana

f. debajo de

g. pocas veces

h. ninguno

_____ **7.** sobre

_____ **8.** abuelo

_____ **9.** ayer

_____ **10.** noche

i. día

j. izquierdo

EXERCISE G

Sam and his brother have returned from visiting a friend's new home. His brother always contradicts what Sam says. Tell what his brother says by using an appropriate antonym in each sentence.

EXAMPLE: Ricky es nuestro amigo.
            Ricky es nuestro **enemigo**.

1. Hay una piscina detrás de la casa.

_____

2. El agua de la piscina está fría.

_____

3. Su hermana está muy contenta.

_____

4. Antes de salir de la casa tomamos un café.

_____

5. Arturo es una persona diligente.

_____

6. Le gusta salir con sus amigos.

_____

7. Viven cerca de la universidad.

_____

8. Nadie estaba en la piscina.

_____

9. Viven en la parte alta de la ciudad.

_____

10. La casa es de color blanco.

_____

EXERCISE H

Answer your parents' questions using the antonym in parentheses.

1. ¿Deseas comer ahora? *(después)*

_____

2. ¿Compras las plumas baratas? *(caras)*

_____

3. ¿Te gusta comer pescado a menudo? *(pocas veces)*

_____

4. ¿Estudias antes de cenar? *(después de)*

_____

5. ¿Vas a vender limonada? *(comprar)*

_____

[3] ANTONYMS (PART II)

WORD / EXPRESSION	ANTONYM
empezar *to begin*	terminar *to end, to finish*
entrar *to enter*	salir (de) *to leave*
este *east*	oeste *west*
fácil *easy*	difícil *difficult, hard*
feo *ugly*	hermoso *beautiful*
feo *ugly*	bonito, lindo *pretty*
fuerte *strong*	débil *weak*
gordo *chubby, fat*	flaco *thin*
grande *large, big*	pequeño *small, little*
hombre *man*	mujer *woman*
invierno *winter*	verano *summer*
levantarse *to stand up*	sentarse *to sit down*
lleno *full*	vacío *empty*
más *more*	menos *less*
mayor *greater, older*	menor *lesser, younger*
mediodía *noon*	medianoche *midnight*
moreno *brunette*	rubio *blond*
mucho *much*	poco *little*
no *no*	sí *yes*

norte	*north*	sur	*south*
nunca	*never*	siempre	*always*
olvidar	*to forget*	recordar	*to remember*
perder	*to lose*	encontrar, hallar	*to find*
perder	*to lose*	ganar	*to win*
pobre	*poor*	rico	*rich*
ponerse	*to put on*	quitarse	*to take off*
pregunta	*question*	respuesta	*answer*
preguntar	*to ask*	contestar, responder	*to answer*
presente	*present*	ausente	*absent*
presente	*present*	pasado	*past*
ruido	*noise*	silencio	*silence*
subir	*to go up*	bajar	*to go down*
tarde	*late*	temprano	*early*
viejo	*old*	joven	*young*
viejo	*old*	nuevo	*new*
vivir	*to live*	morir	*to die*

EXERCISE 1

Select the antonym of the words given. Write the words in the space provided.

1. empezar   lograr, comenzar, terminar   _____

2. mediodía   media, medianoche, remedio   _____

3. mayor   numeroso, menor, medio   _____

4. viejo   nuevo, noveno, nueve   _____

5. encontrar   perder, inventar, desaparecer   _____

6. olvidar   recordar, reconocer, referir   _____

7. moreno   pardo, rubio, rosado   _____

8. norte   sur, este, oeste   _____

9. fuerte   duro, nervioso, débil   _____

10. pregunta   contestar, responder, respuesta   _____

11. más   menor, poco, menos   _____

12. vivir   existir, morir, romper   _____

13. subir   sentir, bajar, poseer   _____

14. nunca   siempre, nadie, algo   _____

15. entrar   sacar, llenar, salir   _____

EXERCISE J

Match the words in column A with their antonyms in column B. Write the letters in the space provided.

A		B
_____ **1.** este		*a.* silencio
		b. mujer
_____ **2.** levantarse		*c.* poco
		d. vacío
_____ **3.** no		*e.* viejo
_____ **4.** ponerse		*f.* contestar
		g. oeste
_____ **5.** mucho		*h.* sí
_____ **6.** hombre		*i.* quitarse
		j. sentarse
_____ **7.** joven		
_____ **8.** preguntar		
_____ **9.** ruido		
_____ **10.** lleno		

EXERCISE K

Laura's grandfather always mixes up his stories. Correct the following one by replacing the words in parentheses with their antonyms.

Ayer vimos una escena *(fea)* _____. *(Enfrente de)* _____ las dos casas
                                          1.   *2.*

hay un espacio *(pequeño)* _____. La niña que vive *(aquí)* _____
                             3.   *4.*

estaba muy *(contenta)* _____. Ella *(compraba)* _____ limonada
                             5.   *6.*

porque hacía *(frío)* _____. Una mujer muy *(alta)* _____ y *(flaca)*
                           7.   *8.*

_____ llegó. Quería *(vender)* _____ una limonada porque era *(cara)*

          9.   *10.*

_____. Tenía *(poco)* _____ dinero y bebió toda la limonada. Ahora

          11.   *12.*

todas las botellas están *(llenas)* _____ y todo el mundo está *(triste)* _____ .

                                       13.   *14.*

EXERCISE L

Adrián's brother never listens to what he says and usually answers his questions foolishly. Answer Adrian's questions negatively, using an antonym for the words in boldface.

EXAMPLE: ¿Es **difícil** la geografía?
                  No, la geografía es **fácil**.

1. ¿Es **bonita** tu amiga?

_____

2. ¿Hay mucha nieve en el **invierno**?

_____

3. ¿Hace calor en el **sur**?

_____

4. ¿Hace sol a **mediodía**?

_____

5. ¿Tienen muchos juguetes los niños **ricos**?

_____

6. ¿Son **grandes** los elefantes?

_____

7. ¿Sacas tú **buenas** notas en las clases?

_____

8. ¿Te gusta el **silencio**?

_____

9. ¿Llegas **temprano** a la escuela?

_____

10. ¿Siempre **encuentras** las llaves?

_____

EXERCISE M

Complete the crossword puzzle with the antonym of the words given.

ACROSS		
2. comprar	**14.** allí	
3. nada	**16.** alegre	
4. delante de	**18.** con	
5. a menudo	**19.** abuelo	
9. alguno	**21.** enemigo	
10. caliente	**22.** diligente	
11. ayer	**23.** corto	
13. alto	**24.** sobre	

DOWN	
1. lejos de	**9.** alguien
3. abajo	**12.** día
6. después	**15.** derecho
7. abrir	**17.** ancho
8. caro	**20.** blanco

MASTERY EXERCISES

EXERCISE N

Match the words in column A with their synonyms in column B and their antonyms in column C. Write the letters in the space provided.

A	B (synonym)	C (antonym)
_____ **1.** alegre	*a.* comenzar	*A.* preguntar
_____ **2.** delante de	*b.* unos	*B.* terminar
_____ **3.** bonito	*c.* diligente	*C.* triste
_____ **4.** amigo	*d.* lindo	*D.* feo
_____ **5.** empezar	*e.* hallar	*E.* ningunos
_____ **6.** a menudo	*f.* feliz	*F.* detrás de
_____ **7.** responder	*g.* contestar	*G.* enemigo
_____ **8.** algunos	*h.* enfrente de	*H.* perezoso
_____ **9.** aplicado	*i.* frecuentemente	*I.* perder
_____ **10.** encontrar	*j.* compañero	*J.* pocas veces

EXERCISE O

Describe the pictures using the following words.

ancho	invierno	mediodía	quitarse
bajar	lleno	menor	rubio
débil	más	menos	subir
estrecho	mayor	moreno	vacío
fuerte	medianoche	ponerse	verano

1. _____   2. _____

3. _____ 4. _____

5. _____

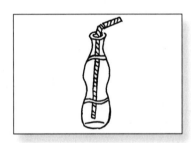

6. _____ 7. _____

8. _____

9. _____

10. _____

11. _____

12. _____

13. _____

14. _____

15. _____

16. _____

17. _____

18. _____

19. _____

20. _____

Chapter 30
Topical (Thematic) Vocabulary

[1] PERSONAL IDENTIFICATION

a. Características físicas

alto, -a *tall*	joven *young*
bajo, -a *short*	lindo, -a *pretty*
bonito, -a *pretty*	moreno, -a *dark-haired, dark-skinned*
delgado, -a *thin*	pelirrojo, -a *redheaded*
feo, -a *ugly*	rubio, -a *fair, blond*
gordo, -a *fat*	trigueño, -a *dark-skinned*
guapo -a *handsome*	viejo, -a *old*

b. Características de la personalidad

aburrido, -a *boring*	independiente *independent*
agradable *pleasant, nice, likable*	inteligente *intelligent*
amable *courteous, kind*	interesante *interesting*
antipático, -a *unpleasant, not nice*	irresponsable *irresponsible*
bueno, -a *good*	malo, -a *bad*
cariñoso, -a *affectionate*	paciente *patient*
desagradable *unpleasant*	popular *popular*
divertido, -a *fun, amusing*	responsable *responsible*
egoísta *selfish*	simpático, -a *friendly, nice, likable*
generoso, -a *generous*	tacaño, -a *stingy*
impaciente *impatient*	tonto, -a *dumb; stupid*

c. Otras palabras

el apellido *last name*	el lugar de nacimiento *place of birth*
el cumpleaños *birthday*	la nacionalidad *nationality*
la dirección *address*	el nombre *name*
la edad *age*	el número de teléfono *telephone number*
la fecha de nacimiento *date of birth*	

EXERCISE A

Select the word in each group that is in a different category from the other three. Write the words in the space provided.

1. gordo, desagradable, lindo, alto _____

2. generoso, divertido, cariñoso, bajo _____

3. paciente, bueno, pelirrojo, independiente   _____

4. tacaño, moreno, rubio, pelirrojo   _____

5. edad, simpático, cumpleaños, fecha de nacimiento   _____

6. egoísta, joven, bueno, popular   _____

7. apellido, tacaño, lugar de nacimiento, dirección   _____

8. aburrido, desagradable, guapo, irresponsable   _____

9. delgado, tonto, viejo, moreno   _____

10. impaciente, responsable, malo, rubio   _____

EXERCISE B

How would you describe yourself? In the left column, make a list of the adjectives that describe your appearance; and in the right column, make a list of five adjectives that describe your personality.

1. _____ 1. _____

2. _____ 2. _____

3. _____ 3. _____

4. _____ 4. _____

5. _____ 5. _____

EXERCISE C

Your new pen pal would like to know more about you. She asks you to write a description of yourself in a minimum of five sentences.

_____

_____

_____

EXERCISE D

You have to exchange a gift you bought but you can't find the salesperson who helped you. In a minimum of five sentences, describe him (her) to the store manager.

_____

_____

_____

_____

_____

_____

_____

EXERCISE E

Mrs. García is talking about Luis and Ricky, her twin grandsons. Their personalities are complete opposites. List at least five adjectives that she would use to describe each boy.

LUIS	RICKY

EXERCISE F

Complete the crossword puzzle with the appropriate Spanish words for the clues given in English.

ACROSS		DOWN	
1. patient	**19.** handsome	**1.** redheaded	**12.** amusing
5. selfish	**20.** age	**2.** good	**13.** thin
7. interesting	**22.** friendly	**3.** ugly	**14.** old
10. name	**25.** bad	**4.** generous	**15.** independent
11. fat	**26.** blonde	**6.** courteous, kind	**21.** address
16. intelligent	**27.** pretty	**8.** tall	**23.** boring
17. dumb	**28.** last name	**9.** stingy	**24.** affectionate
18. young	**29.** dark hair		

[2] HOUSE AND HOME

a. La casa

la alcoba *bedroom*	el estudio *study, den*
el apartamento *apartment*	el garaje *garage*
el ascensor *elevator*	la habitación *room*
el balcón *balcony*	el jardín *garden*
el (cuarto de) baño *bathroom*	el pasillo *corridor, hall*
la casa *house, home*	el patio *courtyard*
la casa particular *private house*	la piscina *swimming pool*
la cocina *kitchen*	el piso *floor, story, apartment*
el comedor *dining room*	la sala *parlor, living room*
el cuarto *room*	la sala de estar *family room*
el desván *attic*	el sótano *cellar, basement*
el dormitorio *bedroom*	el suelo *floor, ground*
la escalera *stairs, staircase*	la terraza *terrace*

b. Los muebles

la alfombra *rug, carpet*	la lámpara *lamp*
el armario *closet*	la mesa *table*
la cama *bed*	los muebles *furniture*
la cómoda *bureau, dresser*	la silla *chair*
la cortina *curtain*	el sillón *armchair*
el escritorio *desk*	el sofá *sofa*

EXERCISE G

In each group, select the word that is *not* thematically in the same category as the other three. Write the words in the space provided.

1. comedor, alcoba, sótano, libro   _____

2. dormitorio, habitación, coche, sala   _____

3. sótano, cama, armario, silla   _____

4. mesa, patio, sofá, cómoda   _____

5. escalera, ascensor, alfombra, piso   _____

6. pasillo, estudio, desván, lámpara   _____

7. terraza, sala, cortina, patio   _____

8. armario, mesa, cómoda, garaje   _____

9. alfombra, apartamento, casa particular, piso   _____

10. garaje, estudio, cama, patio   _____

EXERCISE H

Match the activities in column A with the appropriate room in column B. Write the letters in the space provided.

A	B
___ 1. dormir	*a.* baño
	b. garaje
___ 2. preparar la comida	*c.* alcoba
	d. sala
___ 3. plantar flores	*e.* pasillo
___ 4. lavarse la cara	*f.* cocina
___ 5. nadar	*g.* piscina
___ 6. estacionar el carro	*h.* jardín
	i. estudio
___ 7. estudiar y hacer la tarea	*j.* escalera
___ 8. subir de un piso a otro
___ 9. ir de un cuarto a otro
___ 10. ver la televisión

EXERCISE I

You're planning your dream house. Using the plan below, label the different rooms shown in the floor plan.

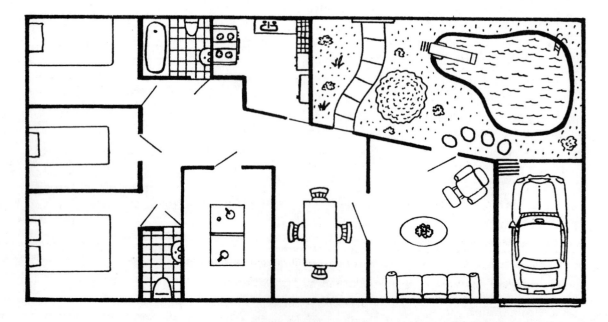

EXERCISE J

Your family is moving to a larger house and you will no longer have to share your room with a sibling. Prepare a list of the furniture and accessories you would like to have in your room.

_____   _____

_____   _____

_____   _____

_____   _____

_____   _____

EXERCISE K

A friend is telling you about her house. If the statement is true, write *Sí*; if it's false, correct it by replacing the word(s) in boldface. Write the correct word(s) in the space provided.

1. Puse una alfombra en **la mesa**.   _____

2. Solamente **una familia** vive en una casa particular.   _____

3. **El suelo** es el cuarto más grande del apartamento.   _____

4. La lámpara y la mesa son **muebles**.   _____

5. Mi madre prepara las comidas en **la escalera**.   _____

6. Mi papá estaciona el carro en **la sala**.   _____

7. Ponemos las cortinas en **las camas**.   _____

8. Mi abuelo se sienta en **la cómoda** para leer el periódico.   _____

9. Guardo la ropa en **el balcón**.   _____

10. Uso **el desván** para ir de un piso a otro.   _____

[3] FAMILY LIFE

la abuela *grandmother*	la hermana *sister*
el abuelo *grandfather*	el hermano *brother*
los abuelos *grandparents*	los hermanos *brothers, brothers and sisters*
el cuñado *brother-in-law*	la hija *daughter*
la cuñada *sister-in-law*	el hijo *son*
la esposa *wife*	los hijos *children, sons and daughters*
el esposo *husband*	la madrastra *stepmother*
la familia *family*	la madre *mother*

la madrina *godmother*	el pariente *relative*
la mamá *mom, mother*	la prima *cousin*
la nieta *granddaugher*	el primo *cousin*
el nieto *grandson*	la sobrina *niece*
la niña *girl*	el sobrino *nephew*
el niño *boy*	el suegro *father-in-law*
la nuera *daughter-in-law*	la suegra *mother-in-law*
el padrastro *stepfather*	la tía *aunt*
el padre *father*	el tío *uncle*
los padres *parents*	los tíos *uncles, aunts and uncles*
los papás *parents*	el yerno *son-in-law*

EXERCISE L

If the statement is true, write *Sí*; if it's false, correct it by replacing the words in boldface. Write the correct words in the space provided.

1. El hijo de mi tío es **mi hermano**.   _____

2. La madre de mi madre es **mi abuela**.   _____

3. La hermana de mi papá es **mi prima**.   _____

4. El yerno de mi abuelo es **mi sobrino**.   _____

5. Yo soy **el hijo** de mi abuelo.   _____

6. Mis abuelos son los suegros de **mis hermanos**.   _____

7. **Mi sobrino** es el hijo de mis padres.   _____

8. Mi madre **es la nuera** de mi padre.   _____

9. **Mis nietos** son los sobrinos de mis papás.   _____

10. Mi padrastro es **el hermano** de mi madre.   _____

EXERCISE M

Match the words in columns A and B logically, following the example. Write the letters in the space provided.

EXAMPLE: padre **hija**

A	B
_____ *1.* abuelos	*a.* padres
_____ *2.* sobrina	*b.* suegra
_____ *3.* yerno	*c.* cuñado
_____ *4.* niño	*d.* nietos
	e. tío

_____ **5.** primos

_____ **6.** hijos

_____ **7.** cuñada

f. madre

g. primas

EXERCISE N

Identify the family relationship in each statement. Write the words in the space provided.

EXAMPLE: La hija de mi padre es mi **hermana**.

1. Los padres de mis tíos son mis_____.

2. El hermano de mi madre es mi_____.

3. Los hijos de mis tíos son los_____de mis padres.

4. El hermano de mi papá es el_____de mi mamá.

5. Mi padre es el_____del padre de mi madre.

6. Mis abuelos maternales son los_____de mi padre.

7. Yo soy el_____de los hijos de mis tíos.

[4] COMMUNITY/NEIGHBORHOOD

a. Areas

el barrio   *neighborhood*

el campo   *country*

el centro   *downtown*

la ciudad   *city*

el pueblo   *town*

el suburbio   *suburbs*

el vecindario   *neighborhood*

b. Los edificios

el aeropuerto   *airport*

el banco   *bank*

la biblioteca   *library*

el café   *coffee shop*

la casa   *house*

la catedral   *cathedral*

el centro comunal   *community center*

el cine   *movies, movie theater*

el correo   *post office*

el edificio   *building*

la escuela   *school*

la estación   *(train) station*

el estadio   *stadium*

el hospital   *hospital*

el hotel   *hotel*

la iglesia   *church*

el museo   *museum*

el palacio   *palace*

el parque   *park*

la piscina   *swimming pool*

el puente   *bridge*

el restaurante   *restaurant*

el teatro   *theater*

la terminal de autobuses   *bus terminal*

el templo   *temple*

la universidad   *university*

c. **Las tiendas**

el almacén *department store*	el mercado *market*
la bodega *grocery store*	la panadería *bakery*
la carnicería *butcher*	la pastelería *pastry shop*
la farmacia *drugstore, pharmacy*	el supermercado *supermarket*
la ferretería *hardware store*	la tienda *store, shop*
la florería *flower shop*	la tienda de ropa *clothing store*
la frutería *fruit store*	la tintorería *dry cleaners*
la lavandería *laundry*	la zapatería *shoe store*

EXERCISE O

In each group, select the word that is *not* related to the other three. Write the words in the space provided.

1. familia, templo, iglesia, catedral _____

2. carnicería, bodega, panadería, templo _____

3. universidad, escuela, fiesta, biblioteca _____

4. lámpara, estación, terminal, aeropuerto _____

5. parque, estadio, piscina, esquina _____

6. almacén, zapatería, hospital, tienda de ropa _____

7. carnicería, puente, panadería, frutería _____

8. cine, museo, teatro, lavandería _____

9. café, edificio, museo, palacio _____

10. casa, centro, palacio, hotel _____

EXERCISE P

Match each activity in column A with the location where it takes place in column B. Write the letters in the space provided.

A	B
_____ 1. comer	*a.* el cine
_____ 2. estudiar	*b.* el hotel
	c. la piscina
_____ 3. comprar estampillas	*d.* el restaurante
_____ 4. ver una película	*e.* la estación
	f. la biblioteca
_____ 5. curar a los enfermos	*g.* el banco

_____ **6.** nadar

_____ **7.** caminar

_____ **8.** buscar un libro

_____ **9.** rezar

_____ **10.** ver un partido

_____ **11.** tomar el tren

_____ **12.** ver una obra de arte

_____ **13.** buscar a un turista

_____ **14.** tomar el autobús

_____ **15.** tomar un café

_____ **16.** cambiar dinero

_____ **17.** viajar en avión

h. el correo

i. el estadio

j. el museo

k. la escuela

l. el café

m. la iglesia

n. el aeropuerto

o. el hospital

p. el parque

q. la terminal

EXERCISE Q

You're running some errands in town. Indicate the stores you'll visit to buy the following items.

1. rosas, claveles y geranios _____

2. refrescos, leche, queso _____

3. jamón, biftec, pollo _____

4. una camisa blanca, una corbata _____

5. manzanas, peras, uvas _____

6. aspirinas, algodón, curitas _____

7. zapatos, pantuflas _____

8. un pastel de cumpleaños _____

EXERCISE R

Read the passage below and determine which store the person should go to.

1. Ramón va a pasar el fin de semana en las montañas con unos amigos. Tiene que comprar un suéter grueso porque va a hacer mucho frío allí. ¿Adónde debe ir Ramón?

_____

2. Vamos a tener invitados a cenar el sábado por la noche. Mi mamá prepara una lista de las cosas que necesita para preparar la cena. ¿Adónde debe ir mi mamá?

_____

3. Susana y Alicia van a pasar las vacaciones en Puerto Rico. Su avión sale a las tres de la tarde. ¿Adónde deben ir las chicas?

_____

4. Pablo está enfermo. El médico le da una receta para una medicina. ¿Adónde debe ir Pablo?

_____

5. Mi prima se casa mañana. La ceremonia de la boda es a las doce.¿Adónde debo ir?

_____

EXERCISE S

You and your family are driving through Mexico in a van. You arrive at a small town around lunchtime. Tell which places the members of your family want to visit in the town.

EXAMPLE: Mi padre **quiere visitar el museo**.

1. Mi madre _____ .

2. Mi hermano _____ .

3. Mi hermana _____ .

4. Mis padres _____ .

5. Mi abuela _____ .

6. Yo _____ .

[5] PHYSICAL ENVIRONMENT

a. La geografía

el cayo _key (Key West)_	el golfo _gulf_
el continente _continent_	la isla _island_
la cordillera _mountain range_	el país _country, nation_
el estado _state_	la península _peninsula_

b. La naturaleza

el aire _air_	el clavel _carnation_
el árbol _tree_	la estrella _star_
el bosque _forest_	la flor _flower_
el campo _country_	la hierba _grass_
el cielo _sky_	la hoja _leaf_

el jardín *garden*
el lago *lake*
la luna *moon*
la lluvia *rain*
el mar *sea*
la montaña *mountain*
el mundo *world*
la naturaleza *nature*
la nieve *snow*

la nube *cloud*
la planta *plant*
la playa *beach, seashore*
el río *river*
la rosa *rose*
el sol *sun*
la tierra *earth, land*
la violeta *violet*

c. Las estaciones y el tiempo

el calor *heat, warmth*
la estación *season*
el fresco *coolness*
el frío *cold*
el grado *degree*
el invierno *winter*
la lluvia *rain*
la nieve *snow*
el otoño *autumn*
la primavera *spring*

el sol *sun*
la temperatura *temperature*
el tiempo *weather*
el verano *summer*
el viento *wind*

hace (calor, fresco, frío, sol, viento)
  it's (hot, cool, cold, sunny, windy)
llover *to rain*
nevar *to snow*

d. Los meses

enero *January*
febrero *February*
marzo *March*
abril *April*
mayo *May*
junio *June*

julio *July*
agosto *August*
septiembre *September*
octubre *October*
noviembre *November*
diciembre *December*

e. Los días

el domingo *Sunday*
el lunes *Monday*
el martes *Tuesday*
el miércoles *Wednesday*

el jueves *Thursday*
el viernes *Friday*
el sábado *Saturday*

EXERCISE T

In each group, select the word that is *not* related to the other three. Write the words in the space provided.

1. mundo, cielo, aire, mercado   _____

2. clavel, lluvia, rosa, violeta   _____

3. tienda, bosque, montaña, campo   _____

4. nieve, viento, estado, lluvia _____

5. playa, ciudad, estado, país _____

6. árbol, planta, hoja, cielo _____

7. primavera, estrella, otoño, invierno _____

8. estación, abril, noviembre, enero _____

9. verano, miércoles, sábado, viernes _____

10. calor, luna, frío, viento _____

11. tierra, lago, río, mar _____

12. cielo, estrella, sol, pueblo _____

13. hierba, flor, mundo, planta _____

14. día, mes, estación, fresco _____

15. tiempo, frío, lluvia, tierra _____

EXERCISE U

If the statement is true, write *Sí*; if it's false, correct it by replacing the word(s) in boldface. Write the correct word(s) in the space provided.

1. Después de abril viene el mes de **mayo**. _____

2. Hace calor en **el invierno**. _____

3. Cuando **hace sol** uso un paraguas. _____

4. El sábado y el domingo son **el fin de semana**. _____

5. Las rosas y las violetas son **árboles**. _____

6. Durante la noche vemos **el sol** en el cielo. _____

7. El verano y el otoño son **meses**. _____

8. El Misisipí es **un lago**. _____

9. California es **un país**. _____

10. Puerto Rico es **una ciudad**. _____

11. Hay edificios altos en **el campo**. _____

12. Vemos muchas estrellas en **el bosque**. _____

13. Nadamos en **el suburbio**. _____

14. Un árbol tiene muchas **nubes**.

_____

15. En el parque hay **un lago**.

_____

EXERCISE V

You're talking about your hometown to your host family in Venezuela. Describe or explain how the following things are where you live.

1. una estación del año

_____

_____

_____

2. tu ciudad o pueblo

_____

_____

_____

3. el mes de febrero

_____

_____

_____

4. los suburbios

_____

_____

_____

5. el cielo en una noche de verano

_____

_____

_____

[6] MEALS / FOOD / BEVERAGES

a. Las comidas

el almuerzo *lunch*	almorzar *to have (eat) lunch*
la cena *supper, dinner*	cenar *to have (eat) supper*
la comida *meal, food*	desayunar *to have (eat) breakfast*
el desayuno *breakfast*	

b. La comida / la bebida

el agua *water*	la naranja *orange*
el alimento *food*	el pan *bread*
el (la) azúcar *sugar*	la papa, la patata *potato*
el café *coffee*	el pastel *pie, pastry*
la carne *meat*	la pera *pear*
la cereza *cherry*	el pescado *fish*
el chocolate *chocolate*	la pimienta *pepper* (spice)
la ensalada *salad*	el pimiento *pepper* (vegetable)
la fruta *fruit*	el pollo *chicken*
la gaseosa *soda, pop*	el postre *dessert*
el helado *ice cream*	el refresco *refreshment, soda*
el huevo *egg*	la sal *salt*
la leche *milk*	la sopa *soup*
la legumbre *vegetable*	el té *tea*
el limón *lemon*	el vino *wine*
la mantequilla *butter*	beber *to drink*
la manzana *apple*	comer *to eat*

EXERCISE W

In each group, select the word that is *not* related to the other three. Write the words in the space provided.

1. fruta, manzana, cereza, puente   _____

2. naranja, azul, ensalada, pera   _____

3. vino, hoja, café, agua   _____

4. queso, pan, huevo, burro   _____

5. almuerzo, cena, chocolate, desayuno   _____

6. sopa, azúcar, pimienta, sal   _____

7. comer, almorzar, caminar, beber   _____

8. pollo, refresco, carne, pescado   _____

9. leche, mantequilla, queso, limón   _____

10. legumbre, postre, helado, pastel   _____

11. té, pescado, chocolate, café   _____

12. cereza, pera, helado, naranja   _____

EXERCISE X

Answer your friend's questions about your eating preferences.

1. ¿Cuál es tu comida favorita?

_____

2. ¿Qué desayunas por la mañana?

_____

3. ¿A qué hora comes el almuerzo?

_____

4. ¿Cuál prefieres, el pollo o el pescado?

_____

5. ¿Qué frutas te gustan?

_____

6. ¿Qué tomas con la cena?

_____

7. ¿Cuál es tu postre preferido?

_____

8. ¿Qué comes mientras ves la televisión?

_____

9. ¿Cuándo comes helado?

_____

10. ¿Por qué comes?

_____

EXERCISE Y

You and some friends are planning a barbecue. List the foods and beverages that you have to buy when you go to the supermarket.

_____

_____

_____

_____

_____

[7] HEALTH AND WELL-BEING

a. El cuerpo

la boca *mouth*	la lengua *tongue*
el brazo *arm*	la mano *hand*
la cabeza *head*	la muela *molar (tooth)*
la cara *face*	la nariz *nose*
el cuerpo *body*	el ojo *eye*
el dedo *finger, toe*	la oreja *ear*
el diente *tooth*	el pelo *hair*
el estómago *stomach*	el pie *foot*
la garganta *throat*	la pierna *leg*
el labio *lip*	

b. Medicina y salud

bien *well*	la medicina *medicine*
el dentista *dentist*	el médico *doctor*
el doctor *doctor*	el paciente *patient*
el dolor *ache, pain*	la receta *prescription*
la enfermedad *illness*	el resfriado *cold (illness)*
la enfermera *nurse*	la salud *health*
enfermo, -a *ill, sick*	doler *to ache*
el hospital *hospital*	tener dolor de *to ache*

EXERCISE Z

In each group, select the word that is *not* related to the other three. Write the words in the space provided.

1. labio, muela, pelo, ascensor   _____

2. médico, cortina, enfermera, hospital   _____

3. sopa, pie, dedo, pierna   _____

4. ojos, postre, nariz, orejas   _____

5. dedo, mano, estómago, brazo   _____

6. comida, medicina, receta, dolor   _____

7. doctor, profesor, dentista, enfermera   _____

8. salud, bien, enfermo, frío   _____

EXERCISE AA

If the statement is true, write *Sí*; if it's false, correct it by replacing the word(s) in boldface. Write the correct word(s) in the space provided.

1. Tengo cinco **dientes** en cada mano. _____

2. Si estoy **enfermo(-a)** mi madre llama al doctor. _____

3. Llevo zapatos en **los pies**. _____

4. Comemos con **la nariz**. _____

5. Usamos **los ojos** para oír. _____

6. Comemos con **los brazos**. _____

7. Una enfermera trabaja en **una tienda**. _____

8. Tomamos **postre** cuando estamos enfermos. _____

9. El resfriado es una clase de **receta**. _____

10. Usamos **la lengua** para hablar. _____

EXERCISE BB

Tell what's wrong with these people. Use *doler* or *tener dolor de* in your responses.

EXAMPLE: Marta no puede oler las flores.
          Le duele la nariz.

1. Roberto no puede comer porque no puede masticar la comida.

_____

2. Mi abuelo tiene dificultad al caminar.

_____

3. José no puede escribir el examen.

_____

4. Graciela no puede hablar.

_____

5. No tengo apetito y no quiero comer nada.

_____

6. Lola no quiere ver la televisión ni leer una revista.

_____

[*8*] EDUCATION

a. La escuela

la alumna *pupil (f.)*	la nota *mark, grade*
el alumno *pupil (m.)*	la página *page*
la asignatura *subject*	la palabra *word*
el autobús escolar *school bus*	el papel *paper*
la bandera *flag*	el párrafo *paragraph*
el bolígrafo *ballpoint pen*	la pizarra *chalkboard*
el borrador *eraser (chalkboard)*	la pluma *pen*
la cafetería *cafeteria*	el profesor *teacher (m.)*
la clase *class*	la profesora *teacher (f.)*
el colegio *school, college*	la prueba *examination, test*
el cuaderno *notebook*	el pupitre *(pupil's) desk*
el diccionario *dictionary*	la regla *rule, ruler*
el dictado *dictation*	las sala de clase *classroom*
el error *mistake, error*	la tarea *assignment*
la escuela (primaria, secundaria) *school (elementary, secondary/high school)*	la tiza *chalk*
el (la) estudiante *student*	la universidad *college, university*
el examen *examination, test*	el vocabulario *vocabulary*
la falta *mistake, error*	aprender *to learn*
la frase *sentence*	contestar *to answer*
la goma *eraser*	enseñar *to teach*
el horario *schedule, program*	escribir *to write*
el lápiz *pencil*	escuchar *to listen (to)*
la lección *lesson*	estudiar *to study*
el libro *book*	explicar *to explain*
el maestro (la maestra) *teacher*	hacer la tarea *to do homework*
el marcador *felt-tip pen*	leer *to read*
la materia *subject*	preguntar *to ask*
la mochila *backpack*	responder *to answer*
	salir bien (mal) *to pass (fail)*

b. Las materias

el álgebra *algebra*	el francés *French*
el arte *art*	la geografía *geography*
las artes industriales *shop*	la geometría *geometry*
la biología *biology*	la historia *history*
las ciencias *sciences*	la informática *computer science*
el coro *choir*	el inglés *English*
el dibujo *drawing*	la música *music*
la economía doméstica *home economics*	la pintura *painting*
la educación física *physical education*	la química *chemistry*
el español *Spanish*	el recreo *recess*
la física *physics*	

EXERCISE CC

In each group, select the word that is *not* related to the other three. Write the words in the space provided.

1. párrafo, dictado, menú, página   _____

2. aprender, enseñar, nadar, escuchar   _____

3. escuela, papel, lección, leche   _____

4. pizarra, clase, cabeza, pupitre   _____

5. manzana, bolígrafo, lápiz, tiza   _____

6. prueba, tarea, examen, salud   _____

7. receta, dibujo, coro, física   _____

8. asignatura, clase, materia, dolor   _____

9. borrador, tiza, cuaderno, pizarra   _____

10. deporte, química, biología, ciencia   _____

EXERCISE DD

Match the words in column A with their respective synonyms or related words in column B. Write the letters in the space provided.

A	B
_____ **1.** falta	*a.* maestro
_____ **2.** escuela	*b.* coro
_____ **3.** profesor	*c.* pizarra
_____ **4.** asignatura	*d.* prueba
_____ **5.** contestar	*e.* error
_____ **6.** examen	*f.* estudiante
_____ **7.** alumno	*g.* responder
_____ **8.** música	*h.* materia
_____ **9.** biología	*i.* colegio
_____ **10.** tiza	*j.* ciencia

EXERCISE EE

Using the drawings below, make a list of the school supplies you have to buy for the new school year.

_____

_____

_____

_____

_____

_____

_____

_____

EXERCISE FF

Answer these questions that a new student from Argentina asks you.

1. ¿Cuántas materias estudias este año?

_____

2. ¿Qué lengua aprendes?

_____

3. ¿Qué clase de ciencia tienes?

_____

4. ¿Tomas una clase de informática?

_____

5. ¿Cómo son los exámenes de la clase de matemáticas?

_____

6. ¿Cúal es tu asignatura favorita?

_____

7. ¿Te gusta tu horario este año?

_____

[9] EARNING A LIVING

a. Las profesiones y los oficios

la abogada, el abogado   *lawyer*

el actor   *actor*

la actriz   *actress*

el agricultor, la agricultora   *farmer*

el / la artista   *artist, entertainer*

la barbera, el barbero   *barber*

el / la bombero   *firefighter*

la carnicera, el carnicero   *butcher*

el / la chófer (chofer)   *chauffeur*

la científica, el científico   *scientist*

el / la comerciante
  businessperson, entrepreneur

la criada   *maid*

el criado   *butler*

el / la dentista   *dentist*

el director, la directora   *director*

el doctor, la doctora   *doctor*

la dueña, el dueño   *owner, boss*

la enfermera, el enfermero   *nurse*

el escritor, la escritora   *writer*

la farmacéutica, el farmacéutico
  pharmacist

el / la gerente   *manager*

el hombre / la mujer de negocios
  businessperson

la ingeniera, el ingeniero   *engineer*

la jefa, el jefe   *supervisor, boss*

la maestra, el maestro   *teacher*

la médica, el médico   *doctor*

el oficio   *occupation*

la panadera, el panadero   *baker*

el / la periodista   *journalist*

el / la piloto   *pilot*

el policía / la (mujer) policía   *police officer*

el profesor, la profesora   *teacher, professor*

el programador / la programadora de
computadoras   *computer programmer*

la sastra, el sastre   *tailor*

la secretaria, el secretario   *secretary*

el / la soldado   *soldier*

la taquígrafa, el taquígrafo   *stenographer*

la veterinaria, el veterinario   *veterinarian*

la zapatera, el zapatero   *shoemaker*

estar desempleado   *to be unemployed*

ganarse la vida   *to earn a living*

trabajar   *to work*

b. Los lugares de trabajo

la barbería *barber shop*	el laboratorio *laboratory*
el consultorio *doctor's office*	la oficina *office*
la corte *court*	la peluquería *hair salon*
la escuela *school*	el salón de belleza *beauty salon*
la fábrica *factory*	la tienda *store*
el hospital *hospital*	la universidad *university, college*

EXERCISE GG

Identify the profession that is associated with the following drawings.

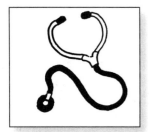

1. _____

2. _____

3. _____

4. _____

5. _____

6. _____

7. _____

8. _____

9. _____

10. _____

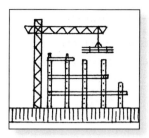

11. _____

12. _____

13. _____

14. _____

15. _____

EXERCISE HH

Use the clues below to identify the professions described. Write the name of the profession in the space provided.

1. Preparo la medicina que el doctor ordena en una receta. _____

2. Defiendo la patria cuando hay una guerra. _____

3. Protejo a las personas. Llevo uniforme. _____

4. Preparo a los jóvenes para el futuro. Me gustan los exámenes. _____

5. Ayudo a los médicos y cuido a los enfermos. _____

6. Hago experimentos. Trabajo en un laboratorio. _____

7. Corto el pelo a los hombres y a las mujeres. _____

8. Trabajo en las películas. Trato de divertir al público. _____

9. Me gusta la vida del campo. Cultivo la tierra y tengo animales como las vacas y los pollos. _____

10. Escribo las noticias todos los días. Las personas compran mi producto diariamente. _____

11. Trato de mejorar la vida con edificios nuevos y puentes. _____

12. Ayudo a las personas cuando tienen dolor de muelas. _____

13. Trabajo en una oficina donde contesto el teléfono y escribo cartas a máquina. _____

14. Reparo la ropa de las personas. Me gusta coser. _____

15. Me fascina volar y siempre llevo a muchas personas de una ciudad a otra. _____

[*10*] LEISURE

el ajedrez *chess*	la grabadora *tape recorder*
el béisbol *baseball*	el instrumento *instrument*
el billar *pool*	la música *music*
el campeón *champion*	el partido *game, match*
la canción *song*	el pasatiempo *pastime, hobby*
el cine *movies*	la película *film, movie*
la cinta *cassette tape*	el programa *program*
el concierto *concert*	el / la radio *radio*
el disco *record*	el teatro *theater*
el disco compacto *CD*	la televisión *television*
las diversiones *amusements*	el tenis *tennis*
el equipo *team*	el tocadiscos *record player*
el fútbol *soccer*	las vacaciones *vacation*

andar en bicicleta *to ride a bicycle*	jugar *to play (a game, sport)*
bailar *to dance*	levantar pesas *to lift weights*
cantar *to sing*	mirar televisión *to watch television*
coleccionar monedas (estampillas, muñecas, insectos) *to collect coins (stamps, dolls, insects)*	nadar *to swim*
	patinar *to skate*
correr *to run*	practicar el judo *to practice judo*
dar un paseo *to take a walk*	sacar fotos *to take pictures*
escuchar *to listen (to)*	salir con los amigos *to go out with friends*
esquiar *to ski*	ser fanático de *to be a fan of*
hacer gimnasia *to do gymnastics*	tocar *to play (music)*
hacer yoga *to practice yoga*	viajar *to travel*
ir de compras *to go shopping*	

EXERCISE II

In each group, select the word that is *not* related to the other three. Write the words in the space provided.

1. leer, disco, tocadiscos, música   _____

2. bailar, cantar, patinar, trabajar   _____

3. película, juego, cine, actriz   _____

4. música, equipo, fútbol, partido   _____

5. esquiar, estudiar, nadar, correr   _____

6. concierto, televisión, escuela, teatro   _____

7. programa, béisbol, tenis, fútbol   _____

8. hacer yoga, levantar pesas, ir de compras, hacer gimnasia   _____

EXERCISE JJ

Identify the pastime that each of these people enjoys most.

1. A Rogelio le gusta conocer otros países y ciudades. Le fascina visitar los museos.

_____

2. Luis siempre me pide los sobres de las cartas que recibo de mi amigo de correspondencia. También le gusta ver las tarjetas postales que recibo de mis amigos cuando visitan otros países.

_____

3. Sarita y Gladys quieren ser bailarinas. Practican mucho y hacen ejercicios especiales.

_____

4. Jorge quiere tener músculos grandes. Es socio de un gimnasio donde hace este ejercicio todos los días.

_____

5. A Enrique le gustan mucho los juegos de mesa. Practica con mucha frecuencia y es el campeón del equipo de la escuela. Prefiere el juego más difícil y exigente.

_____

6. A Sofía le gusta gastar dinero. Compra regalos bonitos para todo el mundo.

_____

7. A Beto le gusta la zoología. Le fascina caminar en el parque y en el bosque. A su hermana no le gustan las cosas que Beto colecciona en sus paseos.

_____

[11] PUBLIC AND PRIVATE SERVICES

autoridad de aqueductos   *water utilities company*

el correo   *mail, post office*

la electricidad   *electricity*

hablar por teléfono   *to speak on the telephone*

hacer una llamada   *to make a call*

llamar   *to call*

la estampilla   *stamp*

el gas   *gas company*

el teléfono   *telephone*

marcar un número   *to dial a number*

pagar el agua (el gas)
to pay the water (the gas) bill

EXERCISE KK

Complete each statement with the appropriate words.

1. Para mandar una carta tengo que comprar_____. Las compro en el

_____.

2. Durante el verano visité un pueblo muy primitivo. Las casas no tienen_____y

tienen que usar el_____del río.

3. Mi tío vive en Buenos Aires. Cada domingo nos_____por teléfono. Es una

llamada de_____. Él no puede_____; tiene que hablar con la

operadora primero.

4. No distribuyen_____en la calle en que vivo hasta las dos de la tarde. Mis padres

reciben mucho_____: cartas, tarjetas postales, revistas y cuentas.

[*12*] SHOPPING

a. Las tiendas

el almacén   *department store, warehouse*
la bodega   *grocery store*
la carnicería   *butcher shop*
el centro comercial   *mall*
la farmacia   *pharmacy, drugstore*
la florería   *florist shop*
la lavandería   *laundry*
la librería   *bookstore*
el mercado   *market*
la mueblería   *furniture store*

la panadería   *bakery*
la papelería   *stationery store*
la pastelería   *pastry shop*
la peluquería   *barbershop, hair salon*
el salón de belleza   *beauty shop*
el supermercado   *supermarket*
la tienda   *store*
la tienda de ropa   *clothing store*
la zapatería   *shoe store*

b. Palabras relacionadas

barato, -a   *cheap, inexpensive*
la caja   *cashier*
caro, -a   *expensive*
el cheque   *check*

el / la dependiente   *salesperson*
el efectivo   *cash*
en especial   *on sale*
la etiqueta   *tag*

la ganga   *sale, bargain*

grande (mediano, pequeño)
  large (medium, small)

el precio   *price*

la queja   *complaint*

rebajado, -a   *reduced*

la talla   *(clothing) size*

el tamaño   *(package) size*

la tarjeta de crédito   *credit card*

ahorrar   *to save*

comprar   *to buy*

devolver   *to return* (an item)

pagar con cheque / tarjeta de crédito
  to pay with check / credit card

pagar en efectivo   *to pay cash*

probarse   *to try (on)*

quedarle bien   *to look well on*

regatear   *to bargain*

vender   *to sell*

¿Cuánto vale (cuesta)?
  How much does it cost?

¿En qué puedo servirle?
  How may I help you?

EXERCISE LL

Match the words in column A with their related words in column B. Write the letters in the space provided.

A	B
_____ **1.** carnicería	***a.*** diccionario
_____ **2.** farmacia	***b.*** ropa limpia
_____ **3.** mueblería	***c.*** calcetines
_____ **4.** librería	***d.*** cortar el pelo
_____ **5.** florería	***e.*** sandalias
_____ **6.** lavandería	***f.*** refrescos
_____ **7.** papelería	***g.*** biftec
_____ **8.** salón de belleza	***h.*** muchos departamentos
_____ **9.** pastelería	***i.*** pan
_____ **10.** tienda de ropa	***j.*** sofá
_____ **11.** bodega	***k.*** tiendas
_____ **12.** centro comercial	***l.*** claveles
_____ **13.** panadería	***m.*** postre
_____ **14.** zapatería	***n.*** tarjetas
_____ **15.** almacén	***o.*** receta

EXERCISE MM

Complete each statement with the appropriate word or expression.

1. En una tienda la persona que atiende al cliente es＿＿＿＿＿＿＿.

2. No tengo ni dinero ni un cheque; voy a pagar con＿＿＿＿＿＿＿.

3. Busco un suéter, ＿＿＿＿＿＿＿grande.

4. Leo el precio del artículo en＿＿＿＿＿＿＿.

5. Estos zapatos cuestan mucho; quiero algo más＿＿＿＿＿＿＿.

6. Este pantalón está＿＿＿＿＿＿＿, ahora cuesta solamente veinte dólares.

7. Pago por las compras en＿＿＿＿＿＿＿.

8. No me gusta este artículo. Quiero hablar con el gerente porque lo tengo que＿＿＿＿＿＿＿.

9. En esta tienda tenemos que pagar el precio indicado; no podemos＿＿＿＿＿＿＿.

10. El perfume viene en dos＿＿＿＿＿＿＿: pequeño o grande.

11. No me gusta el suéter. Voy a＿＿＿＿＿＿＿el suéter a la tienda.

12. Debes＿＿＿＿＿＿＿el suéter antes de salir de la tienda.

[13] TRAVEL

a. Medios de transporte

el autobús *bus*	el coche, el auto *car, automobile*
el automóvil *car, automobile*	el ferrocarril *railroad*
el avión *airplane*	la motocicleta *motorcycle*
el barco *boat*	el tren *train*
la bicicleta *bicycle*	el vapor *steamship*

b. Palabras relacionadas

el aeropuerto *airport*	la maleta *suitcase*
el asiento *seat*	el mapa *map*
el baúl *trunk*	el norte *north*
el billete *ticket*	el oeste *west*
el boleto *ticket*	la parada *bus stop*
el camino *road, way*	el pasillo *aisle*
la entrada *entrance*	el plano (de la ciudad) *(city) map*
la estación *station*	la puerta *gate, door*
el este *east*	la salida *exit*
la fila *row*	el sur *south*

el viaje   *trip, voyage*
el vuelo   *flight*

caminar   *to walk*
hacer la maleta   *to pack*

regresar   *to return*
salir   *to leave, depart*
viajar   *to travel*
volver   *to return*

EXERCISE NN

In each group, select the word that is *not* related to the other three. Write the words in the space provided.

1. avión, sala de clase, bicicleta, coche   _____

2. vapor, ferrocarril, viajar, teatro   _____

3. libro, maleta, baúl, viaje   _____

4. este, pregunta, norte, oeste   _____

5. aeropuerto, calle, parada, estación   _____

6. comer, billete, puerta, boleto   _____

7. tren, vuelo, estación, ferrocarril   _____

8. mapa, calle, plano, número de teléfono   _____

9. asiento, fila, pasillo, baúl   _____

10. vapor, mar, barco, camino   _____

EXERCISE OO

Match the words in column A with their related words in column B. Write the letters in the space provided.

A	B
_____ 1. asiento	*a.* salir
_____ 2. maleta	*b.* aeropuerto
_____ 3. avión	*c.* barco
_____ 4. parada	*d.* puerta
_____ 5. tren	*e.* fila
_____ 6. regresar	*f.* autobús
	g. plano
	h. coche

_____ **7.** mapa

_____ **8.** entrada

_____ **9.** automóvil

_____ **10.** vapor

_i._ baúl

_j._ ferrocarril

EXERCISE PP

Complete each of the sentences with the appropriate word or expression.

1. Ponemos la ropa en _____.

2. El Canadá está al _____ de México.

3. México está al _____ de los Estados Unidos.

4. El avión llega al _____.

5. En el avión me siento en la _____31, _____C.

6. Para subir al avión tengo que mostrar el _____.

7. Una bicicleta con un motor es una _____.

8. En la ciudad uso un _____ para encontrar la calle que busco.

9. Antes de viajar, escojo la ropa para _____.

10. Tomo el autobús en la _____.

[14] ENTERTAINMENT

el actor   *actor*

la actriz   *actress*

el / la artista   *artist, entertainer, performer*

el billete   *ticket*

el boleto   *ticket*

el cine   *movies*

el concierto   *concert*

el estadio   *stadium*

el estreno   *opening (of a performance), showing*

la función   *performance, showing*

el horario   *schedule*

el locutor   *announcer*

la noticia   *news item*

las noticias   *news*

el noticiero   *news broadcast*

la obra   *(theater) work, play*

la película   *film*

la taquilla   *box office*

el teatro   *theater*

hacer cola   *to wait in line*

EXERCISE QQ

Match the words in column A to their related words in column B. Write the letters in the space provided.

	A		B
_____	1. el boleto	a.	el artista
_____	2. la película	b.	el horario
_____	3. la obra	c.	el locutor
_____	4. la taquilla	d.	el cine
_____	5. la función	e.	el teatro
_____	6. el concierto	f.	los deportes
_____	7. el estadio	g.	hacer cola
_____	8. el noticiero	h.	la taquilla

EXERCISE RR

Complete this story with the appropriate word or expression in the list below. Note that the words or expressions are arranged in alphabetical order, not in order of appearance.

billetes	esperar	hacer cola	película
boletos	estadio	horario	taquilla
cine	estreno	locutor	
concierto	función	música	

Sergio invita a Blanca a acompañarle a un _____ de su grupo favorito. Tiene dos

               1.

_____ para el _____ pero no sabe _____ . Tiene

    2.   3.   4.

que recoger los _____ en la _____ del _____ .

               5.   6.   7.

Cuando Sergio y Blanca llegan allí hay mucha gente y tienen que _____ . Mientras

                                                       8.

ellos _____ , escuchan _____ en un radio portátil. El

        9.   10.

_____ anuncia que el avión en que llegaba el grupo favorito de Sergio no va a llegar

    11.

a tiempo y que van a cancelar la _____ . Sergio está enojado y triste pero decide ir

                                      12.

con Blanca a ver una _____ de ciencia ficción en el _____ .

                13.   14.

MASTERY EXERCISES

EXERCISE SS

Ramón's little brother, Pepito, is learning many new words. Write *Sí*, if the sentence is true. If it's false, correct it by replacing the words in boldface with the correct ones.

EXAMPLE:　Los médicos trabajan en **una carnicería**.
　　　　　Los médicos trabajan en **un hospital**.
　OR:　Los médicos trabajan en **un consultorio**.

1. **Hago las maletas** antes de viajar.　　　　　　_____

2. Hay muchos libros en **una florería**.　　　　　_____

3. Compramos pan en **la mueblería**.　　　　　　_____

4. El secretario trabaja en **una oficina**.　　　　_____

5. La química y la historia son **asignaturas**.　　_____

6. Tengo los ojos y **las piernas** en la cara.　　　_____

7. Para **escribir**, uso una pluma o un lápiz.　　　_____

8. Mi padre cocina en **la sala**.　　　　　　　　_____

9. Cuando hace **calor** llevamos abrigo, guantes y botas.　_____

10. La cereza y la pera son **legumbres**.　　　　　_____

EXERCISE TT

You're going on a vocabulary game-show, where you must read each definition on the left and write its corresponding word or words on the right.

EXAMPLE:　libro donde se explican las palabras de una lengua　**un diccionario**

1. persona de pelo negro　　　　　　　　　　_____

2. el cuarto donde duermo　　　　　　　　　_____

3. yo soy su nieta　　　　　　　　　　　　　_____

4. lugar donde se sale a comer　　　　　　　　_____

5. tienda donde se venden flores　　　　　　　_____

6. sinónimo de montaña　　　　　　　　　　_____

7. estación en que hace mucho frío en Norteamérica　_____

8. mes entre septiembre y noviembre　　　　　_____

9. día antes del sábado   _____

10. fruta amarilla que no es dulce   _____

11. parte del cuerpo donde llevo un sombrero   _____

12. lengua que hablan en Perú   _____

13. persona que estudia   _____

14. lugar donde van los enfermos   _____

15. el deporte más popular de Hispanoamérica   _____

16. medio de transporte necesario para ir de México a Argentina   _____

17. artista de cine   _____

18. tienda donde compro libros   _____

19. objeto para escribir en la pizarra   _____

20. palabras que tengo que aprender   _____

Part five
Spanish and Spanish-American Civilizations

ESPAÑA

Islas Baleares

Islas Canarias

MÉXICO

REPÚBLICA
DOMINICANA

PUERTO RICO

CUBA

HONDURAS

GUATEMALA

NICARAGUA

EL SALVADOR

COSTA RICA

VENEZUELA

PANAMÁ

COLOMBIA

ECUADOR

PERÚ

BOLIVIA

PARAGUAY

CHILE

URUGUAY

ARGENTINA

Chapter 31
Spanish Influence in the United States

FIRST SPANISH EXPLORERS

1. **Cristóbal Colón** (Christopher Columbus) is believed to be the Genoese navigator Cristoforo Colombo, who became an explorer for Spain and the first European to reach the New World (1492). He made four voyages, touching on various parts of what is now Spanish America.
2. **Hernán Cortés** conquered Mexico (1519–1521), defeating the Aztecs and their king, Moctezuma.
3. **Francisco Pizarro** conquered Peru (1532–1535), defeating the Incas and their king, Atahualpa. Pizarro founded the city of Lima in 1535.
4. **Juan Ponce de León** was the first Spanish governor of Puerto Rico and the first European to explore what is now Florida (1513) in his search for the Fountain of Youth. He arrived on an Easter Sunday (Domingo de Pascua Florida), therefore naming it Florida.
5. **Álvar Núñez Cabeza de Vaca** shipwrecked on the Texas coast in 1528. He was captured by Native Americans, whom he served as a slave and medicine man. He later escaped and wandered for six years, exploring parts of Texas, Kansas, and New Mexico. After traveling thousands of miles, Cabeza de Vaca finally reached Mexico in 1536. His reports from the Pueblo Indians led to the myth of the "Seven Cities of Cibola."
6. **Francisco Vásquez de Coronado** was the first Spaniard to explore what are now New Mexico and Arizona (1540, including the Grand Canyon) in his search for the supposedly rich and prosperous "Seven Cities of Cibola."
7. **Hernando de Soto** explored much of Georgia, the Carolinas, Tennessee, Alabama, and Oklahoma. He was the first European explorer to reach the Mississippi River (1541), where he was later buried.
8. **Juan Rodríguez Cabrillo** explored the coast of California in 1542.
9. **Vasco Núñez de Balboa** was the first European explorer to reach the Pacific Ocean (1513).

EARLY SPANISH SETTLEMENTS

1. **St. Augustine** (Florida) is the oldest city in the United States. It was established by the Spaniards in 1565.
2. **Santa Fe** (New Mexico) is the oldest capital city in the United States. It was established in 1609.
3. **Spanish missions** were established by priests in the southwestern part of the United States.
   a. **Fray Junípero Serra** was the most famous of the Spanish missionaries. He and his followers established a chain of twenty-one missions from San Diego to San Francisco (1769–1823) along the **Camino Real** (royal road), which is today called Coast Highway 101.
   b. The most famous California missions are **San Juan Capistrano** and **Santa Barbara,** which is called the "Queen of the California Missions."

GEOGRAPHIC NAMES OF SPANISH ORIGIN

1. **States:** California, Colorado, Florida, Montana, Nevada.
2. **Cities:** El Paso, Las Vegas, Los Angeles, Sacramento, Santa Fe, San Francisco.
3. **Rivers:** Brazos (Texas); Colorado (Colorado, Utah, Arizona), Río Grande (New Mexico, Texas).
4. **Mountains:** San Juan (Colorado); Sierra Nevada (California).

SPANISH INFLUENCE IN ARCHITECTURE

1. Many modern American homes and buildings, especially in the southwest, show the influence of the old adobe ranch houses and mission buildings constructed by the Spaniards.
2. **Characteristics of Spanish Architecture**
   a. **Patio** (inner courtyard). An attractive spot for family relaxation, frequently with flowers, shade trees, and an ornamental fountain.
   b. **Reja** (iron grating on windows). Used for security and decoration. In Spanish-speaking countries, it has been a traditional meet-

ing place for sweethearts, with the young lady behind the **reja** and her suitor outside, on the other side of the reja.

c. **Balcón** (balcony). Used for displaying flags during celebrations, watching processions and parades, and sunning flowering plants.

d. **Tejas** (roof tiles). Made of baked clay, red in color.

e. **Arcada** (arcade). A covered passageway along a row of columns in front of commercial buildings. Provides protection from the weather (rain or hot sun) for patrons and strollers.

SPANISH INFLUENCE ON ECONOMIC LIFE

1. **Cattle Raising**
   a. Spaniards brought the first cows, horses, goats, pigs, and sheep to the New World.
   b. From the Spanish cowboy, the American cowboy copied his dress, equipment, vocabulary, and ranching techniques.

2. **Mining**
   Spaniards developed the first gold and silver mines in the New World. Their methods and success influenced the mining industry in America.

SPANISH INFLUENCE ON LANGUAGE

1. Spanish explorers, missionaries, and settlers in North America contributed many Spanish words to our language. Some of these words are identical in English and Spanish. Others have been slightly changed.

2. **Common English Words of Spanish Origin**
   a. **Ranch life:** bronco, chaps (**chaparreras**), cinch (**cincha**), corral, lariat (**la reata**), lasso (**lazo**), mustang (**mesteño**), ranch (**rancho**), rodeo, stampede (**estampida**).
   b. **Foods:** avocado (**aguacate**), banana, barbecue (**barbacoa**), chili (**chile**), potato (**patata**), tomato (**tomate**), vanilla (**vainilla**).

c. **Beverages:** sherry (**Jerez**).

d. **Clothing:** bolero, brocade (**brocado**), mantilla, poncho, sombrero.

e. **Animals and insects:** alligator (**lagarto**), burro, chinchilla, cockroach (**cucaracha**), coyote, llama, mosquito.

f. **Types of people:** cannibal (**caníbal**), comrade (**camarada**), desperado (**desesperado**), padre, peon (**peón**), renegade (**renegado**), vigilante.

g. **Nature:** arroyo, canyon (**cañón**), cordillera, lagoon (**laguna**), mesa, sierra, tornado.

h. **Shipping and commerce:** armada, canoe (**canoa**), cargo (**carga**), contraband (**contrabando**), embargo, flotilla, galleon (**galeón**).

i. **Buildings and streets:** adobe, alameda, hacienda, patio, plaza.

j. **Miscellaneous words:** bonanza, cigar (**cigarro**), fiesta, filibuster (**filibustero**), guerrilla, siesta.

POPULAR MEXICAN FOODS

1. **Tortilla**—a flat, thin cornmeal pancake.
2. **Enchilada**—a rolled tortilla filled with chopped meat or chicken and served with hot chili sauce.
3. **Tamal**—seasoned ground meat or chicken rolled in cornmeal dough, wrapped in corn husks, and steamed.
4. **Chile con carne**—red pepper, chopped meat, and hot chili sauce.
5. **Taco**—a crisp tortilla folded over and filled with seasoned chopped meat or chicken, lettuce, and tomatoes.

POPULAR SPANISH-AMERICAN DANCES

1. **Tango** (Argentina).
2. **Rumba** (Cuba).
3. **Mambo** (Cuba).
4. **Cha-cha-chá** (Cuba).
5. **Merengue** (Dominican Republic).

EXERCISE A

If the statement is true, write *Sí*; if it's false, correct it by replacing the word(s) in boldface. Write the correct word(s) in the space provided.

1. Fray Junípero Serra and his followers established **twenty-seven** missions in California.

twenty-one

2. There are many houses of Spanish-style architecture in the **northwestern** United States.   *southwest*

3. The **American** cowboy copied a great deal from the Spanish cowboy.   *Sí*

4. The Spaniards used **adobe** for building.   *Sí*

5. The **Spaniards** established the cattle-raising industry in the New World.   *Sí*

6. The words *rodeo* and *corral* are related to Spanish **city** life.   *ranch*

7. The oldest city in the United States is **San Diego.**   *St. Augustine*

8. In **New Mexico** there are numerous cities that have Spanish names.   *Sí*

9. The **rejas** of Spanish houses have flowers and trees.   *Patio*

10. A **tamal** is a crisp tortilla filled with meat or beans.   *Enchilada*

EXERCISE B

Match the expressions in column A with their corresponding definitions in column B. Write the letter in the space provided.

	A		B
h	**1.** tango	*a.*	tortilla with chopped meat and chili sauce
j	**2.** De Soto	*b.*	roofing material
i	**3.** Camino Real	*c.*	inner courtyard
f	**4.** Santa Fe	*d.*	covered passageway
e	**5.** Las Vegas	*e.*	city in Nevada
d	**6.** arcada	*f.*	capital city in New Mexico
a	**7.** enchilada	*g.*	Spanish word related to *alligator*
g	**8.** lagarto	*h.*	Argentine dance
c	**9.** patio	*i.*	road connecting the Spanish missions
b	**10.** tejas	*j.*	explorer of the Mississippi River
l	**11.** Ponce de León	*k.*	founder of California missions
k	**12.** Fray Junípero Serra	*l.*	explorer of Florida

EXERCISE C

Complete the following statements.

1. A mountain range in California with a Spanish name is _Sierra Nevada_.

2. A popular dance of the Dominican Republic is the _Merengue_.

3. Two states with Spanish names are _California_ and _Florida_.

4. The river that separates the United States from Mexico is the _Rio Grande_.

5. A popular Cuban dance is the _cha-cha-cha_.

6. An American city with a Spanish name is _Las Vegas_.

7. One of the animals that the Spaniards brought to the New World is the _cows_.

8. The San Juan Mountains are in the state of _Colorado_.

9. A city in Texas with a Spanish name is _El Paso_.

10. The oldest city in the United States is _St. Augustine_.

EXERCISE D

In each group of words, select the word that isn't related to the other three. Write the word in the space provided.

EXAMPLE: rumba, tango, estampida, mambo   **estampida**

1. burro, chinchilla, llama, banana   _____

2. bronco, flotilla, mesteño, rodeo   _____

3. bolero, tornado, arroyo, mesa   _____

4. brocado, tortilla, barbacoa, vainilla   _____

5. sombrero, desesperado, poncho, mantilla   _____

6. patio, hacienda, lazo, alameda   _____

7. taco, tamal, enchilada, bonanza   _____

8. camarada, tomate, patata, chile   _____

9. peón, padre, renegado, embargo   _____

10. armada, contrabando, canoa, sierra   _____

EXERCISE E

Select the words in parenthesis that correctly complete each of the following sentences.

1. (Francisco Pizarro / Juan Ponce de León / Cristóbal Colón) was the first governor of Puerto Rico.

2. (Álvar Núñez Cabeza de Vaca / Hernán Cortés / Hernando de Soto) was the first European explorer to reach the Mississippi River.

3. (Atahualpa / Moctezuma / Cíbola) was the Aztec king conquered by Hernán Cortés.

4. (Fray Junípero Serra / Atahualpa / Juan Rodríguez Cabrillo) was a famous Spanish missionary.

5. (Santa Fe / Santa Barbara / San Francisco) is the oldest capital city in the United States.

6. (San Juan Capistrano / El Paso / St. Augustine) is a famous Spanish mission.

7. The (*tamal* / *rumba* / *cincha*) is a popular Spanish-American dance.

8. The tango is a popular dance from (Mexico / Cuba / Argentina).

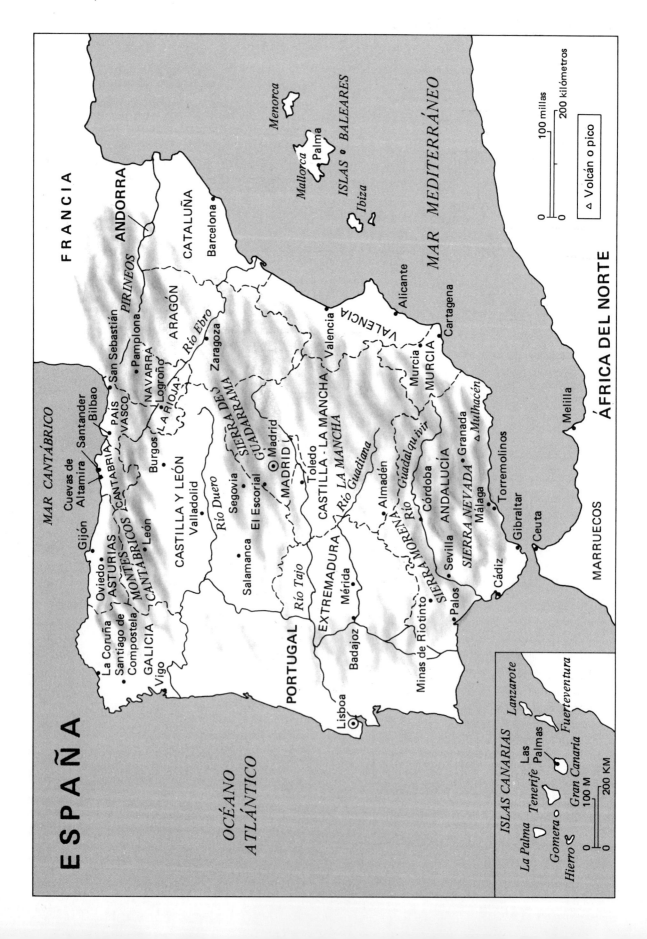

Chapter 32
Geography of Spain

LOCATION OF SPAIN
Located in the southwestern part of Europe, Spain occupies eighty percent of the Iberian peninsula, which it shares with Portugal.

SIZE AND POPULATION
Spain has an area of about 200,000 square miles (four times the size of New York State), and a population of about 40,000,000 inhabitants.

MOUNTAINS
1. The Pyrenees **(los Pirineos)**, in the northeast, separate Spain from France.
2. Cantabrian Mountains **(la Cordillera Cantábrica)** in the northwest.
3. Guadarrama Mountains **(la Sierra de Guadarrama)**, near Madrid.
4. **Sierra Nevada** and **Sierra Morena**, in the south.

RIVERS
1. **El Ebro,** in the northeast, flows into the Mediterranean Sea.
2. **El Tajo,** in the central region, is the longest river. It runs by the city of Toledo.
3. **El Guadalquivir** in the south, is the deepest and most navigable river in Spain. It runs by the cities of Seville **(Sevilla)** and Cordova **(Córdoba).**

OVERSEAS POSSESSIONS
1. The Balearic Islands **(Islas Baleares)** are located in the Mediterranean Sea. They are a popular resort area. **Mallorca** is the largest island in the group.
2. The Canary Islands **(Islas Canarias)** are located in the Atlantic Ocean, off the northwestern coast of Africa.
3. **Ceuta** and **Melilla** are two port cities in Morocco, Africa.

IMPORTANT PRODUCTS
1. Spain is both an industrial and an agricultural country.
2. The **principal agricultural** products are **olives, oranges, grapes, wheat, lemons,** and **cork.**
   a. Spain occupies third place in **wine** production in Europe.
   b. The wines of Jerez (sherry), **Rioja,** and **Málaga** are world-famous.
   c. Spain is one of the world's leading producers of **olive oil.**
3. **Mineral resources** are **coal, iron, mercury, lead,** and **copper.**

REGIONS OF SPAIN
Spain is divided into fifteen regions.

Cantabria, in the north
Galicia, in the northwest
Asturias, in the north, east of Galicia
Basque Country **(País Vasco)**, in the north, bordering the Pyrenees
Navarre **(Navarra)**, in the north
Aragon **(Aragón)**, in the northeast, east of Navarra
Catalonia **(Cataluña)**, in the northeastern corner
Rioja **(La Rioja)**, south of Navarra
Castile and Leon **(Castilla y León)**, in the north central part of the peninsula
Castile–La Mancha **(Castilla–La Mancha)**, in the center
Madrid, in the center, north of Castile–La Mancha
Valencia, in the east
Extremadura, in the west, between Portugal and Castile–La Mancha
Andalusia **(Andalucía)**, in the south

LANGUAGES
1. Spanish **(español,** or **castellano)** is the principal language spoken in Spain.
2. Galician **(gallego)** is spoken in Galicia.
3. Basque **(vascuence)** is spoken in the Basque Country.
4. **Catalán** is spoken in Catalonia.

EXERCISE A

Match the words in column A to their related words in column B. Write the letter in the space provided.

	A		B
i	1. Asturias	a.	Balearic Islands
j	2. Spanish	b.	Atlantic Ocean
h	3. Sierra Morena	c.	Spain's longest river
f	4. Galician	d.	region in the northeast
c	5. Tajo	e.	wine
g	6. Guadalquivir	f.	language spoken in the northwest
e	7. Jerez	g.	most navigable river
b	8. Canary Islands	h.	mountains
d	9. Catalonia	i.	region in the north
a	10. Mallorca	j.	principal language of Spain

EXERCISE B

If the statement is true, write *Sí*, if it's false, correct it by replacing the word(s) in boldface. Write the word(s) in the space provided.

1. The Pyrenees separate Spain from **Portugal**.   France

2. The Mediterranean Sea is situated **west** of Spain.   Sí

3. Spain and Portugal form the **Iberian** Peninsula.   Sí

4. Some Spanish **wines** are world-famous.   Sí

5. Spain has a population of about **60,000,000**.   40,000,000

6. Mallorca is one of the **Canary** Islands.   Balearic

7. The Cantabrian Mountains are in the **south** of Spain.   northwest

8. The most navigable river in Spain is the **Tajo**.   Guadalquivir

9. **Málaga** is an important wine producing country.   Sí

10. The principal language of Spain is **Basque**.   Spanish

EXERCISE C

Select the word or expression that correctly completes each sentence.

1. The (Guadarrama / Pyrenee / Cantabrian) Mountains separate Spain from France.

2. (Apples/ Oranges / Machines) are an important product of Spain.

3. Spain is located in the (southwestern / northeastern / central) part of Europe.

4. Spain has two ports that are situated in (South America / Africa / Mexico).

5. A popular resort area of Spain is (the Balearic Islands / the Canary Islands / Extremadura).

6. The (Tajo / Ebro / Guadalquivir) River passes by Toledo.

7. (Murcia / Aragon / Leon) is in the northwestern part of Spain.

8. An important mineral resource of Spain is (gold / tin / mercury).

9. Spain has an area of (40,000,000 / 200,000 / 1,300) square miles.

10. The (Pyrenee / Guadarrama / Cantabrian) Mountains are near Madrid.

EXERCISE D

Complete the following statements.

1. The _El Tajo_ is the longest river of Spain.

2. The _Balearic Islands_ are islands in the Mediterranean Sea that belong to Spain.

3. _Madrid_ is a region of central Spain.

4. Spain is the one of the world's leading producers of _olive oil_ .

5. _Andalusia_ is a region that covers most of southern Spain.

6. The Cantabrian Mountains are in the _northwest_ part of Spain.

7. Spain consists of _15_ regions.

8. The Sierra Nevada is a mountain range in the _southern_ part of Spain.

9. The regional language of Catalonia is _Catalin_ .

10. A Spanish river that flows into the Mediterranean Sea is _El Ebro_ .

Chapter 33
History of Spain

EARLY INHABITANTS

1. The Iberians **(los iberos)** and the Celts **(los celtas)**, the earliest inhabitants of Spain, united to form the Celtiberians **(los celtíberos)**.
2. The Phoenicians **(los fenicios)** and the Greeks **(los griegos)** established colonies and trading posts in Spain from about the eleventh to the eighth century B.C.
3. The Carthaginians **(los cartagineses)** invaded Spain in the third century B.C.
4. The Romans **(los romanos)**:
   a. defeated the Carthaginians (about 200 B.C.).
   b. ruled Spain for six centuries (until about A.D. 400).
   c. built bridges, aqueducts, and roads.
   d. introduced their language, Latin, from which present-day Spanish is derived.
5. The Visigoths **(los visigodos)** were a Germanic tribe that defeated the Romans and invaded Spain (A.D. 409).
6. The Moors **(los moros)** invaded Spain, defeating the Visigoths in A.D. 711. They ruled large areas of Spain for about seven centuries, and were finally driven out of Spain in 1492. The Moors:
   a. made great contributions in the fields of philosophy, medicine, mathematics, and astronomy.
   b. developed commerce and agriculture and devised an irrigation system by means of a waterwheel called **noria**.
   c. introduced many Arabic words into the Spanish language, mostly those beginning with **al- (algodón, alcalde, álgebra,** and many others).

HEROES OF THE RECONQUEST

1. **Don Pelayo** was the first leader in the Reconquest of Spain from the Moors. He defeated them in the **Battle of Covadonga** (A.D. 718).

2. **El Cid (Rodrigo Díaz de Vivar)**, is Spain's national hero. He continued the struggle against the Moors and captured Valencia from them in 1094.

IMPORTANT RULERS

1. **Fernando** and **Isabel**, known as **los Reyes Católicos** (the Catholic Rulers), completed the Reconquest by driving the Moors from Granada, the last remaining Spanish region under Moorish control (1492). They also financed Columbus's four expeditionary voyages.
2. **Carlos V** (1516–1556), grandson of Fernando and Isabel, was one of the most powerful Spanish kings. During his reign, Spain ruled most of Europe and the New World.
3. **Felipe II,** son of Carlos V. His "Invincible Armada" was defeated in an attempt to invade England in 1588.

NINETEENTH AND TWENTIETH CENTURIES

1. The **War of Independence** (1808–1814) started with a rebellion of the people against French rule under Napoleon.
2. The **Spanish-American War** (1898) between the United States and Spain resulted in the latter's defeat. Spain agreed to give up Cuba, Puerto Rico, the Philippines, and Guam.
3. The **Civil War** (1936–1939) was won by General Francisco Franco and his supporters, who overthrew the republic and set up a dictatorship. At Franco's death (1975), Spain became a constitutional monarchy.
4. In 1975, **Prince Juan Carlos de Borbón** was proclaimed King. In 1982, **Felipe González Márquez** became Prime Minister. Spain joined the European Common Market in 1985.

EXERCISE A

Match the words in column A with their related words in column B.

A		B
__j__	**1.** Pelayo	**a.** early inhabitants of Spain
__g__	**2.** waterwheel	**b.** dictator
__i__	**3.** A.D. 711	**c.** Catholic Rulers
__e__	**4.** el Cid	**d.** Moorish defeat at Granada
__f__	**5.** Felipe II	**e.** Rodrigo Díaz de Vivar
__h__	**6.** 1808	**f.** Invincible Armada
__d__	**7.** 1492	**g.** brought to Spain by the Moors
__a__	**8.** Celtiberians	**h.** War of Independence
__b__	(**9.**) Franco	**i.** Moorish invasion
__c__	**10.** Fernando and Isabel	**j.** Covadonga

EXERCISE B

If the statement is true, write *Sí*; if it's false, correct it by replacing the word(s) in boldface. Write the word(s) in the space provided.

1. The Spanish "Invincible" Armada, at war with England, was defeated in **1588**. — Sí

2. The Moors governed Spain for **two** centuries. — seven

3. The **Celtiberians** established trading posts in Spain. — Phoenicians

4. The **Visigoths** invaded Spain in A.D. 711. — Moors

5. Carlos V was the father of **Felipe II.** — Sí

6. El Cid captured **Valencia** from the Moors. — Sí

7. The **Carthaginians** built bridges and aqueducts in Spain. — Romans

8. Fernando and Isabel completed the Reconquest from the **Moors.** — Sí

9. The **Moors** developed philosophy and the sciences. — Sí

10. The **Phoenicians** conquered the Carthaginians. — Romans

EXERCISE C

Select the word or expression that correctly completes each sentence.

1. The first leader in the Reconquest of Spain was (Franco / **Pelayo** / el Cid).

2. The Spanish-American War took place in (**1898** / 1936 / 1516).

3. Felipe II was the son of (Fernando and Isabel / el Cid / **Carlos V**).

4. The Spanish language is derived from (Portuguese / **Latin** / Basque).

5. The Moors were driven out of Spain in (1588 / 1808 / **1492**).

6. The Romans ruled Spain for (two / **six** / eight) centuries.

7. Many Spanish words that begin with **al-** are of (Greek / **Arabic** / Portuguese) origin.

8. Prince Juan Carlos de Borbón was proclaimed King in (1898 / **1975** / 1982).

9. Columbus's voyages were financed by (Carlos V / **Fernando and Isabel** / Felipe II).

10. Spain's national hero is (don Pelayo / **el Cid** / Franco).

EXERCISE D

a. When did ...

1. the Moors invade Spain? _711 AD_

2. don Pelayo win at Covadonga? _718 AD_

3. Fernando and Isabel recapture Granada? _1492_

4. the Spaniards rebel against Napoleon? _1808 - 1814_

5. England defeat the "Invincible Armada"? _1588_

b. Who ...

6. captured Valencia from the Moors? _El Cid_

7. financed Columbus's voyages? _Fernando + Isabel_

8. was the father of Felipe II? _Carlos V_

9. built the Alhambra? _Moors_

10. overthrew the Spanish republic in 1939? _Franco_

Chapter 34
Important and Interesting Places in Spain

1. Madrid is Spain's capital and largest city (population: approximately 4,500,000). In Madrid and its vicinity there are many interesting places to visit, among which are:
   a. **el Prado,** a world-famous art museum.
   b. the Royal Palace **(el Palacio Real),** one of the most luxurious palaces in Europe, built in the eighteenth century. The Spanish royal family lived there until King Alfonso XIII was forced to leave the country. The palace is now a museum.
   c. **la Puerta del Sol,** the central plaza of Madrid. Streets originate from it in all directions, to all parts of the city.
   d. **el Escorial,** a huge building combining a palace, art museum, monastery, library, and burial place for Spanish kings. It was built between 1563 and 1584 by order of Felipe II.
   e. the Valley of the Fallen **(el Valle de los Caídos),** an enormous monument in memory of the soldiers who died in the Spanish Civil War (1936–1939).

2. **Barcelona,** the principal city of **Catalonia** and the second largest city in Spain (population about 4,000,000). Spain's main industrial city, it has been an important seaport for more than two thousand years. It contains unique works by master architect Gaudí. Many Spanish books are printed in Barcelona.

3. Seville **(Sevilla),** in Andalusia **(Andalucía),** located on the bank of the Guadalquivir River. Seville is one of Spain's most picturesque cities for its gypsies and flamenco dancing.
   a. the Cathedral of Seville **(la Catedral de Sevilla),** the largest in Spain, and one of the largest in the world. Some historians believe it contains the tomb of Columbus.
   b. **la Giralda,** the tower of the Cathedral of Seville, an admirable example of Moorish architecture.

4. **Valencia,** located in a rich agricultural region on the Mediterranean coast called the "garden of Spain," is a leading export center for oranges and rice.

5. **Granada,** a picturesque city in the south; the last Moorish possession in Spain, recaptured by the Christians in 1492. The famous Moorish palace, the **Alhambra,** attracts visitors from everywhere.

6. **Toledo,** a famous medieval city on the **Tajo River** (near Madrid). It is important in metalworking, especially fine steel and exquisite jewelry. Toledo was the home of the famous painter **El Greco,** and contains many of his works.

7. Salamanca, site of the **University of Salamanca,** the oldest in Spain, and among the oldest and best universities of Europe. It was established in the thirteenth century.

8. Cordova **(Córdoba),** on the **Guadalquivir River.** During the tenth and eleventh centuries it was the Moorish capital of Spain and one of the most important cultural centers of Europe. The city's main tourist attraction is the Mosque **(la Mezquita**—a Muslim place of worship), built in the eighth century and converted into a Roman Catholic cathedral in 1238.

9. **Burgos,** home of **el Cid,** Spain's national hero. **The Cathedral of Burgos,** one of the finest in Europe, contains his tomb.

10. **Bilbao,** a seaport in the north, where some of Spain's most important mines and steelyards are located.

11. **Segovia,** an ancient city in central Spain. A Roman aqueduct known as the Bridge **(el Puente),** built under the Roman Emperor Trajan (A.D. 53–117), is still in use today.

EXERCISE A

If the statement is true, write *Sí;* if it's false, correct it by replacing the word(s) in boldface. Write the word(s) in the space provided.

X Barcelona is an important seaport on the **Atlantic Ocean.** _Mediterranean_

2. The Royal Palace is in **Segovia.** _Madrid_

3. The largest cathedral in Spain is located in **Seville.**   *Sí*

4. Valencia and Bilbao are important **regions** of Spain.   *ports*

5. The Escorial was built by order of **Carlos V.**   *Felipe II*

6. **Madrid** is located on the Guadalquivir River.   *Cordova*

7. **Granada** was the last Moorish possession in Spain.   *Sí*

8. Toledo was the home of **El Greco.**   *Sí*

9. Cordova was an important cultural center in the **nineteenth** century.   *10th & 11th*

10. The aqueduct of Segovia is an important **Moorish** monument.   *Roman*

EXERCISE B

Select the word or expression that correctly completes each sentence.

1. A burial place for kings is located in the (Cathedral of Burgos / Valley of the Fallen / Escorial).

2. The Alhambra is located in (Granada / Bilbao / Salamanca).

3. An important mining area of Spain is located near (Segovia / Madrid / Bilbao).

4. The Valley of the Fallen is near (Barcelona / Madrid / Burgos).

5. Cordova is famous for its (castle / mosque / university).

6. The oldest university in Spain is located in (Toledo / Madrid / Salamanca).

7. The second largest city of Spain is (Sevilla / Barcelona / Madrid).

8. Valencia is famous for its (minerals / wines / oranges).

9. The (Prado / Giralda / Alhambra) is a famous art museum in Madrid.

10. The population of Madrid is about (2,000,000 / 4,500,000 / 37,000,000).

EXERCISE C

Match the words in column A with their related words in column B. Write the letter in the space provided.

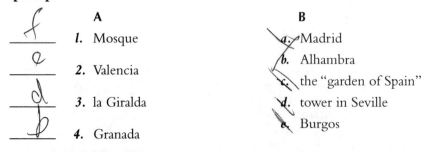

	A		B
_f_	**1.** Mosque	**a.**	Madrid
_c_	**2.** Valencia	**b.**	Alhambra
_d_	**3.** la Giralda	**c.**	the "garden of Spain"
_b_	**4.** Granada	**d.**	tower in Seville
		e.	Burgos

_____ *a* **5.** Puerta del Sol

_____ *e* **6.** el Cid

_____ *i* **7.** Toledo

_____ *j* **8.** books

_____ *h* **9.** Salamanca

_____ *g* **10.** Bilbao

f. Muslim temple
g. steel-manufacturing center
h. university
i. medieval city
j. Barcelona

EXERCISE D

Complete the following statements.

1. The cities of Seville and Cordova are located on the ___Guadalquivir___ River.

2. ___Granada___ is Spain's most picturesque city.

3. ___Valley of the Fallen___ is a monument to the soldiers who died in the Spanish Civil War.

4. The central plaza of Madrid is called ___La Puerta del Sol___

5. ___Cordova___ was one of the most important cultural centers of Europe during the tenth century.

6. Many Spanish kings are buried in ___el Escorial___ .

7. ___Madrid___ is the capital of Spain.

8. A very important industrial city of Spain is ___Barcelona X Bilbao___

9. Toledo is located on the ___Tajo___ River.

10. Granada was recaptured from the Moors in the year ___1492___ .

Chapter 35
People and Customs of Spain

FRANCIA
PORTUGAL
ESPAÑA
Barcelona
Madrid
Islas Baleares
ITALIA
Sevilla

NAMES

1. **Family Names**
   a. Spaniards have at least two family names (the father's family name followed by the mother's).

   Pedro Ortega Gómez

   This name would be filed under **Ortega** because the father's name is considered more important.
   b. When a woman marries, she keeps her family name and takes on her husband's preceded by **de.** Thus, **Pedro's** wife, whose maiden name was **Elena López Suárez,** would be:

   Elena López de Ortega

   NOTE: The mother's family names of both **Pedro** and **Elena** are omitted.
2. **Saint's Day (el Día del Santo).** Most people in Spain (and in the rest of the Spanish-speaking countries) have as their given name, the name of a saint. They generally celebrate their saint's day instead of, or in addition to, their birthday.

CUSTOMS

1. **La tertulia** is an informal social gathering for meeting and chatting with friends. It often extends well past midnight.
2. **La siesta** is an afternoon nap or rest following the noon meal. Many stores are closed at this time.
3. The lottery **(la lotería)** is a government-controlled game whose earnings are used to finance many services, such as public assistance for orphans or widows.

RELIGIOUS HOLIDAYS

1. Christmas **(Navidad)** is one of the most important religious holidays in Spain. Christmas trees are not used. Instead, each home has its nativity scene **(nacimiento),** clay figures representing the scene of the birth of Christ. On Christmas Eve **(Nochebuena)** people attend a midnight mass **(Misa del Gallo).** Children receive gifts on January 6, the Day of the Three Wise Men **(Día de los Reyes Magos).** The **Reyes Magos** play the same role in Spanish life as Santa Claus.

2. Easter **(Pascua Florida)** is celebrated throughout Spain and Spanish America. Holy Week **(Semana Santa)** is observed the week before, with solemn ceremonies. The Holy Week celebration in Seville is world-famous.
3. Carnival **(Carnaval)** is a celebration that occurs during the last three days before Lent.
4. All Souls' Day **(Día de los Muertos)** is observed solemnly on November 2. People visit the graves of dead relatives and friends.

NATIONAL HOLIDAYS

1. May 2 commemorates the uprising of the Spaniards against French rule (1808). It is Spain's national holiday.
2. October 12 corresponds to Columbus Day. It is called **El Día de la Hispanidad** or **El Día de la Raza.**

TYPICAL FOODS AND BEVERAGES

1. **Arroz con pollo,** yellow rice with chicken, popular in Spain and Spanish America.
2. **Paella,** yellow rice with chicken and seafood.
3. **Cocido,** beef stew that is popular among farmers and laborers.
4. **Chocolate,** thick hot cocoa, usually served at breakfast with **churros,** a kind of cruller.
5. **Horchata,** cold drink made with crushed toasted almonds or sesame seeds, water, and sugar.

REGIONAL DANCES

1. Andalusia: bolero, fandango, flamenco. Generally accompanied by a guitar.
2. Aragon: jota.
3. Catalonia: sardana.

PICTURESQUE CHARACTERS

1. **The tuna** is a group of strolling musicians, usually university students, who play romantic and lively music. This is a tradition that exists since the sixteenth century.
2. **The Gypsies (los gitanos)** are found mostly in the south, especially around Seville and Granada. It is believed that they came from northern India. Their language is called *Romani*.

EXERCISE A

Match the words in column A with their related words in column B. Write the letter in the space provided.

	A		B
d	1. Saint's Day	a.	Aragon
e	2. Carnival	b.	afternoon nap
i	3. flamenco	c.	beverage
h	4. Holy Week	d.	birthday celebration
b	5. siesta	e.	Lent
a	6. jota	f.	Santa Claus
f	7. Three Wise Men	g.	midnight mass
j	8. tertulia	h.	Easter
c	9. horchata	i.	Andalucia
g	10. Christmas	j.	social gathering

EXERCISE B

Select the word or expression that correctly completes each statement.

1. A popular Spanish dish is (sardana / paella / tertulia).

2. Spaniards usually have (horchata / tea / chocolate) at breakfast.

3. The lottery is managed (by the church / privately / by the government).

4. Instead of Christmas trees, Spaniards usually have a (basket / bull / nativity scene) set up in the house.

5. The jota is a Spanish (dance / musical instrument / dish).

6. The Spanish national holiday is (May 2 / October 12 / November 2).

7. A gathering for the purpose of talking is a (nacimiento / tertulia / cocido).

8. The city of (Seville / Valencia / Granada) is famous for its Holy Week celebration.

9. Spanish children receive their Christmas gifts on (December 16 / December 25 / January 6).

10. Spaniards visit the cemeteries on (their saint's day / All Soul's Day / Christmas Day).

EXERCISE C

Complete the following sentences.

1. The *fandango* is a regional dance of _Andalusia_ .

2. Juan López Serrano marries Dolores Moreno Ortega. The wife's full name is now

   Dolores Moreno ~~de Serrano~~ López *(Ortega)*

3. Juan and Dolores have a son, Carlos, whose full name is _Carlos ~~López~~ Moreno Serrano_ .

4. Christmas eve is called _Nochebuena_ in Spain.

5. A group of university students who sing in the streets is called a _the tuna_ .

6. A typical dish of Spain is _Cocido_ .

7. A _nacimiento_ is a Nativity scene.

8. The uprising against the French took place on _May 2_ , 1808.

9. A regional dance of Catalonia is the _sardana_ .

10. _El Día de la Hispanidad_ is celebrated on October 12.

EXERCISE D

Define each of the following.

1. arroz con pollo _yellow rice w/ chicken_

~~2.~~ dos de mayo _____

3. Reyes Magos _Santa Claus_

4. cocido _beef stew popular among farmers + laborers_

5. nacimiento _Nativity Scene_

6. Día de la Raza _Columbus Day_

7. tertulia _informal social gathering for meeting + chatting w/ friends_

8. misa del gallo _midnight mass for Christmas_

9. Nochebuena _Christmas Eve_

10. gitano ___Gypsies fand mostly in the south___

11. Día del Santo ___Saints Day___ ~~~~

12. siesta ___afternoon nap ~~after~~ midday meal___

13. churros ___kind of cruller___

14. la tuna ___group of strolling musicians___

15. horchata ___cold drink made w/ crushed toasted almonds or sesame seeds, water, + sugar___

Chapter 36
Spanish Literature, Science, and the Arts

WRITERS

1. **Middle Ages**
   a. **Juan Ruiz,** known as **Arcipreste de Hita** (1283–1351), *El libro de buen amor.*
   b. **Fernando de Rojas** (?–1541), *La Celestina* (or *Comedia de Calisto y Melibea*) 1499.
   c. Anonymous, *Lazarillo de Tormes* (1554).
2. **Golden Age (Siglo de Oro [1560–1680])**
   a. **Miguel de Cervantes** (1547–1616), one of Spain's greatest novelists, wrote the world-famous novel *El ingenioso hidalgo don Quijote de la Mancha.*
   b. **Lope de Vega** (1562–1635), one of Spain's leading dramatists, wrote hundreds of plays.
   c. **Pedro Calderón de la Barca** (1600–1681), the last great figure of the Golden Age, wrote the famous play *La vida es sueño (Life Is a Dream).*
3. **Nineteenth and Twentieth Centuries**
   a. **Benito Pérez Galdós** (1843–1920), another great Spanish novelist, among the most famous of the nineteenth century. He wrote *Marianela.*
   b. **Vicente Blasco Ibáñez** (1867–1928), famous novelist who wrote *The Four Horsemen of the Apocalypse (Los cuatro jinetes del Apocalipsis)* and *Blood and Sand (Sangre y arena).* He also wrote many novels about Valencia, of which the most famous is *La barraca.*
   c. **Jacinto Benavente** (1866–1954), famous dramatist, winner of the Nobel Prize for Literature in 1922.
   d. **Juan Ramón Jiménez** (1881–1958), famous poet, winner of the Nobel Prize for Literature in 1956.
   e. **Federico García Lorca** (1898–1936), famous poet and dramatist whose works deal with folkloric and traditional themes. His plays *Bodas de sangre* and *La casa de Bernarda Alba* continue to be presented in the theater. He died tragically during the Spanish Civil War.
   f. **Vicente Aleixandre** (1898–1984), renowned essayist and poet, winner of the Nobel Prize for Literature in 1977.
   g. **Camilio José Cela** (1916–   ), famous novelist of contemporary Spain, winner of the Nobel Prize for Literature in 1989.
   h. **Carmen Laforet** (1921–   ), famous contemporary novelist whose novel *Nada* deals with life in Spain immediately after the Civil War.
   i. **Ana María Matute** (1926–   ), famous contemporary novelist whose works have received numerous national prizes.

SCIENTISTS

1. **Santiago Ramón y Cajal** (1852–1934), winner of the Nobel Prize for Medicine in 1906, for his studies on the structure of the nervous system.
2. **Juan de la Cierva** (1895–1936), aeronautical engineer who invented the autogyro, the forerunner of the helicopter, in 1923.
3. **Severo Ochoa** (1905–   ), winner of the Nobel Prize for Medicine (1959) for his studies on heredity.

PAINTERS

1. **Doménico Theotocopulos,** known as **El Greco** (1541–1614), sixteenth century Greek painter who settled in Toledo, where many of his works can still be found. Most of his paintings deal with religious themes.
2. **Diego Velázquez** (1599–1660), considered by many to be one of Spain's greatest painters. He was court painter to Felipe IV (seventeenth century). His most famous work is *Las meninas.*
3. **Francisco Goya** (1746–1828), among the greatest Spanish painters of the eighteenth and nineteenth centuries. His work attacks the social and political decay of the period.
4. **Pablo Picasso** (1881–1973), one of the outstanding painters of the twentieth century, and the founder of cubism, a style of painting in which figures are deconstructed into geometric forms.
5. **Joan Miró** (1893–1983), one of the greatest painters of abstract art of the twentieth century.
6. **Salvador Dalí** (1904–1989), an outstanding twentieth-century painter of surrealist art.

COMPOSERS AND MUSICIANS

1. **Isaac Albéniz** (1860–1909), composer of music for the piano.

2. **Manuel de Falla** (1876–1946), one of Spain's greatest composers and foremost representatives of modern Spanish music.
3. **José Iturbi** (1896–1980), famous pianist, composer, and conductor.
4. **Andrés Segovia** (1893–1987), among the most famous guitarists, gave many concerts all over the world.
5. **Pablo Casals** (1876–1973), cellist of international fame.
6. **Plácido Domingo** (1941–   ), **José Carreras** (1947–   ), **Monserrat Caballé** (1933–   ) are opera singers of international fame.
7. **Julio Iglesias** (1943–   ), famous singer of popular music.

EXERCISE A

If the statement is true, write *Sí;* if it's false, correct it by replacing the word(s) in boldface. Write the word(s) in the space provided.

1. Andrés Segovia was a world-famous **pianist**.   *guitarists*

2. Pablo Casals was one of Spain's greatest **composers**.   *cellist*

3. **Blasco Ibáñez** wrote *The Four Horsemen of the Apocalypse*.   *Sí*

4. Lope de Vega was one of Spain's leading **poets**.   *dramatists*

5. **Ramón y Cajal** invented the autogyro.   *Juan de la Cierva*

6. **Cervantes** was one of the greatest Spanish novelists.   *Sí*

7. José Carreras is a famous **painter**.   *opera singers*

8. **Velázquez** was the founder of cubism.   *Picasso*

9. **Carmen Laforet** wrote plays about Spanish folklore.   *Lorca*

10. **Dalí** won a Nobel Prize for Literature.   *Benavente*

EXERCISE B

Match the names in column A with their related words in column B. Write the letter in the space provided.

	A		B
g	1. Plácido Domingo	*a.*	twentieth-century dramatist
e	2. Calderón	*b.*	religious paintings
f	3. Ramón y Cajal	*c.*	*Las meninas*
b	4. Albéniz	*d.*	*El ingenioso hidalgo don Quijote de la Mancha*
a	5. Jacinto Benavente	*e.*	Golden Age dramatist
h	6. Blasco Ibáñez	*f.*	studies of the nervous system
		g.	tenor

_____ b   **7.** El Greco

_____ d   **8.** Miguel de Cervantes

_____ c   **9.** Diego Velázquez

_____ i   **10.** Pablo Picasso

h. novels about Valencia

i. cubism

j. composer

EXERCISE C

Select the word or expression that correctly completes each statement.

1. The Golden Age occurred during the (eighteenth and nineteenth / nineteenth and twentieth / sixteenth and seventeenth) centuries.

2. One of the most famous Spanish composers is (Pablo Picasso / Manuel de Falla / Pablo Casals).

3. A Spanish novelist who won the Nobel Prize was (Ana María Matute / Camilo José Cela / Federico García Lorca).

4. The last great dramatist of the Golden Age was (Velázquez / Calderón / Cervantes).

5. The autogyro was invented by (Juan de la Cierva / Severo Ochoa / Juan Miró).

6. Juan Ramón Jiménez was a famous (poet / musician / painter).

7. (Lope de Vega / Plácido Domingo / Andrés Segovia) was a great Spanish guitarist.

8. One of the greatest painters of eighteenth-century Spain was (Francisco Goya / Diego Velázquez /Salvador Dalí).

9. One of the greatest novelists of Spain was (Miguel de Cervantes / José Carreras /Vicente Aleixandre).

10. Severo Ochoa received a Nobel Prize in the field of (literature / medicine / economics).

EXERCISE D

Complete the following statements.

1. A sixteenth-century painter who lived in Toledo was ___Greco___ .

2. An author who wrote about Spain after the Civil War is ___Laforet___ .

3. ___Iturbi___ was a famous pianist and orchestra leader.

4. *Sangre y arena* was written by ___Ibáñez___ .

5. ___Velázquez___ was court painter to Felipe IV.

6. ___Barca___ is the author of *La vida es sueño*.

7. _____Galdos_____ was among the most famous novelists of the nineteenth century.

8. _____Aleixandre_____ won the Nobel Prize for Literature in 1977.

9. _____Miro_____ earned his fame as a painter of abstract art.

10. _____Monsserat Caballe_____ is a famous Spanish soprano.

EXERCISE E

a. Who wrote ...

1. *El ingenioso hidalgo don Quijote de la Mancha?* _____Cervantes_____

2. *La Casa de Bernarda Alba?* _____Lorca_____

3. *Nada?* _____Laforet_____

4. about Valencia? _____Ibáñez_____

5. hundreds of plays? _____Vega_____

b. Who was ...

6. Joan Miró? _____artist_____

7. one of Spain's greatest composers? _____Falla_____

8. Santiago Ramón y Cajal? _____scientists_____

9. the father of cubism? _____Picasso_____

10. Francisco Goya? _____painter_____

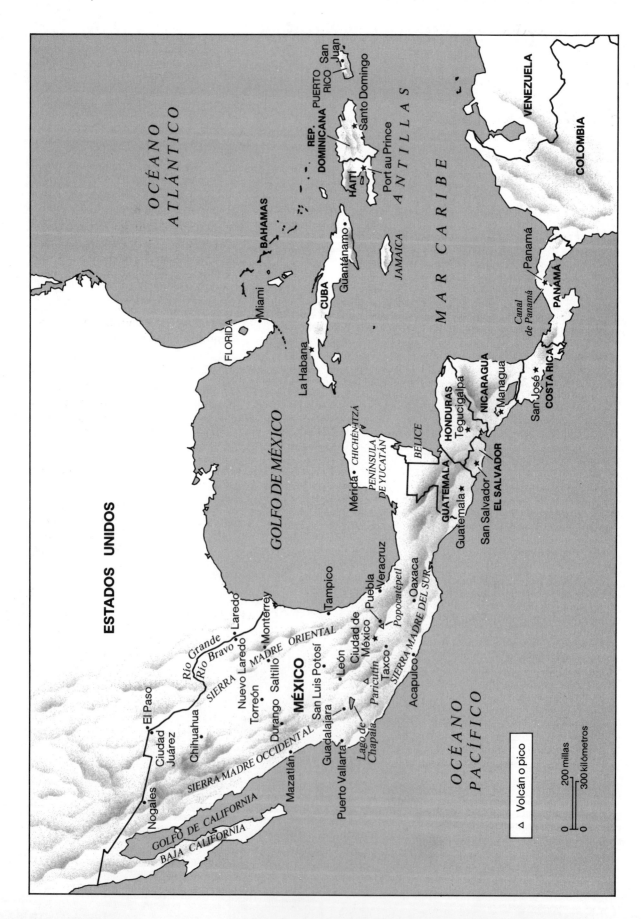

Chapter 37
Geography of Spanish America

COUNTRIES AND THEIR CAPITALS

1. In North America

   Mexico (capital: **Federal District of Mexico**) is directly south of the United States of America, bordering the states of Texas, New Mexico, Arizona, and California; our nearest Spanish-American neighbor. Land of the **Aztecs** and the **Mayas,** two of the most advanced Native-American civilizations.

2. In Central America
   a. **Costa Rica** (capital: **San José**) is one of the most progressive countries in Central America. It has good environmental laws and no army.
   b. **El Salvador** (capital: **San Salvador**) is the smallest country in Central America.
   c. **Guatemala** (capital: **Guatemala City**) is the main producer of *chicle,* used in the manufacture of chewing gum. Guatemala was the center of the old Mayan empire.
   d. **Honduras** (capital: **Tegucigalpa**) has important mineral and timber resources. Exports mainly bananas and coffee.
   e. **Nicaragua** (capital: **Managua**) is the largest country in Central America. Exports cotton and textiles, coffee and sugarcane.
   f. **Panama** (capital: **Panama City**) is an isthmus joining Central and South America. The Panama Canal is located there.

3. In the Caribbean (Antilles)
   a. **Cuba** (capital: **Havana**) is the largest island of the Caribbean.
   b. **Dominican Republic** (capital: **Santo Domingo**), together with French-speaking Haiti, forms the island of Hispaniola.
   c. **Puerto Rico** (capital: **San Juan**) is a commonwealth of the United States. The smallest of the Greater Antilles, it's also called **Borinquen,** its native name.

4. In South America
   a. **Argentina** (capital: **Buenos Aires**) is the largest Spanish-speaking country in South America.
   b. **Bolivia** (two capitals: **La Paz** and **Sucre**) is the only country in South America without an outlet to the sea. Although Sucre is the official capital, La Paz is the actual seat of government.
   c. **Colombia** (capital: **Bogotá**) is the only South American country with seacoasts on both the Atlantic and Pacific Oceans.
   d. **Chile** (capital: **Santiago**) is the longest and narrowest country in South America.
   e. **Ecuador** (capital: **Quito**) is crossed north to south by two parallel ranges of very high volcanic peaks, part of the Andes Mountains. The **Galápagos Islands** belong to Ecuador.
   f. **Paraguay** (capital: **Asunción**) has a large Native-American population. Paraguay produces soybeans and packed meats; also produces **yerba mate,** a popular tea used widely in Argentina.
   g. **Peru** (capital: Lima) The land of the Incas, a Native-American civilization that flourished centuries before the arrival of Europeans in America.
   h. **Uruguay** (capital: Montevideo) is the smallest Spanish-speaking country in South America.
   i. **Venezuela** (capital: Caracas) is the richest oil-producing country in South America; is also the birthplace of Simón Bolívar, "The Liberator."

   NOTE: Some countries are not mentioned here because their cultural heritage is not Spanish but French (Haiti, Martinique, Guadeloupe, French Guiana); English (Belize, Jamaica, Trinidad and Tobago, Guyana), Portuguese (Brazil); or Dutch (Surinam).

GEOGRAPHIC FEATURES

1. Mountain Ranges
   a. **The Andes** extend the entire length of South America along the west coast. There are many high peaks; the highest, **Aconcagua,** has an altitude of nearly 23,000 feet (more than four miles), and it is the highest peak in the Western Hemisphere. There are many other peaks nearly as high.
   b. **The Sierra Madre** (Mexico) consists of two parallel mountain chains, the **Sierra Madre Oriental** (Eastern) and the **Sierra Madre Occidental** (Western), with a great plateau between them.

2. Principal Rivers
   a. The **Orinoco** (Venezuela) is the longest single river in Spanish America. (The

MAR CARIBE

OCÉANO
ATLÁNTICO

Barranquilla
Cartagena

La Guaira
★ Caracas

LLANOS

Río Orinoco

Medellín

VENEZUELA

GUYANA

GUAYANA
FRANCESA

SURINAM

★ Bogotá

Río Magdalena

COLOMBIA

Ecuador

Quito ★
△ Cotopaxi
△ Chimborazo

• Guayaquil

ECUADOR

Río Amazonas

LOS ANDES

PERÚ
Callao
Lima

BRASIL

Cuzco

Lago
Titicaca

★ La Paz

BOLIVIA

★ Brasilia

LOS ANDES

Desierto de Atacama

GRAN CHACO

Río Paraguay

Río de Janeiro

OCÉANO
PACÍFICO

PARAGUAY
Asunción ★

Iguazú

Tucumán

Río Paraná

CHILE

Córdoba

Aconcagua

Viña del Mar
Valparaíso

Rosario

URUGUAY

Santiago

Buenos Aires ★

★ Montevideo

OCÉANO
ATLÁNTICO

Islas Juan
Fernández
(Ch.)

Río de la Plata

PAMPAS

ARGENTINA

PATAGONIA

0   300 millas
0   500 kilómetros

△ Volcán o pico

Estrecho
De
Magallanes

Islas Malvinas
(Falkland Islands)
(Ing.)

Tierra del Fuego

Cabo de
Hornos

Amazon River, which is more than twice as long, is in Brazil.)

b. The **Río de la Plata** (between Uruguay and Argentina) has the capitals of both countries, Argentina and Uruguay, on its banks.

c. The **Paraná–Paraguay** System is formed by the Paraná and Paraguay Rivers. It connects with the **Río de la Plata,** to form the chief water outlet from the interior regions to the sea.

d. The **Magdalena** (Colombia) crosses the whole country from south to north; it is an important means of transportation.

3. **Climate**

a. **Argentina, Uruguay, Paraguay,** and **Chile** are in the South Temperate Zone. Northern Mexico is in the North Temperate Zone. Southern Mexico and the rest of Spanish America lie in the tropics (Torrid Zone).

b. Most cities located in the tropics, except the ones at high altitudes, are very warm.

ANIMAL LIFE

1. Birds

a. The **condor** is a carrion-eating bird from the Andes; probably the largest among flying birds.

b. The **quetzal** is a brilliantly colored bird of Central America. It is the national emblem of Guatemala, and gives name to its monetary unit.

2. **Wool-Bearing Animals**

a. **Alpaca, guanaco, llama, vicuña** (in the Andes).

b. **Sheep** (mainly in Argentina and Uruguay).

3. **Beasts of Burden**

a. The **burro** is the most common beast of burden in Spanish America.

b. The **llama** is the main beast of burden of the Andean countries (Peru, Ecuador, Bolivia).

IMPORTANT PRODUCTS

1. Some of the products that Spanish America gives to the world are potatoes, corn, tomatoes, chocolate, vanilla, pineapples, peanuts, pecans, and cashew nuts.

2.
AGRICULTURAL PRODUCTS	MAIN PRODUCERS
apples and peaches	Chile
bananas	most Central-American countries
beef	Argentina, Uruguay
cacao bean (used in manufacturing chocolate)	Ecuador, Venezuela
coffee	Colombia, Venezuela
sugar	Cuba, Dominican Republic
corozo nuts (used in manufacturing buttons)	Ecuador
tobacco	Cuba
wheat	Argentina, Uruguay

3.
MINING AND CHEMICAL INDUSTRIES	MAIN PRODUCERS
copper	Chile, Peru
emeralds	Colombia
nitrates (used for fertilizer)	Chile
petroleum	Venezuela, Mexico
platinum	Colombia
silver	Mexico, Peru
tin	Bolivia

EXERCISE A

If the statement is true, write *Sí*; if it's false, correct it by replacing the word(s) in boldface. Write the correct word(s) in the space provided.

1. Two important products of Venezuela are **petroleum** and **coffee.**   *Sí*

2. Lima is the capital of **Argentina.**   ~~~~ Perú

3. **Santiago** is the capital of Colombia.   Bogotá

4. Costa Rica and Honduras produce many **bananas.**   Sí

5. The Parana River flows into the **Pacific Ocean**.   Atlantic

6. Spanish is the language of **six** countries in South America.   9

7. **Montevideo** is the capital of Venezuela.   Caracus

8. The condor lives in the **Andes**.   Sí

9. Mexico and Peru produce **emeralds**.   silver

10. There are **six** countries in Central America.   Sí

EXERCISE B

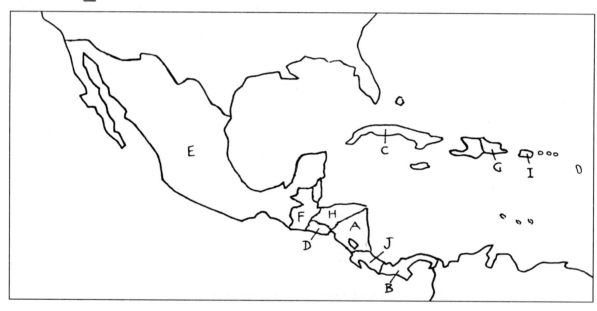

In the map above, identify each of the following countries by writing its corresponding letter in the space provided.

B   1. Panama   F   6. Guatemala

I   2. Puerto Rico   E   7. Mexico

J   3. Costa Rica   C   8. Cuba

H   4. Honduras   A   9. Nicaragua

D   5. El Salvador   G   10. Dominican Republic

EXERCISE C

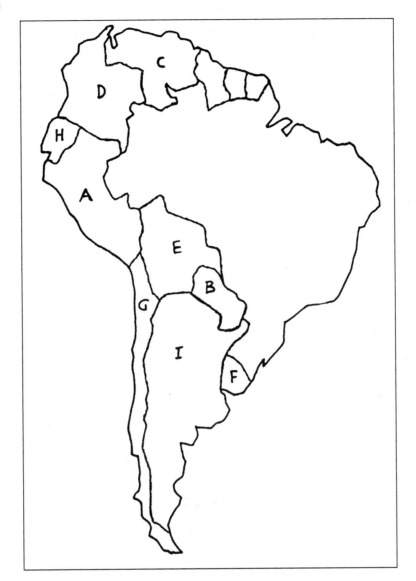

In the map above, identify each of the following countries by writing its corresponding letter in the space provided.

E *1.* Bolivia

I *2.* Argentina

G *3.* Chile

H *4.* Ecuador

F *5.* Uruguay

D *6.* Colombia

A *7.* Peru

B *8.* Paraguay

C *9.* Venezuela

EXERCISE D

Match the words in column A with their corresponding definitions in column B. Write the letter for the definition in the space provided.

	A		B
_e_	1. Sierra Madre	a.	river in Colombia
_g_	2. corozo nuts	b.	capital of Nicaragua
_j_	3. yerba mate	c.	used to manufacture chocolate
_f_	4. Aconcagua	d.	fabric borne by the alpaca
_i_	5. tin	e.	mountains in Mexico
_a_	6. Magdalena	f.	highest peak in the Western Hemisphere
_b_	7. Managua	g.	used to manufacture buttons
_c_	8. cacao	h.	bird of the Andes
_d_	9. wool	i.	element found in Bolivia
_h_	10. condor	j.	popular tea from Paraguay

EXERCISE E

Write the word that is needed to complete each statement.

1. The longest river in Venezuela is the _Orinoco_.

2. The Andes are situated in _on the west coast of South America_.

3. The quetzal is found mainly in _Central America_.

4. The main beast of burden in the Andes is the _llama_.

5. In Chile, Argentina, and Uruguay it is cold in the months of _June, July, August._

6. The capital of Costa Rica is _San José_.

7. The only country in South America without an outlet to the ocean is _Bolivia_.

8. The country crossed north to south by two parallel ranges of peaks is _~~Mexico~~ Ecuador_.

9. The richest oil-producing country of South America is _Venezuela_.

10. The ingredient used to manufacture chocolate is _cacao_.

Chapter 38
Famous Names in Spanish America

NATIONAL HEROES OF SPANISH AMERICA

1. **Simón Bolívar** (1783–1830) was one of the main figures in the struggle for South American independence from Spain. Called **El Libertador** (the Liberator), he won independence for the northern part of South America. **Bolivia** was named in his honor.
2. **José de San Martín** (1778–1850) was an Argentinian general who won independence for the southern part of South America, including Argentina and Chile.
3. **Bernardo O'Higgins** (1778–1842) was a Chilean general who helped San Martín in the liberation of Chile. O'Higgins became the first president of Chile.
4. **Antonio José de Sucre** (1795–1830) defeated the Spanish army in the battle of Ayacucho (Peru), the last battle for South American Independence (1824).
5. **Miguel Hidalgo** (1753–1811) was a Mexican priest and patriot who began the struggle for Mexican independence (1810).
6. **Benito Juárez** (1806–1872) fought against Archduke Maximilian, Emperor of Mexico. Juárez was later called the "Abraham Lincoln of Mexico."
7. **José Martí** (1853–1895) was a famous Cuban poet and patriot who died fighting for Cuban independence from Spain.

WRITERS

1. **Andrés Bello** (1781–1865) was a Chilean poet, critic, and a leading intellectual of Spanish America. He wrote *Gramática de la lengua castellana*.
2. **Domingo Faustino Sarmiento** (1811–1888) was an Argentinian educator and statesman, known as the "Schoolmaster President." He wrote *Facundo*, which deals with the life of a **gaucho** (Argentinian cowboy) leader.
3. **Ricardo Palma** (1833–1919) wrote *Tradiciones peruanas*, a collection of stories about Peru during colonial times.

4. **Rubén Darío** (1867–1916) was born in Nicaragua. One of the greatest poets of Spanish America, he helped create a new poetic style called "modernism."
5. **Mariano Azuela** (1873–1952) was a Mexican novelist who wrote *Los de abajo*, a novel about the Mexican Revolution of 1910–1920.
6. **Gabriela Mistral** (1889–1957) was a Chilean poet who won the Nobel Prize for Literature in 1945.
7. **Rómulo Gallegos** (1884–1969) was a Venezuelan novelist and statesman who wrote *Doña Bárbara*, a novel about life on the plains of Venezuela.
8. **Miguel Ángel Asturias** (1899–1974) was a Guatemalan novelist whose books describe the suffering caused by the local dictator and by the big "Yanqui" companies. He received the Nobel Prize for Literature in 1967.
9. **Pablo Neruda** (1904–1973) was a Chilean poet and diplomat who received the Nobel Prize for Literature in 1971.
10. **Gabriel García Márquez** (1928–   ) is a Colombian novelist who wrote *Cien años de soledad*, the history of an imaginary town in Colombia. He received the Nobel Prize for Literature in 1982.
11. **Octavio Paz** (1914–   ) is a Mexican poet and essayist who received the Nobel Prize for Literature in 1990.

PAINTERS

1. **Diego Rivera, José Clemente Orozco,** and **David Alfaro Siqueiros** are the three most important painters of Mexico. All three specialized in mural painting, and all treated political and social topics.
2. **Cesáreo Bernaldo de Quirós,** of Argentina, painted scenes of gaucho life.

COMPOSERS AND MUSICIANS

1. **Carlos Chávez** was a famous Mexican composer and orchestra conductor.
2. **Claudio Arrau** was a famous Chilean pianist.

EXERCISE A

Identify each of the following names by writing the corresponding letter in the space provided.

a. patriot   b. writer   c. painter   d. composer–musician

_____ **1.** Mariano Azuela	_____ **9.** Diego Rivera
_____ **2.** Andrés Bello	_____ **10.** Bernardo O'Higgins
_____ **3.** Rubén Darío	_____ **11.** Carlos Chávez
_____ **4.** Rómulo Gallegos	_____ **12.** Claudio Arrau
_____ **5.** Antonio José de Sucre	_____ **13.** Cesáreo Bernaldo de Quirós
_____ **6.** Benito Juárez	_____ **14.** Miguel Ángel Asturias
_____ **7.** Gabriela Mistral	_____ **15.** José Clemente Orozco
_____ **8.** Octavio Paz	

EXERCISE B

Match the names in column A with their related words in column B. Write the letters in the space provided.

A

_____ **1.** Juárez

_____ **2.** Sarmiento

_____ **3.** San Martín

_____ **4.** Martí

_____ **5.** García Márquez

_____ **6.** Darío

_____ **7.** Orozco

_____ **8.** Palma

_____ **9.** Bolívar

_____ **10.** Rivera

B

a. novelist

b. great Spanish-American poet

c. *Tradiciones peruanas*

d. Schoolmaster President

e. murals

f. Mexican patriot

g. painter

h. Argentina's independence

i. Cuban patriot

j. "the Liberator"

EXERCISE C

Select the name, title, or word that correctly completes each statement.

1. (Siqueiros / Neruda / Martí) was the second writer to win a Nobel Prize for Chile.

2. (Juárez / Hidalgo / San Martín) was called the "Abraham Lincoln of Mexico."

3. One of the greatest Spanish-American poets was (Ricardo Palma / Rubén Darío / Rómulo Gallegos).

4. (*Doña Bárbara* / *Facundo* / *Los de abajo*) is a novel about the Mexican Revolution.

5. (Claudio Arrau / Bernardo O'Higgins / Gabriela Mistral) was a famous Chilean pianist.

6. Diego Rivera was a famous (musician / novelist / painter).

7. The last battle in the struggle for South American independence took place at (Lima / Ayacucho / Mexico).

8. (Gabriela Mistral / Jose Martí / Andrés Bello) won the Nobel Prize for Literature.

9. The first president of Chile was (Sucre / O'Higgins / Azuela).

10. Sarmiento wrote (*Facundo* / *Cien años de soledad* / *Tradiciones peruanas*).

EXERCISE D

a. In the space provided, write a name that would fit each definition.

1. Mexican painter   _____

2. Argentine educator   _____

3. Spanish-American novelist   _____

4. Spanish-American poet   _____

5. country named for Bolívar   _____

6. Mexican composer   _____

7. a Mexican Nobel Prize winner   _____

8. a Colombian Nobel Prize winner   _____

b. Tell who wrote the following titles.

9. *Facundo*   _____

10. *Doña Bárbara*   _____

11. *Cien años de soledad*   _____

12. *Tradiciones peruanas*   _____

13. *Los de abajo*   _____

14. *Gramática de la lengua castellana*   _____

EXERCISE E

Complete the following statements.

1. One of Nicaragua's most famous poets is _____ .

2. San Martín won independence for Chile and _____ .

3. The Mexican movement for independence from Spain was begun by _____ .

4. Bernaldo de Quirós painted scenes of the life of the _____ .

5. The Spanish army was defeated by Sucre at the battle of _____ .

6. José Clemente Orozco was a Mexican _____ .

7. José Martí was killed in the war for the independence of _____ .

8. The Chilean general who helped San Martín win independence for Chile is _____ .

INTERESTING PLACES IN MEXICO

1. The Federal District of Mexico (**Distrito Federal de México**) is the capital of Mexico. It was the original capital of the Aztec empire (**Tenochtitlán**). Today it is a large and modern city, the largest Spanish-speaking city in the world.

   a. The Metropolitan Cathedral (**Catedral Metropolitana**) is the largest and oldest cathedral on the North American continent.

   b. The Sun Stone (**La Piedra del Sol**) is an ancient stone inscribed with the Aztec calendar. It is found at one of the most beautiful museums in the world, the Museum of Anthropology (**Museo Antropológico**).

   c. **Chapultepec** is a large, beautiful park with an impressive castle.

   d. The Palace of Fine Arts (**Palacio de Bellas Artes**) contains a beautiful theater and art museum.

   e. **Ciudad Universitaria** is the site of the National University, the oldest university of the North American continent.

   f. **Popocatépetl** and **Ixtaccíhuatl** are picturesque volcanoes overlooking the Federal District of Mexico.

   g. **Xochimilco** is a town near the Federal District famous for its floating gardens.

2. **Taxco** is one of Mexico's most picturesque cities. The Spanish colonial atmosphere is still preserved. Taxco is famous for its silver.

3. **Cozumel** and **Cancún** are fashionable seaside resorts, which are in the region of Mayan temples, such as **Chichén-Itzá, Uxmal,** and **Palenque.**

INTERESTING PLACES IN CENTRAL AND SOUTH AMERICA

1. **Monteverde** (Costa Rica), rain forest.
2. **Tikal** (Guatemala), Mayan ruins.
3. **Buenos Aires** (Argentina), one of the most beautiful capitals in the world.
4. **Lima** (Peru) is the capital and main industrial and cultural center of Peru. The University of San Marcos, the oldest university in South America, is located here.
5. **Cuzco** (Peru) is the ancient capital of the Incas. Nearby are the famous Inca ruins of Machu-Picchu.
6. **Bogotá** is the capital and most important cultural center of Colombia. It has many excellent examples of colonial architecture.
7. **Quito** is the capital and principal textile center of Ecuador. It is located almost at the equator, but it has a pleasant climate due to its high altitude (nearly 10,000 feet).
8. **Lake Titicaca** is located in the Andes Mountains between Bolivia and Peru. It is the highest navigable lake in the world.
9. The Iguazú Falls (**Las Cataratas del Iguazú**) are spectacular waterfalls located between Argentina and Brazil; they are higher than the Niagara Falls.
10. Christ of the Andes (**El Cristo de los Andes**) is a giant statue of Christ located in the Andes Mountains, on the border between Chile and Argentina. It was erected to commemorate the peaceful settlement of a boundary dispute.

EXERCISE A

Match each of the tourist attractions in column A with its description in column B. Write the letter in the space provided.

A	B
_____ 1. Monteverde	*a.* floating gardens
_____ 2. Tenochtitlán	*b.* seaside resort
	c. Mayan ruins in Guatemala
_____ 3. Cristo de los Andes	*d.* statue

_____   **4.** Popocatépetl   **e.** rain forest

_____   **5.** Cuzco   **f.** original Aztec capital

                                                  g. lake

_____   **6.** Iguazú   **h.** volcano in Mexico

                                                  i. Inca capital

_____   **7.** Xochimilco   **j.** waterfall

_____   **8.** Cancún

_____   **9.** Titicaca

_____   **10.** Tikal

EXERCISE B

If the statement is true, write _Sí;_ if it's false, correct it by replacing the word(s) in boldface. Write the word(s) in the space provided.

1. The **Piedra del Sol** is a famous theater in Mexico.   _____

2. The city of **Quito** is located near the equator.   _____

3. The University of San Marcos is located in **Bolivia.**   _____

4. Bogotá is the capital of **Colombia.**   _____

5. Taxco is a picturesque city in **Argentina.**   _____

6. **Chichén-Itzá** is a famous beach in Mexico.   _____

7. **Iguazú Falls** are located between Bolivia and Peru.   _____

8. The largest Spanish-speaking city in the world is **Buenos Aires.**   _____

9. The oldest university in North America is located in **Peru.** _____

10. The ruins of Machu-Picchu are located near **Cuzco.**   _____

EXERCISE C

Complete the following statements.

1. The volcanoes _Popocatépetl_ and _Ixtaccíhuatl_ are located near _____ .

2. The highest navigable lake in the world is _____ .

3. The oldest university in South America is located in _____ .

4. _El Cristo de los Andes_ commemorates the settlement of a dispute between Argentina and

_____ .

5. The famous rain forest in Costa Rica is _____ .

6. The oldest university in Mexico is _____ .

7. Quito has a pleasant climate because of its _____ .

8. Between Brazil and Argentina there is a waterfall called _____ .

9. Cozumel is a seaside resort in _____ .

10. Cuzco was the ancient capital of the _____ .

EXERCISE D

Identify the country where each of the following is located.

1. Palacio de Bellas Artes _____

2. Cuzco _____

3. Cataratas del Iguazú _____

4. Bogotá _____

5. Cancún _____

6. Titicaca _____

7. Buenos Aires _____

8. Piedra del Sol _____

9. Tikal _____

10. Lima _____

PEOPLE OF SPANISH AMERICA

Most Spanish-American countries have several different racial groups. The four principal groups are:

1. **Whites,** descendants of Spanish settlers and other European immigrants (from Italy, Germany, England, Ireland, and the Slavic countries).
2. **Native Americans,** found in great numbers in many Spanish-American countries, especially in Mexico, Central America, Ecuador, Bolivia, Paraguay, and Peru. Most are descendants of the Aztecs, the Mayas, and the Incas.
3. **Blacks,** descendants of Africans who were brought to Spanish America for heavy labor. They are most numerous in the Caribbean.
4. **Mestizos** (people of mixed European and Native-American ancestry), the largest racial group in many Spanish-American countries.
5. **Mulattos** (people of mixed European and African ancestry), most numerous in the Caribbean.

NATIONAL HOLIDAYS

1. **October 12 (El Día de la Raza),** corresponds to Columbus Day and is celebrated throughout the Spanish-speaking world.
2. **September 16,** the Mexican national holiday that commemorates the beginning of the rebellion against Spain (1810).
3. **May 5,** commemorates the Mexican freedom struggle against France and Maximilian, the emperor of Mexico.

RELIGIOUS HOLIDAYS

1. Christmas **(Navidad)** is one of the most important religious holidays in Spanish America.
2. **Las Posadas** (December 16-24) is a Mexican celebration that takes place during the nine days before Christmas. Children break piñatas (colorful figures containing candy, fruit, and toys).
3. Carnival **(Carnaval)** is a celebration that takes place before Lent.
4. Easter **(Pascua Florida)** is celebrated throughout Spanish America.

5. All Souls' Day **(El Día de los Muertos)** is celebrated on November 2 and is observed solemnly throughout the Spanish-speaking world. It is also known as **El Día de los Difuntos.**

PICTURESQUE TYPES

1. **El charro,** the typical Mexican cowboy.
2. **La china poblana,** the female companion of the charro.
3. **El mariachi,** a group of Mexican street singers.
4. **El gaucho,** the cowboy of the Argentine **pampas** (plains).

CLOTHING

In the cities, people generally dress as we do in the United States. However, one often sees traditional dress, especially during holiday celebrations.

1. **El sarape** is a bright colored Mexican blanket (serape). It is worn by men and women, slung over the shoulders.
2. **El poncho** is a cape worn by the Mexicans, gauchos, and other Spanish Americans, as protection from the cold and the rain.
3. **El rebozo** is a shawl worn by Mexican women.
4. **El sombrero de jipijapa** (Panama hat) is a high-quality straw hat made in Ecuador, not in Panama.

SPORTS AND SPECTACLES

1. Soccer **(el fútbol)** is a very popular game in most Spanish-speaking countries.
2. **Jai-alai** is a game that originated in the Basque country of Spain. This sport is popular in Spain, Mexico, Venezuela, Cuba, as well as Connecticut and Florida. Jai-alai is somewhat similar to handball.
   a. **El frontón** is a three-walled court on which jai-alai is played.
   b. **La cesta** is a curved basket strapped to the player's wrist, in which the ball is caught and thrown against the wall.
3. Bullfights **(las corridas de toros)** are prohibited in some Spanish-American countries, but they are still popular in Mexico, Peru, Colombia, and Venezuela.

EXERCISE A

Match the words in column A with their related words in column B. Write the letter in the space provided.

	A		B
f	1. charro	a.	jai-alai
i	2. Día de los Muertos	b.	Lent
e	3. Las Posadas	c.	candy
d	4. gaucho	d.	Argentina
g	5. fútbol	e.	Christmas
a	6. frontón	f.	china poblana
j	7. sarape	g.	soccer
b	8. Carnaval	h.	Columbus Day
c	9. piñata	i.	November 2
h	10. Día de la Raza	j.	blanket

EXERCISE B

If the statement is true, write *Sí;* if it's false, correct it by replacing the word(s) in boldface. Write the correct word(s) in the space provided.

1. The **incas** were the dominant Native American culture in Mexico.   Sí

2. **El Día de los Muertos** is celebrated in Mexico.   Los Posadas

3. The cowboy of Argentina is the **charro**.   gaucho

4. The gauchos wear **ponchos** as protection from the rain.   Sí

5. Panama hats are made in **Panama**.   Ecuador

6. **El Día de la Raza** is celebrated in Spanish America and Spain.   Sí

7. **Jai-alai** originated in the Basque country in Spain.   Sí

8. Bullfights are popular in **Mexico**.   Sí

9. *Las Posadas* occur immediately **after** Christmas.   before

10. A **corrida** is a Mexican blanket.   sarape

EXERCISE C

Select the word or expression that correctly completes each sentence.

1. Mexican women wear a shawl called a (~~rebozo~~ / poncho / cesta).

2. In (Argentina / ~~Bolivia~~ / Uruguay) most of the inhabitants are Indians.

3. A three-walled court is used for (bullfighting / ~~jai-alai~~ / soccer).

4. One of the most important religious holidays in Spanish America is (~~Navidad~~ / Día de los Muertos / Carnaval).

5. The Mexican street singers are called (charros / gauchos / ~~mariachis~~).

6. The Mexican national holiday is (November 2 / October 12 / ~~September 16~~).

7. A person of mixed Native American and European ancestry is called a (china poblana / ~~mestizo~~ / sarape).

8. On May 5, Mexicans commemorate the rebellion against (~~Maximilian~~ / Bolívar / Martí).

9. El Día de la Raza corresponds to (All Soul's Day / Easter / ~~Columbus Day~~).

10. On November 2, Spanish Americans celebrate (Christmas / ~~All Soul's Day~~ / Easter).

EXERCISE D

Define each of the following.

1. mestizos ___people of mixed European + Native American ancestry___

2. Día de la Raza ___Oct. 12 corresponds to Colombus Day___

3. cesta ___curved basket strapped to a jai-alai player's wrist___

4. sarape ___colorful mexican blanket___

5. frontón ___3 walled court where jai-alai is played___

6. mariachi ___group of mexican street singers___

7. gauchos ___Argentine cowboy of the (pampas) plains___

8. piñata ___colorful figure containing candy, fruit, + toys___

9. china poblana ___female companion of the charro___

10. poncho ___cape worn to be protected by the rain.___

Part six

Comprehensive Testing:
Speaking, Listening, Reading, Writing

ESPAÑA
Islas Baleares

Islas Canarias

MÉXICO

REPÚBLICA
DOMINICANA
PUERTO RICO

CUBA
HONDURAS
NICARAGUA

GUATEMALA
EL SALVADOR
COSTA RICA
PANAMÁ

VENEZUELA

COLOMBIA

ECUADOR

PERÚ

BOLIVIA

PARAGUAY

CHILE
URUGUAY
ARGENTINA

INFINITIVE	PRESENT	COMMAND	PRETERITE	IMPERFECT	FUTURE
venir *to come*	**vengo**	**ven** / no **vengas** } (tú)	**vine**	venía	**vendré**
	vienes	**venga** (Ud.)	**viniste**	venías	**vendrás**
	vienes	**vengamos** (nosotros)	**vino**	venía	**vendrá**
	venimos	venid / no **vengáis** } (vosotros)	**vinimos**	veníamos	**vendremos**
	venís		**vinisteis**	veníais	**vendréis**
	vienen	**vengan** (Uds.)	**vinieron**	venían	**vendrán**
ver *to see*	**veo**	ve / no veas } (tú)	**vi**	**veía**	veré
	ves	vea (Ud.)	**viste**	**veías**	verás
	ve	veamos (nosotros)	**vio**	**veía**	verá
	vemos	ved / no veáis } (vosotros)	**vimos**	**veíamos**	veremos
	veis		**visteis**	**veíais**	veréis
	ven	vean (Uds.)	**vieron**	**veían**	verán

[5] PUNCTUATION

Spanish punctuation, though similar to English, has the following major differences:

(a) Questions are preceded by an additional question mark, in inverted form (¿).

¿Quién es?　　　　　　　*Who is it?*

(b) Exclamatory sentences are preceded by an additional exclamation point, in inverted form.

¡Qué día!　　　　　　　*What a day!*

(c) The comma is not used before a conjunction (**y, e, o, u,** or **ni**) in a series.

Hay clases el lunes, el martes　　*There are classes on Monday, Tuesday,*
y el miércoles.　　　　　　*and Wednesday.*

(d) Cardinal numbers are set off by periods, and decimal numbers by commas.

3,5 (tres coma cinco)　　　　*3.5 (three point five)*
1.200 (mil doscientos)　　　*1,200 (twelve hundred OR one thousand two hundred)*

(e) Final quotation marks precede commas and periods; however, if the quotation marks enclose a complete statement, they follow the period.

Cervantes escribió　　　　*Cervantes wrote*
«Don Quijote».　　　　　*"Don Quijote."*

«Escribe pronto.» Con esas　　*"Write to me soon." With those words*
palabras terminé mi carta.　　*I ended my letter.*

[6] SYLLABICATION

Spanish words are divided at the end of a line according to units of sound or syllables.

(a) Syllables generally begin with a consonant and end with a vowel. The division is made before the consonant.

te-**n**er   di-**n**e-**r**o   a-**m**e-**r**i-ca-**n**o   re-**f**e-**r**ir

(b) Ch, ll, and **rr** are never divided.

pe-**rr**o   ha-**ll**a-do   di-**ch**o

(c) If two or more consonants are combined, the division is made before the last consonant, except in the combinations **bl, br, cl, cr, dr, fl, fr, gl, gr, pl, pr,** and **tr.**

trans-**p**or-te   des-**c**u-bie**r**-to   con-**t**i-nuar   al-**b**er-**c**a

BUT

ha-**bl**ar   a-**br**ir   des-**cr**i-bir   a-**pr**en-**d**er

(d) Compound words, including words with prefixes and suffixes, may be divided by components or by syllables.

sur-a-me-ri-ca-no   OR   su-ra-me-ri-ca-no
mal-es-tar   OR   **ma**-les-tar

[7] STRESS

In Spanish, word stress follows three general rules.

(a) Words ending in a vowel, **n,** or **s** are stressed on the next-to-the-last syllable.

esc**ue**la   de**sas**tre   **jo**ven   se**ño**res

(b) Words ending in a consonant that is not **n** or **s** are stressed on the last syllable.

compren**der**   ala**bar**   reci**bir**   se**ñor**

(c) All exceptions to the above rules have an accent mark on the stressed syllable.

sábado   **jó**venes   **Adán**   **Cé**sar   fran**cés**

Spanish-English Vocabulary

The Spanish-English Vocabulary is intended to be complete for the context of this book.

Nouns are listed in the singular. Regular feminine forms of nouns are indicated by **(–a)** or the ending that replaces the masculine ending: **abogado(-a)** or **alcalde(-esa)**. Irregular noun plurals are given in full: **voz** *f.* voice; (*pl.* **voces**). Regular feminine forms of adjectives are indicated by **-a**.

ABBREVIATIONS

adj.	adjective	*m.*	masculine
f.	feminine	*m./f.*	masculine or feminine
inf.	infinitive	*pl.*	plural
irr.	irregular	*sing.*	singular

abajo below, downstairs
abierto open
abogado(-a) lawyer
abrigo *m.* overcoat
abrir to open
abuela *f.* grandmother
abuelo *m.* grandfather
aburrido bored; boring
acá here
acabar to end; **acabar de** to have just
acompañar to accompany
acostarse (ue) to go to bed
actor *m.* actor
actriz *f.* actress
acuerdo *m.* agreement; **estar de acuerdo** to agree
además besides; in addition
adiós good-bye
admirar to admire
¿adónde? where to?
aeropuerto *m.* airport
afeitar: afeitarse to shave
aficionado(-a) fan, devotee
agrio, -a sour
agua *f.* water
ahí there
ahora now
ahorrar to save
aire *m.* air; **al aire libre** outdoors, in the open

ajedrez *m.* chess
alcalde(-esa) mayor
alcoba *f.* bedroom
alemán, (*f.* **alemana**) German
alfombra *f.* rug, carpet
algo something
algodón *m.* cotton
algún some
alguno someone
alimento *m.* food
almacén *m.* department store
almohada *f.* pillow
almorzar (ue) to have (eat) lunch
alquilar to rent
alto, -a tall; high
alumno(-a) student, pupil
amable nice
ancho, -a wide
andar (*irr.*) to walk, go
anillo *m.* ring
año *m.* year
anoche last night
ansioso, -a anxious
anteayer the day before yesterday
anteojos *m. pl.* eyeglasses
antes de before
antiguo old; ancient
antipático unpleasant, disagreeable

anuncio *m.* announcement
apagar: apagarse to extinguish, put out
aparecer (zc) to appear
apellido *m.* family name, last name
aplicado, -a diligent, studious
aprender to learn
aquel, –ella that; (*pl.* **aquellos, -ellas** those)
aquí here
árbitro *m.* referee, umpire
árbol *m.* tree
arena *f.* sand
arete *m.* tree
armario *m.* closet
arreglar to arrange; to fix
arriba above, upstairs
arroz *m.* rice
ascensor *m.* elevator
asiento *m.* seat; **tomar asiento** to sit down
asignatura *f.* class, subject
asistir (a) to attend
aspiradora *f.* vacuum cleaner; **pasar la asipadora** to vacuum
atracción *f.* (amusement) ride
aula *f.* (el aula) classroom
ausente absent
autobús *m.* bus

457

automóvil (auto) *m.* automobile, car
avión *m.* airplane; **en avión** by plane
ayer yesterday
ayudar to help
azúcar *m. / f.* sugar

bailar to dance
baile *m.* dance
bajar to go down; to descend; to lower
bajo, -a low; short
balcón *m.* balcony
banco *m.* bank; bench
bandera *f.* flag
bañar: bañarse to take a bath, bathe
barato, -a cheap, inexpensive
barbero(-a) barber
barco *m.* boat
barrio *m.* neighborhood
basura *f.* garbage
batido, -a shaken; **leche batida** milkshake
baúl *m.* trunk
beber to drink
bebida *f.* drink; beverage
beca *f.* scholarship
biblioteca *f.* library
bien well
biftec *m.* beefsteak
billete *m.* ticket
billetera *f.* wallet
boca *f.* mouth
boda *f.* wedding
bodega *f.* grocery store
boleto *m.* ticket
boliche *m.* bowling
bolígrafo *m.* ballpoint pen
bolsa *f.* bag, purse
bombero *m.* fireman
bondad *f.* kindness; **tener la bondad de** please . . .
bonito, -a pretty
borrador *m.* (chalkboard) eraser

borrar to erase
bosque *m.* forest, woods
brazo *m.* arm
broma *f.* joke
bueno, -a good
bufanda *f.* scarf
buscar (qu) to look for
butaca *f.* armchair

¿cuál? (*pl.* **¿cuáles?**) which?, what?
¿cuánto, -a? how much?; *pl.* **¿cuántos, -as?** how many?
caballo *m.* horse
cabeza *f.* head
cacto *m.* cactus
cada each, every
cadena *f.* chain
caer (*irr.*) to fall; **caerse** to fall down
caja *f.* box; cashier
calcetín *m.* sock
caliente hot
calle *f.* street
calor *m.* heat; **hace calor** it is hot
cama *f.* bed; **guardar cama** to stay in bed
cámara *f.* camera
camarero(-a) waiter
cambiar to change
caminar to walk
camino *m.* road, path
camión *m.* truck
camiseta *f.* t-shirt
campana *f.* bell
campeón (*f.* **campeona**) champion
campesino(-a) *m.* farmer
campo *m.* country, countryside
canción *f.* song
cansado, -a tired
cantante *m./f.* singer
cantar to sing
cara *f.* face
cárcel *f.* prison

cariñoso, -a loving, affectionate
carne *f.* meat
carnicería *f.* butcher shop
carnicero(-a) butcher
caro, -a expensive; dear
carrera *f.* career; race
carro *m.* car
carrusel *m.* carrousel
carta *f.* letter
cartel *m.* poster
cartera *f.* wallet, purse
caso *m.* case; **hacer caso de** to pay attention to, to heed
castañuelas *f. pl.* castanets
catedral *f.* cathedral
celebrar to celebrate
celoso, -a jealous
cena *f.* dinner; supper
cenar to eat supper
centro *m.* center; downtown; **centro comercial** mall
cepillar to brush; **cepillarse** to brush oneself
cerca de near; close to
cerdo *m.* pork
cereza *f.* cherry
cerrado, -a closed
cerrar (ie) to close
cesar (de) to stop
chaqueta *f.* jacket
chofer (also **chófer**) *m. / f.* driver
chuleta *f.* chop; **chuleta de cerdo** pork chop
cielo *m.* sky
cien (ciento) one hundred
científico,(-a) scientist
cine *m.* movie theater, movies
cinta *f.* tape
cinturón *m.* belt
cita *f.* appointment, date
ciudad *f.* city
ciudadano(-a) *f.* citizen
claro, -a light (color)
clase *f.* class; kind, type
clavel *m.* carnation
clima *m.* climate

coche *m.* car

cocido, -a cooked; **bien cocido** well cooked (done)

cocina *f.* kitchen

cocinar to cook

cocinero(-a) cook

cola *f.* line; tail

colegio *m.* school

colocar to place, to put

comedor *m.* dining room

comenzar (ie) to begin; to start

comer to eat

comerciante *m. / f.* merchant, businessperson

cómico, -a comical, funny

comida *f.* food; meal

como as, like; **¿cómo?** how?, what?

cómoda *f.* bureau, dresser

cómodo, -a comfortable

compañero(-a) friend, pal

compartir to share

competencia *f.* competition

compra *f.* purchase; **ir de compras** to go shopping

comprar to buy

concurso *m.* contest

conducir (zc) to drive; to lead

confesar (ie) to confess

conocer (zc) to know (someone), to be familiar with (something)

consejero(-a) adviser

consentido, -a pampered, spoiled

construir (y) to build

contador(-ora) accountant

contar (ue) to count; to tell

contento, -a happy, content

contestar to answer

contra against

coro *m.* chorus

correo *m.* mail; post office

correr to run

correspondencia *f.* correspondence; **amigo por correspondencia** pen pal

cortar to cut

corte *f.* court, tribunal

cortés polite

cortina *f.* curtain

corto, -a short

cosa *f.* thing

coser to sew

costar (ue) to cost

creer (y) to believe; to think

criado(-a) servant

crudo, -a raw

cuaderno *m.* notebook

cuadro *m.* painting, picture

cuando when; **de vez en cuando** from time to time, sometimes; **¿cuándo?** when?

cuarto *m.* room; quarter, fourth; **una cuarta parte de** a quarter of, a fourth of

cubeta *f.* pail

cubrir to cover

cuchara *f.* spoon

cucharita *f.* teaspoon

dalia *f.* dahlia

dama *f.* lady; **jugar a las damas** to play checkers

dar (*irr.*) to give; **darse la mano** to shake hands

debajo de beneath, under

deber to owe; should, ought to

débil weak

decidir to decide

decir (*irr.*) to say; to tell

decorar to decorate

dedo *m.* finger, toe

defender (ie) to defend

dejar to leave; to allow; **dejar de** to fail to; to stop; to neglect to

delante de in front of

delgado thin, skinny

demasiado too much; excessively; too

dentro de within

dependiente(-a) salesperson

deporte *m.* sport

deportista *m. / f.* athlete

derecha *f.* right; **a la derecha** to the right

derretido, -a melted

desaparecer (zc) to disappear

desayunarse to have (eat) breakfast

descansar to rest

describir to describe

descubrir to discover

desear to wish; to want

desilusionado, -a disappointed

despacio slowly

despertador *m.* alarm clock

despertar (ie) to wake (someone) up; **despertarse** to wake up

después de after

desván *m.* attic

detrás de behind

devolver (ue) to return; to give back

día *m.* day

dibujar to draw

diccionario *m.* dictionary

dictado *m.* dictation

diente *m.* tooth

dificultad *f.* difficulty

dinero *m.* money

dirección f. address

disco *m.* record

disculpa *f.* excuse, apology; **pedir disculpa** to ask for forgiveness, apologize

diseño *m.* design

distancia *f.* distance; **larga distancia** long distance

distribuir (y) to distribute

diversión *f.* amusement

divertido, -a fun; funny, amusing

divertir (ie) to amuse; **divertirse (ie)** to enjoy oneself, have fun

dividir to divide

doler (ue) to be painful, to cause sorrow

dolor *m.* ache, pain
domingo *m.* Sunday
donde where; **¿dónde?** where?
dormir (ue) to sleep;
   dormirse to fall asleep
dormitorio *m.* bedroom
dueño(-a) owner, boss
dulce *m.* sweet, candy
durante during
durar to last, endure
duro, -a hard

echar to throw; to throw out,
   dismiss; **echar de menos** to
   miss (someone or something)
edad *f.* age
edificio *m.* building
egoísta *m. / f.* selfish person;
   adj. selfish
emocionante exciting
empezar (ie) to begin, start
encantar to like a lot, love; **me
   encanta** I like it a lot, I love it
encontrar (ue) to find; to meet
enero January
enfermedad *f.* sickness, illness
enfermero(-a) nurse
enfermería *f.* infirmary
enfermo, -a sick, ill
enfrente opposite, facing
ensalada *f.* salad
enseñanza *f.* teaching
enseñar to teach
entender (ie) to understand
entonces then
entrada *f.* entrance; ticket
entrar (en) to enter
entre between, among
entrenador(-ora) *m.* coach,
   trainer
entrevista *f.* interview
equipaje *m.* baggage
equipo *m.* team
escalera *f.* staircase, stairs
esconder to hide
escribir to write

escritor(-ora) writer
escritorio *m.* desk
escuchar to listen (to)
escuela *f.* school
ese, -a that; *pl.* **esos, -as** those
espalda *f.* back (body)
esperar to wait for; to hope
esposa *f.* wife
esposo *m.* husband
esquiar to ski
esquina *f.* corner
estación *f.* season; (train) station
estadio *m.* stadium
estado *m.* state
estampilla *f.* stamp
estante *m.* shelf
estar to be
este *m.* east
este, -a this; (*pl.* **estos, -as** these)
esto this
estómago *m.* stomach
estrecho, -a narrow
estrella *f.* star
estreno *m.* opening (of a performance), show
etiqueta *f.* label, tag
excursión *f.* trip
explicar to explain
extranjero *m.* foreign; **al
   extranjero, en el extranjero**
   abroad

fábrica *f.* factory
falda *f.* skirt
falta *f.* mistake, error
faltar to lack, need
fanático(-a) fan
farmacéutico(-a) pharmacist
farmacia *f.* drugstore, pharmacy
fascinar to fascinate
favor *m.* favor; **por favor** please
fecha *f.* date (*month, day, and
   year*)
feliz happy
feroz ferocious
ferrocarril *m.* railroad

fiesta *f.* party; holiday
fijarse (en) to pay attention,
   to note
fila *f.* row
flan *m.* custard
flor *f.* flower
florería *f.* flowershop
fotografía *f.* photograph; **sacar
   fotografías** to take pictures
frecuencia *f.* frequency; **con
   frecuencia** frequently
fresa *f.* strawberry
frijol *m.* bean
frío *m.* cold; **frío, -a** (*adj.*) cold
frutería *f.* fruit store
fumar to smoke
función *f.* performance, show
funcionar to function; to work
galleta *f.* cracker
gallo *m.* rooster
gana *f.* desire, will; **tener ganas
   de (cantar).** to feel like
   (singing)
ganar to win, earn; **ganarse la
   vida** to earn a living
garaje *m.* garage
garganta *f.* throat
gaseosa *f.* soda pop
gastar to spend; **gastar dinero**
   to spend money
gasto *m.* expense
gato(-a) cat
gemelos *m. pl.* twins
geranio *m.* geranium
gerente *m. / f.* manager
globo *m.* balloon
goma *f.* (pencil or ink) eraser
gozar (de) to enjoy
grabadora *f.* recorder
gracias *f. pl.* thanks; thank you
grado *m.* degree, grade
graduarse (ú) to graduate
gran great
grande large, big
granja *f.* farm
gritar to shout

grueso, -a thick
guante *m.* glove
guapo handsome
guayaba *f.* guava
guerra *f.* war
guía *m.* guide
gustar to please
gusto *m.* pleasure; **mucho gusto** my pleasure

habitante *m. / f.* inhabitant
hablar to speak
hacer to do; to make
hacha *f.* (**el hacha**) ax
hacia toward
hallar to find
hambre *f.* hunger; **tener hambre** to be hungry
hasta until; as far as; up to
helado *m.* ice cream
hermana *f.* sister
hermano *m.* brother
hielo *m.* ice
hierba *f.* grass
hija *f.* daughter
hijo *m.* son
historia *f.* history; story
historietas *f. pl.* comics book, comic strip
hoja *f.* leaf
hombre *m.* man
hora *f.* hour; **¿a qué hora?** at what time?
horario *m.* schedule
horno *m.* oven
hoy today
huevo *m.* egg

ida y vuelta *f.* round trip
iglesia *f.* church
importar to matter
incluir (y) to include
independiente independent
ingeniero(-a) engineer
inglés English
insistir (en) to insist on

invierno *m.* winter
invitado(-a) guest
ir to go; **irse** to go away
isla *f.* island

jabón *m.* soap
jalea *f.* jelly
jamón *m.* ham
japonés (*f.* **japonesa**) Japanese
jardín *m.* garden
jaula *f.* cage
jefatura *f.* headquarters
jefe(-a) chief, boss
joven *m. / f.* young person
juego *m.* game
jueves *m.* Thursday
jugada *f.* play
jugador(-a) player
jugar (ue) to play
jugo *m.* juice
juguete *m.* toy
junto together
justo, -a fair, just
juventud *f.* youth

labio *m.* lip
ladrar to bark
ladrido *m.* bark
ladrillo *m.* brick
lago *m.* lake
lana *f.* wool
lápiz *m.* pencil; (*pl.* **lápices**)
largo, -a long
lavandería *f.* laundry
lavar to wash; **lavarse** to wash (oneself)
lección *f.* lesson
leche *f.* milk
lechuga *f.* lettuce
leer (y) to read
legumbre *f.* vegetable
lejos (de) far (from)
lengua *f.* tongue; language
lento, -a slow
levantar to lift; **levantarse** to get up

libra *f.* pound
librería *f.* bookstore
libro *m.* book
limón *m.* lemon
limpiar to clean
limpio, -a clean
listo, -a ready; **estar listo** to be ready; **ser listo** to be clever, smart
llamada *f.* call; hacer **una llamada** to make a call
llamar to call; **llamarse** to be named, be called
llave *f.* key
llegada *f.* arrival
llegar to arrive
lleno, -a full
llevar to carry; to take; to wear
llorar to cry
lluvia *f.* rain
locutor(-ora) announcer
luego then, next; afterwards; **hasta luego** until then, good-bye
lugar *m.* place
luna *f.* moon
lunes *m.* Monday

madrastra *f.* stepmother
madre *f.* mother
madrina *f.* godmother
maestro(-a) teacher
maleta *f.* suitcase
mal badly
malo, -a bad
maltratar to mistreat
manera f. way, manner; **de ninguna manera** no way
mano *f.* hand
mantequilla *f.* butter
manzana *f.* apple
mañana tomorrow
máquina *f.* machine
mar *m.* sea
marcador *m.* felt-top marker

marcar (un número) to dial (a number)

marco *m.* frame

martes *m.* Tuesday

más more; plus

máscara *f.* mask

materia *f.* subject

mayor older; oldest

medianoche *f.* midnight

medio, -a half

mediodía *m.* noon, midday

medir (i) to measure

mejor better

melancólico, -a sad

melocotón *m.* peach

memoria *f.* memory; **de memoria** by heart

menor younger; minor

menos less; except

menudo tiny, minute; **a menudo** often, frequently

mercado *m.* market

mes *m.* month

mesa *f.* table

mesero(-era) waiter

miedo *m.* fear; **tener miedo** to be afraid, fear

miércoles *m.* Wednesday

mil one thousand

millón *m.* million

mirar to look

mismo same

mitad *f.* half

mochila *f.* knapsack

molestar to bother, to annoy

moneda *f.* coin

mono *m.* monkey

montaña *f.* mountain

montar to ride; **montar en bicicleta** to ride a bicycle

moreno, -a brunette; dark-skinned

morir (ue) to die

mostrar (ue) to show

mozo (-a) waiter

mucho, -a a lot

mueble *m.* piece of furniture; **muebles** *m. pl.* furniture

muela *f.* molar (tooth)

mujer *f.* woman

mundo *m.* world; todo **el mundo** everybody

muñeca *f.* doll

nada nothing; **de nada** you're welcome

nadar to swim

naranja *f.* orange

nariz *f.* nose; (*pl.* **narices**)

natación *f.* swimming

naturaleza *f.* nature

Navidad *f.* Christmas

negro, -a black

nevar (ie) to snow

ni neither; **ni... ni...** neither . . . nor . . ., either

nieta *f.* granddaughter

nieto *m.* grandson

nieve *f.* snow

ninguno none, not any

niña *f.* girl, child

niño *m.* boy, child

noche *f.* night; esta noche tonight

nombre *m.* name

norte *m.* north

nota *f.* grade; note

noticia *f.* news item; (*pl.* **noticias** news)

noticiero *m.* news broadcast

novia *f.* girlfriend; bride

novio *m.* boyfriend, groom

nube *f.* cloud

nuera *f.* daughter-in-law

nuevo, -a new; **de nuevo** again

nunca never

obedecer (zc) to obey

obra *f.* work, play

ocupado, -a busy

oeste *m.* west

oficio *m.* occupation

ofrecer (zc) to offer

oído *m.* ear

olmo *m.* elm tree

olvidar to forget

oración *f.* sentence

orden *f.* order

oreja *f.* ear

oro *m.* gold

orquídea *f.* orchid

oscuridad *f.* darkness

oso *m.* bear; **oso de peluche** teddy bear

otoño m. autumn, fall

otro other, another

oveja *f.* sheep

paciente *m. / f.* patient

padrastro *m.* stepfather

padre *m.* father

padrino *m.* godfather

pagar to pay (for)

página *f.* page

país *m.* country

pájaro *m.* bird

palabra *f.* word

palacio *m.* palace

pálido, -a pale

palomitas (de maíz) *f.* popcorn

pan *m.* bread

panadería *f.* bakery

panadero(-a) baker

pantalón *m.* pants, trouser

pantufla *f.* slipper

pañuelo *m.* handkerchief

papa *f.* potato; **papas fritas** French fries

papá *m.* father, dad

papel *m.* paper

para for, in order to

parada *f.* stop

paraguas *m. sing. & pl.* umbrella

parecer (zc) to seem

pared *f.* wall

pariente *m.* relative

parque *m.* park

párrafo *m.* paragraph

parte *f.* part; **en ninguna parte** nowhere
particular private
partido *m.* game, match
partir to leave; to depart
párvulo(-a) child; **escuela de párvulos** nursery school
pasado, -a past; **el año pasado** last year; **la semana pasada** last week
pasar to pass; to spend (time)
pasatiempo *m.* hobby, pastime
paseo *m.* stroll; outing
pasillo *m.* hall; aisle
pastel *m.* cake
pastelería *f.* pastry shop
patata *f.* potato
patín *m.* skate
patinar to skate
patio *m.* courtyard
pato *m.* duck
patria *f.* native land, fatherland, motherland
pavo *m.* turkey; **pavo real** peacock
pedazo *m.* piece
pedir (i) to ask for; to request; to order (food)
peinar to comb; **peinarse** to comb one's hair
peine *m.* comb
pelear to fight
película *f.* film
pelirrojo, -a redheaded
pelo *m.* hair
pelota *f.* ball
peluquería *f.* hairdresser's, barbershop
pensar (ie) to think; to intend
pequeño, -a small
pera *f.* pear
perder (ie) to lose; to waste; to miss (train, bus, and so on)
perezoso, -a lazy
periódico *m.* newspaper
periodista *m. / f.* reporter

permiso *m.* permission; **con permiso** excuse me
permitir to permit; to allow
perro *m.* dog
pesa *f.* weight; **levantar pesas** to lift weights
pescado *m.* fish *(food)*
pescar to fish
pez *m.* fish
pie *m.* foot; **a pie** on foot; **de pie** standing
piedra *f.* stone
pierna *f.* leg
pimienta *f.* pepper *(spice)*
pimiento *m.* pepper *(vegetable)*
piña *f.* pineapple
pintura *f.* paint; painting
piscina *f.* swimming pool
piso *m.* floor, story (building)
pizarra *f.* chalkboard
plano *m.* map (city)
plátano *m.* plantain
plato *m.* plate; dish
playa *f.* beach
pluma *f.* pen
pobre poor
poco little
poder *(irr.)* to be able; can, may
policía *m. / f.* police officer
pollo *m.* chicken
poner *(irr.)* to put; **poner la mesa** to set the table; **ponerse** to put on (clothing)
porque because; **¿por qué?** why?
por for, by, through; times; **dividido por** divided by
poseer (y) to possess; own
postre *m.* dessert
practicar (qu) to practice
precio *m.* price
preferir (ie, i) to prefer
pregunta *f.* question
preguntar to ask
premio *m.* prize; award
prendedor *m.* pin

preocupado, -a worried
preparar to prepare
preparativo *m.* preparation
prestado, -a lent; **pedir prestado** to borrow
prestar to lend; **prestar atención** to pay attention
primavera *f.* spring
primero, a first
primo (-a) cousin
prisa *f.* hurry, haste; **de prisa** quickly; **tener prisa** to be in a hurry
producir (zc) to produce
programador(-ora) programmer
prometer to promise
pronóstico *m.* forecast
pronto soon; **de pronto** suddenly
propina *f.* tip
propio,-a own
próximo, -a next
proyecto *m.* project
prueba *f.* test, exam
pueblo *m.* town
puente *m.* bridge
puerta *f.* door, gate
pulsera *f.* bracelet
punto *m.* point; **en punto** sharp (time)
pupitre *m.* (pupil's) desk

que who, whom, which, that; than; **¿qué?** what?, which?; **¡qué... !** what a . . . !, how . . . !
quedar to be left; **quedarse** to stay, remain
queja *f.* complaint
querer *(irr.)* to want; wish; to love
querido, -a dear
queso *m.* cheese
quien who, whom; **¿quién?** who?, whom?; **¿de quién?** whose?

química *f.* chemistry
quitar to take away; **quitarse** to take off (clothing)

rama *f.* branch
rato *m.* while; (short) time; **pasar un buen rato** to have a good time
razón *f.* reason; **tener razón** to be right
receta *f.* recipe; prescription
recibir to receive
reconocer (zc) to recognize
recordar (ue) to remember
recreo *m.* recess
recuerdo *m.* remembrance; souvenir
referir (ie) to tell; to narrate
refresco *m.* refreshment; soft drink, soda
regalo *m.* gift, present
regatear to bargain
regla *f.* ruler; rule
regresar to return
reloj *m.* watch; clock
remar to row
remedio *m.* remedy; **no hay más remedio** it can't be helped
reñir (i) to quarrel; to scold
reparar to repair, mend
reparto *m.* cast
repente *m.* sudden movement; **de repente** suddenly
repetir (i) to repeat
resfriado *m.* cold *(illness)*
resolver (ue) to solve; to resolve
responder to answer
responsable responsible
respuesta *f.* answer
reunión *f.* meeting
revista *f.* magazine
rezar to pray
rico, -a rich
río *m.* river

rompecabezas *m. sing. & pl.* puzzle
romper to break
ropa *f.* clothing
rosado, -a pink
rubio, -a blonde
ruido *m.* noise

sábado *m.* Saturday
saber *(irr.)* to know
sabroso, -a delicious
sacar to take out; **sacar fotografías** to take photos
sal *f.* salt
sala *f.* living room
salchicha *f.* sausage, frankfurter
salida *f.* exit, departure
salir to go out; to leave; **salir bien** (mal) to pass (fail)
salón *m.* room, salon; **salón de belleza** beauty shop; **salón de clases** classroom
salsa *f.* sauce
saltar to jump
salud *f.* health
saludar to greet
saludo *m.* greeting; regards
sandía *f.* watermelon
santo(-a) saint
sastre(-a) tailor
sed *f.* thirst; **tener sed** to be thirsty
seda f. silk
segundo, -a second
semana *f.* week
señor *m.* mister, sir
señora *f.* madam, missus
señorita *f.* miss, young lady
sentado, -a seated
sentarse (ie) to sit down
sentir (ie) to regret; to be sorry; **sentirse** to feel sorry
ser *(irr.)* to be
serpiente *f.* snake
servilleta *f.* napkin

servir (i) to serve
siempre always
siguiente following; **al día siguiente** on the following day
silbar to whistle
sillón *m.* chair
simpático, -a nice
sin without
sobre on top of, over
sobrina *f.* niece
sobrino *m.* nephew
sol *m.* sun
solamente only
soldado *m. / f.* soldier
solo alone
sonar (ue) to sound; to ring
sopa *f.* soup
sorprendido, -a surprised
sorpresa f. surprise
sótano *m.* basement, cellar
subir to go up, climb; to raise
suburbio *m.* suburb
sucio, -a dirty
suelo *m.* ground; floor
sufrir to suffer
sur *m.* south

tacaño, -a stingy
talla *f.* (clothing) size
tamaño *m.* size
también also, too
tampoco neither, not either
tanto so much, as much; **no es para tanto** it is not a big deal
taquígrafo(-a) stenographer
taquilla *f.* box office
tardar to delay
tarde *f.* afternoon; evening; late
tarea *f.* assignment; chore
tarjeta *f.* card; **tarjeta postal** post card
teatro *m.* theater
tela *f.* cloth; fabric
telenovela *f.* soap opera

televisión *f.* television (industry); television (set)

televisor *m.* television set

temprano early

tenedor *m.* fork

tener *(irr.)* to have

tercero, -a third

tercio *m.* third *(fraction)*

terminal *f.* terminal; **terminal de autobuses** bus terminal

terminar to finish; to end

tía *f.* aunt

tiempo *m.* time; weather; **a tiempo** on time

tienda *f.* store

tierra *f.* earth, land

tigre(-esa) tiger

tintorería *f.* dry cleaner

tío *m.* uncle

tirar to throw

tiza *f.* chalk

tocadiscos *m.* record player

tocar (qu) to touch; to play (a musical instrument); **tocar (a uno)** to be one's turn

todavía still, yet

todo, -a all

tomar to take; to drink

tonto, -a dumb, foolish

trabajar to work

trabalenguas *m. pl.* tongue twister

traducir (zc) to translate

traer *(irr.)* to carry; to bring

traje *m.* suit; **traje de baño** bathing suit

tratar (de) to try to

travieso, -a naughty, mischievous

triste sad

tulipán *m.* tulip

uña *f.* nail (body)

unos, -as *pl.* some

usar to use; to wear

uva *f.* grape

vaca *f.* cow

vacío, -a empty

valer *(irr.)* to be worth

valor *m.* value

vapor *m.* steamship

vaso *m.* glass

vecino(-a) neighbor

vender to sell

venir *(irr.)* to come

venta *f.* sale; **en venta** on sale

ventana *f.* window

ver *(irr.)* to see; to watch

verano *m.* summer

verdad *f.* truth

verde green

vestido *m.* dress

vestir (i) to dress; **vestirse** to get dressed

veterinario(-a) veterinarian

vez *f.* time; **otra vez** again; **a veces** sometimes; **en vez de** instead of

viajar to travel

viaje *m.* trip; **hacer un viaje** to travel

vida *f.* life

viejo, -a old

viento *m.* wind; **hacer viento** to be windy

viernes *m.* Friday

visitar to visit

vista *f.* sight

vivir to live

vivo, -a vivid, bright *(colors)*

volar (ue) to fly

volver (ue) to return; to come (go) back

voz *f.* voice; *pl.* **voces**

ya already

yerno *m.* son-in-law

zapatería *f.* shoe store

zapatero *m.* shoemaker

zapato *m.* shoe

zoológico *m.* zoo

The English-Spanish Vocabulary includes only those words that occur in the English-to-Spanish exercise.

able: to be able poder *(irr.)*; **to be able to** poder + *inf.*
about de, acerca de
absent ausente; **to be absent** estar ausente
acquaint: to become acquainted with conocer a
activity actividad *f.*
address dirección *f.*
after después de
afternoon tarde *f.*; **in the afternoon** por la tarde; PM de la tarde
again de nuevo; otra vez
age edad *f.* **your age** su edad *(irr.)*
agree: to agree with estar de acuerdo con
airplane avión *m.;* **by plane** en avión
airport aeropuerto *m.*
alone solo; **to be alone** estar a solas, estar solo
always siempre
amusing divertido
angry enojado
animal: stuffed animal animal de peluche *m.*
another otro
answer contestar, responder
any ninguno, ninguna
anyone alguien
appear aparecer (zc)
arrive llegar (gu)
art arte *f.* (el arte)

ask preguntar; **to ask a question** hacer una pregunta; **to ask for** pedir (i)
assignment tarea f.
attend: to attend school asistir / ir a la escuela
August agosto *m.*
avenue avenida *f.*
awake despierto; **to awaken (wake up)** despertarse *(ie)*

bank banco *m.*
bath baño m.; **to take a bath (bathe)** bañarse
beach playa f.
beautiful hermoso, bello
because porque
become llegar (gu) a ser; ponerse *(irr.)* + *adj.;* hacerse *(irr.)*
bed cama f.; **to go to bed** acostarse (ue)
before antes de
begin empezar (ie, c), comenzar (ie, c)
behind detrás de
better mejor
bicycle bicicleta f.
big grande
birthday cumpleaños *m.*
black negro
blue azul
boring aburrido
born: to be born nacer (zc)
box caja f.
boy niño, muchacho *m.*

boyfriend novio *m.*
breakfast desayuno *m.;* **to have (eat) breakfast** desayunarse
bring traer *(irr.)*
brother hermano *m.*
bus autobús *m.*
business negocio *m.*
but pero
by por; **by (bus, train)** en (autobús, tren)

call llamada *f.;* **to call** llamar
camp campamento *m.*
car auto *m.*, carro *m.*, coche *m.*
card tarjeta *f.;* **credit card** tarjeta de crédito
careful cuidadoso; **to be careful** tener cuidado
celebrate celebrar
chair silla *f.*
change cambio; **to change** cambiar
check cheque *m.;* **traveler's check** cheque de viajero *m.*
chicken pollo *m.*
childhood niñez *f.*
city ciudad *f.*
class clase *f.*
close cerrar (ie)
clothes ropa *f.*
coach entrenador *m.*
cold frío; **to be cold (weather)** hacer frío; **to be cold (person)** tener frío

comb peine *m.*; **to comb one's hair** peinarse
come venir *(irr.)*
company compañía *f.*
computer computadora *f.*
confess confesar (ie)
cook cocinar
cost costar (ue)
counselor consejero *m.*, consejera *f.*
count contar (ue)
country país *m.*; **countryside** campo *m.*
cry llorar

dance baile *m.*; **to dance** bailar
dark oscuro
day día *m.*
deal: a great deal mucho
decide decidir
defend defender (ie)
desk (pupil's) pupitre *m.*; escritorio *m.*
dictionary diccionario *m.*
difficult difícil
dinner cena *f.*
directly directamente
disagreeable desagradable
disappear desaparecer (zc)
discover descubrir
do: to do hacer
dog perro *m.*
doll muñeca *f.*
door puerta *f.*
downtown centro *m.*
dress vestido *m.*; **to get dressed** vestirse (i)
during durante

each cada
early temprano
earn ganar
eat comer; **to eat breakfast** desayunar; **to eat dinner** cenar; **to eat lunch** almorzar
electronic electrónico

employee empleado *m.*, empleada *f.*
end: to end terminar
English inglés *m.*
enjoy divertirse (ie, i)
evening noche *f.*
every cada, todos los, todas las
everyone todos; todo el mundo
everything todo, todas las cosas
exercise ejercicio *m.*
explain explicar (qu)

face cara *f.*
fall caer *(irr.)*; **to fall down** caerse
family familia *f.*
father padre *m.*
favorite favorito
feel sentir(se) (ie, i); **to feel like** tener ganas de
few unos
fifth quinto
film película *f.*
find encontrar (ue), hallar
fine fino; bien; *(weather)* hacer buen tiempo
first primero
flower flor *f.*
fly volar (ue)
follow seguir (i)
food comida *f.*
football fútbol *m.*
for para
forget olvidar
free libre
friend amigo *m.*, amiga *f.*

game partido *m.*; juego *m.*
get up levantarse
gift regalo *m.*
girlfriend novia *f.*
give dar *(irr.)*
go ir *(irr.)*; **to go away** irse *(irr.)*
gold oro *m.*
good bueno
grade nota *f.*, calificación *f.*
grandfather abuelo *m.*

grandmother abuela *f.*
great gran
green verde
greet saludar
ground suelo *m.*
guitar guitarra *f.*
gym gimnasio *m.*
gymnastics gimnasia *f.*

half mitad *f.*; **one-half** (un) medio
happily alegremente
happy contento, alegre
have tener *(irr.)*; **to have to** tener que + *inf.*
hear oír *(irr.)*
here aquí, acá
hide esconder(se)
home casa *f.*; **at home** en casa
hot caliente
hour hora *f.*
how ¿cómo?
hunger hambre *f.* (el hambre); **to be hungry** tener hambre
hurry prisa *f.*; **to be in a hurry** tener prisa

ill enfermo
include incluir (y)
insist: to insist on insistir en
intend pensar (ie) + *inf.*
interesting interesante
island isla *f.*

just justo; **to have just** acabar de + *inf.*

key llave *f.*
kitchen cocina *f.*
know saber *(irr.)*; conocer (zc); **to know how** saber + *inf.*

last último; **last (month, year)** (el mes, el año) pasado
late tarde
learn aprender
leave irse *(irr.)*; dejar

library biblioteca *f.*
like gustarle (a uno)
line cola *f.*, fila *f.*
listen escuchar
little (quantity) poco; *(size)* pequeño
live: to live vivir
long largo
look: to look at mirar; **to look for** buscar (qu)
lose perder (ie)
lot: a lot mucho
loud en voz alta; **louder** en voz más alta
love querer *(irr.)*
luck suerte *f.*; **to be lucky** tener suerte
lunch almuerzo *m.*; **to have (eat) lunch** almorzar (ue, c)

magazine revista *f.*
make hacer *(irr.)*
man hombre *m.*
many muchos, muchas; **how many?** ¿cuántos?, ¿cuántas?
matter asunto *m.*; **what's the matter?** ¿qué tiene?
meal comida *f.*
mean querer decir
meet conocer (zc), encontrar (ue)
member miembro *m.*, socio *m.*
midnight medianoche *f.*; **at midnight** a medianoche
minute minuto *m.*
miss echar de menos
Monday lunes *m.*
money dinero *m.*
month mes *m.*
more más
morning mañana *f.*; **in the morning** por la mañana
most más
mother madre *f.*
mountain montaña *f.*
movies cine *m.*

much mucho; **too much** demasiado; **how much?** ¿cuánto?
music música *f.*

name nombre *m.*; **to be named** llamarse
near cerca (de)
need necesidad *f.*; **to need** necesitar, hacerle falta (a uno), faltarle (a uno)
nervous nervioso
never nunca
new nuevo
newspaper periódico *m.*
nice simpático
night noche *f.*; **at night** por la noche
no ninguno, ninguna, ningún; **no longer** ya no
no one nadie
noise ruido *m.*
noon mediodía; **at noon** al mediodía
north norte *m.*
now ahora
number número *m.*; **telephone number** número de teléfono

obey obedecer (zc)
October octubre
offer ofrecer (zc)
often a menudo
old viejo; **to be . . . years old** tener... años *(irr.)*
open abierto
or o, u; ni
other otro

parents padres *m. pl*
park parque *m.*
party fiesta *f.*
passport pasaporte *m.*
patience paciencia *f.*
pay pagar (gu); **to pay attention** prestar atención; **to pay attention to** hacerle caso a *(irr.)*

pen pluma *f.*; **ballpoint pen** bolígrafo *m.*
people gente *f.*; personas *f.*; **young people** jóvenes *m. pl.*
photograph fotografía *f.*; **to take pictures** sacar fotografías
phrase frase *f.*
pilot piloto *m.*
place lugar *m.*
plan: to plan pensar + *inf.*
play: to play (music) tocar (qu); **(game)** jugar (ue, gu)
pleasant agradable, simpático
please por favor; tener la bondad de, hacer el favor de
point punto *m.*
police policía *f.*
pool piscina *f.*
popcorn palomitas *f. pl.*
poster cartel *m.*
practice practicar (qu)
prefer preferir (ie, i)
pretty bonito
produce producir (zc)
program programa *m.*
purse bolsa *f.*
put poner *(irr.)*; **to put on** ponerse

quarter cuarto; **one quarter** un cuarto, una cuarta parte

rapid rápido; **rapidly** rápidamente
rare raro
rarely raramente
read leer (y)
recognize reconocer (zc)
record disco m.
red rojo
remember recordar (ue)
repeat repetir (i)
respond responder, contestar
rest descansar
return volver (ue), regresar; *(give back)* devolver (ue)

rice arroz *m.*
ride: to ride a bicycle montar en bicicleta
room cuarto *m.*, habitación; **roommate** compañero de cuarto
row fila *f.*; **to row** remar
rule regla *f.*

salary sueldo *m.*; salario *m.*
Saturday sábado m.
save ahorrar
school escuela *f.*, colegio *m.*; **high school** escuela secundaria
scold reñir (i)
sea mar *m.*
seat asiento *m.*; **seated** sentado
second segundo
see ver *(irr.)*
seem parecer (zc)
sell vender
serve servir (i)
several varios
sharp *(time)* en punto
shoe zapato *m.*
short corto
show mostrar (ue), enseñar
silly tonto
sing cantar
sister hermana *f.*
sit sentarse (ie)
skit escena *f.*
sky cielo *m.*
sleep dormir (ue, u); **to fall asleep** dormirse (ue, u); **to be sleepy** tener sueño
small pequeño
snow nieve *f.*; **to snow** nevar (ie)
soccer fútbol *m.*
soda refresco *m.*, gaseosa *f.*
some alguno, algún, unos, unas; **sometimes** a veces
song canción *f.*
soon pronto

soup sopa *f.*
Spanish español *m.*
spend (time) pasar; **(money)** gastar
spoiled consentido
star estrella *f.*
start empezar (ie, c), comenzar (ie, c)
station estación *f.*
stay quedarse; **to stay in bed** guardar cama
still todavía
stop dejar de + *inf.*
store tienda *f.*
street calle *f.*
strict estricto
student alumno *m.*, alumna *f.*, estudiante *m. / f.*
study estudiar
suitcase maleta *f.*
summer verano *m.*
sun sol *m.*; **to be sunny** hacer sol
Sunday domingo *m.*
sweater suéter *m.*

table mesa *f.*
take tomar; **to take pictures** sacar fotografías
tall alto
teacher maestro *m.*, maestra *f.*, profesor *m.*, profesora *f.*
team equipo *m.*
tell decir *(irr.)*; **to tell about** referir (ie, i) de; **to tell the truth** decir la verdad
tennis tenis *m.*
test prueba *f.*, examen *m.*
that ese, esa; aquel, aquella
there ahí, allí, allá; **there is (there are)** hay
thing cosa *f.*
think pensar (ie)
thirst sed *f.*; **to be thirsty** tener sed
this este, esta

those esos, esas; quellos, aquellas
through por
Thursday jueves *m.*
ticket boleto *m.*, billete *m.*, entrada *f.*
time (hour) hora *f.*; **(in a series)** vez *f.* *(pl.* veces); tiempo; **on time** a tiempo; **to have a good time** divertirse (ie), pasar un buen rato
tired cansado; **to be tired** estar cansado
today hoy
together junto
tomorrow mañana
tonight esta noche
tooth muela *f.*, diente *m.*; **toothache** dolor de muela
train tren *m.*
translate traducir (zc)
travel viajar
tree árbol *m.*
trip viaje *m.*; **to make (take) a trip** hacer un viaje *(irr.)*
try tratar de
Tuesday martes *m.*
turn turno *m.*; **to be one's turn** tocarle (a uno)
typewriter máquinilla *f.*

understand comprender, entender (ie)
university universidad *f.*
use usar

vacation vacaciones *f. pl.*
very muy
visit visitar
voice voz *f.*; *(pl.* voces)

wait esperar
walk caminar, andar *(irr.)*; **to take a walk** dar un paseo
wallet cartera *f.*
want desear, querer *(irr.)*

wash lavar; **to wash oneself** lavarse

watch reloj *m.*; **to watch** mirar

wear llevar, usar; ponerse *(irr.)*

weather tiempo *m.*

Wednesday miércoles *m.*

week semana *f.*

well bien

what? ¿qué?

when cuando; **when?** ¿cuándo?

where donde; **where?** ¿dónde?; **(from) where?** ¿de dónde? **(to) where?** ¿adónde?

while mientras

white blanco

whom ¿a quién?

whose ¿de quién?

why ¿por qué?

wide ancho

win ganar

wind viento *m.*; **to be windy** hacer viento

with con; **with me** conmigo

without sin

woods bosque *m.*

word palabra *f.*

work trabajo *m.*; **to work** trabajar

worry preocupación *f.*; **to be worried** estar preocupado

write escribir

wrong: to be wrong no tener razón

year año *m.*

yesterday ayer

young joven; **younger** menor

Index